Smart Women and Small Business

How to Make the Leap from Corporate Careers to the Right Small Enterprise

Ginny Wilmerding

WILEY

John Wiley & Sons, Inc.

Published by John Wiley & Sons, Inc., Hoboken, New Jersey.
Published simultaneously in Canada.

For general information on our other products and services or for technical support, please contact our Customer Care Department within the United States at (800) 762-2974, outside the United States at (317) 572-3993 or fax (317) 572-4002.

Wiley also publishes its books in a variety of electronic formats. Some content that appears in print may not be available in electronic books. For more information about Wiley products, visit our web site at www.wiley.com.

Author Note Regarding Names and Numbers:
In almost every personal anecdote related in this book, real names and actual numbers have been used. In a very few cases, a person's name has been changed or omitted to protect her privacy. Examples or stories stated to be hypothetical are the only ones not based on actual interviews or the author's experience.

Library of Congress Cataloging-in-Publication Data:

Wilmerding, Ginny, 1969–
    Smart women and small business : how to make the leap from corporate careers to the right small enterprise / Ginny Wilmerding.
        p.   cm.
    Includes index.
    ISBN-13: 978-0-471-77868-4 (cloth)
    ISBN-10: 0-471-77868-0 (cloth)
    1. Self-employed women—United States.   2. Businesswomen—United States.
3. Women-owned business enterprises—United States.   4. Vocational guidance for women—United States.   I. Title.
HD6072.6.U5W55   2006
658.1'10820973—dc22

                                                                                    2006011037

Printed in the United States of America.
10 9 8 7 6 5 4 3 2 1

For my parents,
who taught me the virtues of
small business and self-employment,
despite my career girl ambitions

CONTENTS

Contents

Contents

FOREWORD

Deborah Moore, C.B.I.
Sunbelt Business Advisors Network

*F*or the past 10 years I've owned a business brokerage and mergers and acquisitions company in Pennsylvania that is part of a national network (of which I am also an owner). Sunbelt Business Advisors Network has grown to become the largest business brokerage firm in the world, with over 300 offices. We assist business owners in selling their privately held businesses, and we help buyers evaluate those companies.

When I got an unexpected call from Ginny Wilmerding last fall, I spoke with her for nearly an hour and subsequently invited her to come and meet with me in Pennsylvania. I immediately sensed that her book had the potential to propel many women into entrepreneurial action and also to make positive impacts on the brokerage and franchising industries. Helping men and women find small businesses to secure their financial freedom is what our industry is all about. I read Ginny's book and loved the way she made the small business world so accessible and full of options.

I myself owned three small businesses prior to getting into brokerage, and over the years I've mentored a number of women who needed help with their careers or wanted to know how I got started. One of the reasons I chose to open a business brokerage firm as my next venture was to help more women get into business. I wanted to take the mystery out of business ownership for women seeking to be entrepreneurs.

Although my practice has been successful and has led me to places I'd never thought possible, I have helped only a few women become business owners, and I've been surprised at how few women approach me about becoming one. The number of women who inquire about buying a business at my firm is less than 5 percent, and the number of those who actually succeed is even less than that.

On behalf of my firm, Sunbelt Business Advisors, I helped establish an initiative within the International Business Brokerage Association (IBBA) to encourage business ownership among women. I've always been on the lookout for grassroots efforts that would open women's minds to the advantages of the small business world and alternatives to starting companies from scratch.

I became an owner of the Sunbelt national network in 2002 when five Sunbelt office owners from around the country, including myself (I was the only woman), orchestrated a franchisee buyout of the company. I became one of the five charter board members (and again, the only woman) for Sunbelt Business Advisors Network, based in Charleston, South Carolina. On that board with me was the charismatic original founder of Sunbelt, Ed Pendarvis. He liked to joke with me that "There's not one yes-man on our board, and there's certainly not a yes-woman!"

It was Ed who gave me the opportunity to open the first Sunbelt office in the northeastern United States 10 years ago. Today, at least 8 percent of Sunbelt's brokerage offices are women-owned. Five years after I opened my first office, Sunbelt gave me the "Office of the Year" Award. That same year, I received the national ATHENA Foundation Award as well as the Governor's award for being one of the top 50 business women in the state. In 2005 I became the first woman president of the Pennsylvania Association of Business Brokers. I mention these honors to draw attention not to myself but to the huge opportunities for women in the world of small business.

I wish this book, *Smart Women and Small Business*, had been available 12 years ago, when I was exploring options for myself. I remember being a little guppy in a big, male pond. I was fortunate enough to have received the support and encouragement from my husband Bill to leave my corporate job in telecommunications and find the business that channeled my experience and talents, and *so can you*. There's no need to take or stay in a job that's a poor match for your interests, desires, experience, or capabilities.

Have you looked at other women entrepreneurs and wondered, "How did they do it?" In writing this book, Ginny has scoured the country for inspiring examples of women, not unlike you, who have carved out interesting niches for themselves in the small business world. She has also shared her own small business experiences. This book is a tremendous asset for women who are looking for a way to evaluate whether business ownership is for them, and for those who are already navigating business plans, due diligence, and financing.

I admire Ginny for her research and her commitment to get the word out, to inspire, influence, and assist women in harnessing their entrepreneurial spirit. It is my hope that this book becomes a small business classic. I think of Ginny and her book as a master gardener that will plant the seed of entrepreneurship in you. Don't miss out on a fantastic way to channel your skills and talents in the small business world. You won't look back.

D.M.

Reading, Pennsylvania
March 15, 2006

PREFACE

I wrote this book because it did not exist, and there was a huge need for something like it. As a consumer of small business advice books, I found many volumes that struck a chord with me personally and helped me come to the conclusion that small business offers the perfect fit for millions of midcareer businesswomen (and I recommend many of those titles in this book). However, none of the small business books that really impressed me were written from a female point of view, and none of the nonfiction titles about women's disillusionment with their careers or struggle to make time for family had anything innovative to say about the allure of small business. Nothing I read gave would-be women entrepreneurs the sense of multiple choice (not just start, but buy, join, franchise, consult, or partner) that I feel is critical.

Over the last five years, I've been putting the pieces together in my own mind of what a single concise volume could offer to women like me and you, and this is that book. I wrote it because I had something to say, ideas that I felt compelled to articulate for the benefit of all the women who are dreaming entrepreneurial dreams.

Before John Wiley & Sons offered me a publishing contract, my future editor Laurie Harting pitched my book proposal to a number of decision makers at her firm. Laurie told me later that all of the *women* at that meeting could be seen nodding their heads in recognition at the concepts in the book. I feel indebted to Laurie and those women for recognizing the commonality of women's professional angst and desires and realizing that I had something innovative to say.

My editor and her colleagues took a chance on me even though I'm not a famous columnist, prominent corporate executive, or conference speaker with a national platform to reach potential readers. And actually, that is a crucial point. I speak with authority simply because *I'm one of you*—a smart, go-getting business woman—and because I've experienced many of the things I write about in this book. In my prior careers, I've owned, operated, and consulted for decidedly non-high-tech small businesses; I've worked for big corporations, both American and foreign; I've held high-level positions in high-tech start-up companies (that no longer exist); and I've spent some of my prime career years not working at all. I'm also a parent of two children, and some of the entrepreneurial wisdom I've collected over the years comes from my daily struggles to manage a household and family.

Like many of the readers of this book, I've had interruptions and twists and turns to my business career that make me, on paper, an interesting but nontraditional candidate for jobs. But I've grown uninterested in selling myself by reputation, pedigree, or resume accomplishments. I'm not really compelled to prove myself in the corporate world. Indeed, more and more I desire to emulate my father, a small businessman and real estate investor who can actually boast that he never, ever put together a resume. He has led an independent, noncareerist, successful professional life as a small businessperson. A self-made man, he retired early, and his retirement income comes not from a pension plan but from an income stream he built over the years from his various business investments. He's well respected and well known in his community, and he has always had time for family and hobbies. In some ways, I want just what he has had . . . but there's a difference: I want the female version of it.

I want the satisfaction and economic success that come with being a successful business owner, but caring for my family is an equally important if not higher priority than providing for them. Here, my mother sets a good example—her second career as a real estate agent allowed her to be present for me every day after school. Like my mother, I don't have a wife at home to attend to family and household needs; I *am* the wife.

Moreover, like many other women, I have a broad array of motives for being a self-employed business owner, and wealth creation is not at the tip-top of my list (but it's *on* the list!).

This book does not presume affluence or dual-income households. Whether I am affluent or of modest means, I do, after all, want a *life*. However, this book does emphasize one of the wonderful realities of being self-employed: You can choose how fast you want your business to grow and how hard you will work. You must also accept the consequences of that choice. I want the freedom to work intensely if I so choose, but I also want the freedom to pursue a more modest return if it allows me to spend more time with my family or simply preserve my sanity. What I want for you, the reader, is to find the small business that's right for you and to operate it in such a way that it delivers the financial rewards you're seeking. I also want to help you avoid the trap of being in a business that delivers such minimal financial returns that it's not worth your time.

I've been struck over the last few years by how many women want what I want, yet aren't going after it and don't know where to start. The small business world is filled with both women and men, but there's certainly no national PR campaign or recruitment effort to get our best and brightest career women to give it all up for small business. The popular media instead seem forever focused on comparing women's progress in the corporate world to that of men, and lamenting that it still seems to be a man's world up in the highest echelons.

The down-to-earth world of business brokers and small business transactions, in contrast, is rarely featured in newspapers and magazines. But that world, too, is populated mostly by men, and those men's clients are also largely male. All this, despite the fact that women can relate better to the small business pitch than most men, and that they are hungrier than ever for solutions to the business career quandary! Women need ideas other than just turning their hobby into a business in their guest room—mostly because those businesses start small and stay small and can't support them. This hunger for solutions actually presents a market opportunity (and labor opportunity) for business brokers, business owners, and franchisors, but most don't see it.

Who This Book Is For

I'd conjecture that the profile of my women readers looks something like this: You're educated, talented, business-minded women with at least 10 years of work experience under your belt. You're interested in building on your past corporate or professional work experience to do something entrepreneurial and not necessarily corporate. You've been intrigued for some time by the idea of running your own business. You'd like to set some finite limits on the amount of time you're willing to devote to work, because most of you have other responsibilities (chief among them family) and interests or avocations. Some of you are working but disillusioned; others have left the work force and are trying to figure out how to reenter it.

No matter how high your level of formal education, if you're a smart woman with good business sense, this book is for you. Higher education degrees and rarefied social standing are not prerequisites for success in the world of small business. You may be drawn to this book because you've worked in support roles in small companies, seen the mistakes your business-owner bosses have made, and determined that you could do it better if only given a chance. Some of you may have cringed at the typically male way your employer runs the show, and something tells you that a female approach to the business might improve performance.

Not explicitly represented in my audience is the younger, extremely driven career woman, because, as a prominent female professor at Harvard Business School pointed out to me, this book's message "won't capture their attention." Most of them aren't ready to listen to it. But "ten years out," she said, it's another story. With a little more real-life experience, they'll be open-minded enough to focus on alternatives to the high-powered jobs for which they were groomed. Privately, I hold out hope for that forward-looking younger reader, too.

I've been told by many women I've interviewed or talked to about this book that "The timing is just right for your book," "This is a cutting-edge, modern dilemma," and "There is a huge demand for books that help women reenter the work force." I do not disagree, but I also consider the topic quite retro.

Certainly, the desire to have fulfilling work, and at the same time a happy home life, is not new. Dual-income households have been the norm for a while. For many decades now, women have had the opportunity to be well-educated, and both they and society at large have expected them to play a huge role in the economy—and in their families. Likewise, women business owners and entrepreneurs are commonplace these days. There is nothing brand-new about offering help and advice to women who want to find their place in the business world.

What is brand-new, however, is giving women multiple options to chew on in one book, and packaging that advice with helpful gender-specific insight. Why haven't mainstream media picked up on the nuance of small business choices for women? Why haven't national organizations like the Small Business Administration (SBA), in their outreach to women, loudly advocated buying businesses or franchises as an alternative to starting companies from scratch? I believe it's because there are widespread misconceptions about both the affordability and riskiness of those options versus start-ups—especially among women.

What's Inside This Book

While somewhat philosophical in the beginning, this book gets down to business in fairly short order. In Chapter 1, I zero in on some tricky issues for women that are background themes to the book, including the difference between *professional* and *business* orientation, women's attitudes toward money and risk, and their expressions of ambition. Chapter 2 is about entrepreneurial career planning; it advocates a paradigm shift among women who may have never considered small business to think of it as a worthy target of their highest career ambitions. Chapter 3 imparts the secret that business brokers and serial business owners have always known: Buying a business is much easier than starting one (even if you don't have deep pools of capital); and Chapter 4 offers practical advice on finding, evaluating, and closing on the right business.

Chapter 5 gives still more options—acquiring a franchise or a territory for a direct sales company. Chapter 6 explains how one can work for, consult for, or partner with existing business owners rather than buying a company outright. Chapter 7 illuminates the family company option for those who could possibly consider working with, partnering with, or taking over a business from a relative. It's not until Chapter 8 that would-be entrepreneurs will read about starting a company from scratch; although that is a natural choice for many, most would be wise to consider other alternatives first.

Chapter 9 is filled with advice on how women can best prepare themselves and their businesses to obtain financing. Chapter 10 is about the benefits and tricky challenges of operating a business with partners, especially other women. Chapter 11 brings together the main ideas of the book and urges readers to get started on their own search. And the appendixes, finally, offer a tool kit and sample documents to help women think through and plan for their transition into small business.

This book is not an academic paper or even a business case, although I've worked in academic business research, appreciate the empirical approach, and have referenced such sources throughout. Rather than third-person commentary that leaves the student to draw her own lessons, *Smart Women and Small Business* offers observation, analysis, advice, and common sense. In writing this book, I've interviewed more than 50 women and experts and have written about their experiences as well as my own in anecdotal form. The simple goal of our collective voices is to educate and inspire.

Other books aim to raise awareness of the difficulties women face in their careers, and in so doing to advocate societal change. This book does not. Now, don't get me wrong. I laud those who advocate for either corporate policy changes or government programs that would make it easier for women to balance family and work and remain in their chosen career tracks. I also hasten to point out how many *men* need and would benefit from such reforms. But can we really wait around for political solutions to our career challenges? Probably not in our prime career lifetimes.

Smart Women and Small Business urges women not to wait around for public action but instead (or in addition) to act on a personal level and take their lives and business careers into their own hands . . . and into the realm of small business.

CHAPTER ONE

The Business Mind-Set: Your Key to Success

*L*et's get philosophical. Why, exactly, are you thinking of doing something entrepreneurial? Do you crave the feeling of achievement of doing something on your own? Are you looking for a better, more flexible lifestyle? Are you tired of working for someone else? Are you finding it difficult to get a new job? Are you disillusioned with the job you've got? Do you have a passion that you'd like to turn into a profession?

Valid reasons, all of these. So . . . do you have the right mind-set to succeed? That's harder to answer. Before you explore the possibilities for a successful second career in small business, explore your state of mind and your readiness to operate in a different way.

Begin by asking yourself these questions:

- Are you business minded or simply professionally oriented?
- Have you given yourself permission to care about making money?
- Do you know how to think about risk?
- Are you comfortable expressing your business ambition?
- How important is lifestyle choice in choosing your next gig?

Business Orientation

I've often wondered why there aren't more women out there who identify their professional interest as simply "business." Somehow, we are much more inclined to describe our professional interests in terms of industry (banking, pharmaceuticals, consumer products, advertising) or department (marketing, finance, PR, HR, operations, administration) than in terms of business potential. Our first jobs are usually in established companies, where we learn to work on a team, to be professional, to perform our small part in making a corporation successful. But is this the same as learning about the basics of business? Most certainly not. Yet, because we've worked in for-profit corporations, we tend to think of ourselves as being business oriented.

Is it possible that we're so focused on doing a job well that we give scant thought to business survival basics such as profitability, cash flow management, meeting payroll, and selling enough products or services to stay in business? (Would your reply to that be, like so many others', "Hmm, that's possible, but that's someone else's job, not mine"?) And what does this portend for our quest to break out of the larger corporate world and do something entrepreneurial?

The first step we have to go through in the mind-set change is to acknowledge that professional excellence and business excellence are not synonymous.

Take, as an example, the case of a woman I know named Sarah. She feels proud of her business success: She's producing a top-quality product that some big-name customers want to buy, she has a team of happy employees and sales reps, and she loves what she does. What Sarah is slow to realize or loath to admit, however, is that her products are priced under market, her employees are being compensated far better than she's able to compensate herself (though she's bearing all the risk), and her neglect of financial management could threaten her happiness in the event of a crisis.

Sarah needs to trade in a bit of her professionalism for true business orientation, and she may need to shake that feeling that focusing on the bottom line is crass or boring. Let's face it: Being a financial success is usually the only way that a small business can grow larger. It's also a means to an end. Profits enable you to treat employees well, if that's what's important to you, or maybe to pursue some other, higher calling. Yet women are often guilty of downplaying the profitability mandate.

Being openly greedy about becoming rich in business is generally considered in poor taste, but when men do it, they're usually laughed off or even encouraged by other men rather than incurring disapproving looks. I'll never forget one moment during my stint as vice president of business development for a much-hyped, well-funded online service for children in the late 1990s (where, incidentally, very few parents worked because the hours were so intense). It was the day that we finally launched the beta version of our product, and there was a company celebration. Exhausted employees who were passionate about their work and this company were dancing and laughing and drinking, and I remarked to the founder of the company, "You must be so proud." Instead of agreeing that this was a huge highlight in the company's history as well as his own, he turned to me and said that the milestone meant very little to him. What he cared about and was waiting for, he said, was the IPO—going public on the stock market (and, therefore, getting rich). I was appalled, despite those stock options in the file drawer that I hoped would be worth something one day.

This entrepreneur was focused on quickly creating great personal wealth, not on building a profitable company with staying power. His intentions, too, were in the wrong place. He indulged himself in grand ideas when he, too, should have been training himself to be more business oriented. Not surprisingly, the business failed after four years.

Even if it doesn't come naturally at first, business orientation can be learned. It's just another form of discipline.

Women's Attitudes toward Money

Our culture somehow deemphasizes to women the basics of business and making money. If you identify yourself as a business-oriented woman, do yourself a favor: Give yourself permission to care about making money. This is essential to getting off to the right start in an entrepreneurial career, and it is the second change in mind-set that I advocate.

Isabella Califano, co-founder of the women's active apparel company Chickabiddy, reflected that "The biggest problem for women is that they are not taught to understand money. They are told to find a career they love, as opposed to understanding money and business. Men are taught to be aware of how to make money." Isabella discovered this for herself when she left a creative job at an ad agency to launch her own line of surf wear for women. She knew from her previous job how to market clothes and how to create a brand—valuable business skills, to be sure—but found out on the job that she knew very little about cash flow and running the day-to-day finances of what was really a manufacturing company. She quickly came up to speed, however, and when I talked to her she described herself as "really into finances." Still, after years of hard work, she was taking home only a modest amount of money and struggling to increase the size of her staff.

In *The Old Girls Network: Insider Advice for Women Building Businesses in a Man's World*, the three female authors state flatly, "We would argue that collectively, women are far less powerful than men, a situation that stems in part from how we deal with money, how we earn money, and how we think about money. . . . Not many of us were told, let alone encouraged, that we could express ourselves through the medium of business. We were not told that by creating and selling products and services we could manifest our ingenuity, our intelligence, our independence; that we could do good for others and have a fully realized life."[1]

Being Realistic about Risk

Part of thinking about money in a productive way is being realistic about risk; this is the third challenge for you in creating a business mind-set. Not only do we need to have a sense of how much or how little risk is appropriate to take on, but we also need to develop an instinct for how taking certain risks can be very beneficial, while engaging in other risky behaviors can seriously disadvantage our businesses. What fouls up many women (and men, too) is that they don't always understand when they are taking on risk and whether a certain amount of risk is acceptable, perhaps even advantageous to their businesses.

For example, you may agree to buy a small business for a fair price but need to finance the purchase through a loan. It's not risky to take on this debt if you know that the payments have been spaced out in a way that's affordable to the business, but it is risky to agree to a repayment schedule that's too aggressive. Or let's say you want to start a business from scratch. It's not too risky to give up your job and invest $25,000 of your own money if you've got industry experience, have written a thorough business plan, and have secured a contract for your first product or service. But it is risky to quit your job and rack up $25,000 in credit card debt to produce a glossy brochure and build a product prototype if you not only haven't done that up-front work but also have no additional cash reserves. (For that matter, it may be riskier to quit your job and spend $5,000 on your business idea than it is to spend $25,000, because $5,000 may not get you all the way there).

Our tolerance for risk varies from woman to woman; there's no magic threshold for all of us. But naiveté about risk can be a killer. Being completely risk averse is also very limiting. Deborah Moore of Sunbelt Business Advisors Network, the largest business brokerage firm in the world, says, "I see women tear deals apart because they don't know how to evaluate risk. They're looking for security, so they tiptoe into a new venture, unwilling to put much money up front. They limit themselves, being so risk averse, and are blinded to a reasonable analysis of risk versus reward." In the area of risk assessment, a little bit of savvy goes a long way.

Career Ambition versus Life Ambition

The fourth change in mind-set we may have to undergo is to come to terms with our own ambition, which may look a lot different than it did when we were first out of school. When Ania Camargo and Electa Sevier teamed up to start a consulting firm together six years ago, they

5

agreed that they'd become more holistic about their ambitions since their early career days: "In our first meeting, when we were thinking of going into business together, we both agreed: We don't want successful careers, we want successful *lives*." What this meant to them was being picky about clients, working flexible and shorter hours with minimal travel, charging market rates, and keeping their company small (just the two of them).

What's commendable about Ania and Electa is that they articulated what they were striving for at the beginning of their business venture. But I don't think I heard them use the word *ambition*.

Anna Fels, a psychiatrist and Cornell faculty member, published an article in the April 2004 *Harvard Business Review* entitled, "Do Women Lack Ambition?" She found that the term itself conjured up negative characteristics that the women she interviewed did not want to associate with themselves, terms like *egotism, selfishness, self-aggran-dizement*, or "the manipulative use of others for one's own ends." Women especially seem to struggle with the idea that the expression of ambition is selfish.

In her book *Creating a Life*, Sylvia Ann Hewlett quotes a 35-year-old stay-at-home mother named Cindy living in Raleigh, North Carolina, who sums it up this way: "Men are always accusing me of being greedy when I say I want it all. But I'm not talking about bells and whistles. I'm talking about the basics: love and work. What sane person doesn't want that?"[2] In fact, it is not wrong or crazy to want both of these things.

Does entrepreneurial ambition look different from corporate ambition, or even community ambition? I'd say that it does. There's much more emphasis on personal choice (and consequences), independent problem solving and decision making, and responsibility and commitment. In a private company, only you and your closest advisers know how you are doing financially, but the fact remains that you can measure your success by your tangible results—no more performance reviews or concern over titles. It's exhilarating, but it can also be daunting. Other women usually react positively and admiringly toward women who own their own business or consult or work for others on their own terms. They'll root for you in a way they may not have if you were climbing the corporate ladder. Even if they don't want to do it themselves, they want to live vicariously through you!

As Ania and Electa said, their business goals are hard to separate from their life goals. That is their choice; another choice could be to pursue high-potential, high-growth businesses, possibly placing a lower priority on lifestyle and personal goals. By and large, this book is for the large audience of women who are seeking income, independence, flexibility, and balance in their businesses—not for those seeking to build high-profile companies or great wealth. Gary Schine, author of *How to Succeed as a Lifestyle Entrepreneur: Running a Business without Letting It Run Your Life*, would call these women *lifestyle entrepreneurs*.

But don't expect to find this term in many small business books. "The fact that lifestyle choice and not money is the main reason entrepreneurs become entrepreneurs is barely dealt with by those who write books on small business or otherwise dispense small business advice," remarks Schine.[3] Why? Americans are very work oriented, and an explicit focus on lifestyle is viewed as a luxury. Moreover, the American model for success at work calls for achievement above all else, rather than happiness, balance, or a feeling of significance or legacy.[4]

And you thought peer pressure was over after you got out of high school! Ambition is unseemly, being profit oriented is unfeminine, and to choose a lifestyle business is to deny your full potential! (I hope you're rolling your eyes now.) Just remember that ambition is a personal choice. Realize how societal expectations influence your behavior and thinking, but follow the path that's right for you. And decide up front how much relative importance to give to lifestyle when you're evaluating opportunities.

Envision Your Future—Find a Female Role Model

As women do, we talk about and share our stories, discussing the gap between youthful expectations of our future careers and the reality of our adult lives, which often is more complicated than we envisioned it to be.

We analyze the truth of our lives with other women—in groups of friends, on talk shows, in books, on web sites. We're fascinated by other women who have done what we dream of doing.

Yet, figuring out whether the timing is right for a new career or business is a personal and private challenge, and our friends can play no more than supporting roles. Sometimes it takes someone we don't even know to inspire us to take action. In this book you'll meet many other women like yourself who worked in many different roles before taking the plunge into small business.

Take, for example, Linda Gay, a former vice president at Merrill Lynch who bought a Foot Solutions franchise in Princeton, New Jersey, in the fall of 2003. She reflected on her participation in a franchising conference just after setting up shop: "It's funny. Now I know I'm part of a huge group of people I never knew existed!" In her case, that meant corporate refugees, many of whom were women, who found that running a franchise was a perfect match for what they found gratifying: economic independence and getting away from corporate politics.

Linda had imagined doing something noncorporate for a long time but was afraid of failure; a big psychological barrier for her was the lack of a business idea. Once she faced her fear and did some research, she began to realize that she actually had a lot of options—and role models. She acknowledges that "This is something I couldn't have done twenty years ago," but now she's in a different place mentally, and she feels very gratified and happy. "I'm now of the opinion that it's actually riskier to stay in a corporate job than to go out on my own!" Making the switch has been an adjustment for her financially, but her second year sales are already 60 percent higher than her first, and she remarks, "Guess what? I can live on a whole lot less, and it's not even painful."

Your goal, of course, should be to determine whether *you* have the right kind of ambition to strike out on your own. Give yourself permission to be ambitious again, but by all means, make the choice that really suits you. If you can't picture yourself starting a company from scratch, or don't have the money to consider buying one, have you considered consulting for or working for a small business as the first step? You can achieve similar levels of independence and flexibility, with drastically lower levels of responsibility and commitment. If you get that far mentally, then consider the vast array of franchises that exist today. If that's too intimidating, what about becoming an independent consultant for a direct sales company such as Creative Memories or the Carlisle Collection? (Read about them in Chapter 5.) Do you have a family business you could consider joining or buying into? The possibilities are myriad.

Let's get started on the journey. Stick with me and you'll soon determine for yourself which option is right for you.

CHAPTER TWO

Business Career Planning:
A New Way to Work Smart

*I*f you were drawn to read this book, chances are that you were a high achiever in your high school and/or college years. Back then, you would've described yourself as smart, ambitious, and career-oriented. You dreamed abstractly of the job and career you would have, knowing that in your generation women had finally achieved a level playing field with men in the workplace. The types of careers you envisioned were as varied as your interests—business and industry, law, medicine, academics or teaching, public service, and so on. At a certain point, you probably began honing in on possible business careers. Maybe you imagined working for a Fortune 500 company (preferably one recognized as being a good place for women to work) or joining some type of professional service firm.

Gravitating toward a job that offers solid business experience and exposure to the ways of the corporate world was the smart thing to do at that point in your life. Large businesses offer opportunities to learn an industry, develop and launch new products, observe strategic decision making, and be trained in operational skills. But what's smart for your career when you're first starting out is totally different from what's smart for your career when you're older and looking for a change in lifestyle and perhaps work style, too.

Today, you're either (1) stalled or somewhat dissatisfied with your career, (2) trying to reenter the workforce after some time off, or (3) wanting to pursue an entrepreneurial dream you've had for a long time. You may have also realized that you were never presented with a clear-cut career path in business like those who chose medical, legal, or academic professions. Or, if you did choose a business profession with a rigid career trajectory (finance, consulting, even corporate law), your job may be so demanding that part-time employment, flexible hours, or job sharing are not easy options. Sometimes you feel positively breathless as you balance your work, family, and personal interests day to day, with no time to spare.

What all my readers have in common is that you dream about working for yourself, and you're wondering if doing so will change your life for the better. You are either working for a master, and *that master isn't you*, or you're trying to reestablish yourself in the working world and questioning what you really want to do. Your previous career gave you great experience for whatever you decide to do next. But it's all right to step off that track if you're not happy or if you feel you've already proved yourself.

It sounds like you could benefit from some career planning help.

Career Planning—Then and Now

Think back to your final year as a student. Your school probably had a Career Services office that organized recruiting opportunities on campus for graduating seniors. There was societal, financial, and parental pressure to get on a stable, professional career track that was recognized almost by sound bite ("I work in marketing at Procter & Gamble"; "I'm a director of product development at IBM"; "I'm in sales and trading with Fidelity"; "I'm a management consultant"; "I'm an account executive with J. Walter Thompson").

Did anyone ever encourage you then to look for a job in a traditional small business? Did small businesses advertise job openings at your college? Would you have sought out a job in a company with, say, fewer than 10 employees that was importing foodstuffs, designing brochures and newsletters, offering landscaping services, providing temporary staffing, or selling refurbished medical equipment? Would you have wanted to work in a restaurant, a retail store, or a Mailboxes Etc.? Would you have wanted your first job to be in a small, family-run business? Maybe, but probably not.

If you can think back to that time in your life, you can remember how you probably would have reacted to such suggestions: negatively, dismissively. You were thinking big, and these kinds of businesses were not on your radar screen — they sounded too small-time.

But it's unlikely that small businesses were looking for you, either, for several reasons. Most small businesses don't have big training programs or the time to train people, and therefore prefer to hire experienced staff. Second, small companies find it harder to offer competitive salaries or comprehensive benefits; the people who make good money are usually the owners. Finally, they're certainly not big enough to join organized recruiting efforts at universities. Let's face it, newly minted college graduates and small businesses are not usually a great fit for each other.

By the time you are in the middle phase of your career (or even after you have left your career for a while to have a family), your perspective is different. Ann Gray, whom you'll read about in Chapter 9, remembers the exact moment when she realized that she simply wasn't that interested in big-company problems anymore. Not only have your interests changed, but the resources you have at your fingertips have changed, too.

Phase Two Career Goals

In planning for the future, you'll reach your goals faster if you're clear about what you're striving for and why. Most of the women I interviewed for this book concurred that their career goals have changed quite a bit since they first started working. Did we all start with unrealistic goals? I would rather call us naïve about the complexities of life—which is just to say that we were once young!

So, if you're no longer shooting for the moon in your corporate career, how would you articulate your professional aims? Maybe something like this: "My new goals for a redefined, successful phase two career are to achieve a happy medium in my life by being my own boss (or close to it); to play a part in determining the pace at which my company will grow; to operate with a high degree of responsibility and challenge while working flexible or part-time hours; and to be compensated fairly." Yes, that sounds nice!

What You Were Looking for Then	*What You Are Looking for Now*
A chance to work hard and prove yourself.	Control over your work life and schedule.
Experience that would look good on your resume.	Pride and self-esteem about what you do.
A good salary relative to peers.	Decent compensation that makes your efforts seem worthwhile.
Mentors in your chosen field of work.	Female role models.

Ironically, it's a time like now when you really need a Career Services office. Women are probably most in need of help and guidance at about a third to halfway through our productive professional years. This is when we may find ourselves at a crossroads with nowhere near the kind of career planning resources that we had when young.

One industry that has successfully marketed itself to women facing a professional crossroads is real estate brokerage, which has attracted a huge number of middle-aged women in recent decades. Like our sisters who went into real estate, most of us are less able and less willing to move for a job, travel for a job, or work 80-hour weeks. These limitations and preferences lead many of us to think that we're unemployable or that our choices are few. Some of us continue working in a less than ideal job because we're afraid we cannot create a better situation for ourselves. But we can.

SMART WOMAN PROFILE
Finding Out Who Your Friends Are

Hsiu-Lan Chang, now 54 and the owner of a FastFrame framing franchise in Brookline, Massachusetts, was the epitome of a glamorous international career woman. Born in Hong Kong and raised in Japan, she spoke five languages and capitalized on those language skills to move to Europe, initially as a CEO-level interpreter but later moving into a successful career in financial services, in sales and strategic negotiations. During her 20 years in Paris, she worked for Pierre Cardin and then spent several years with German investment bank Matushka Gruppe. Chang married a man from Monaco and for a time raised her two sons there; she and her husband subsequently divorced. In the mid-1990s, when her older son wanted to attend college in the United States, she moved to Boston and became the director of global marketing and sales for Batterymarch Financial Management.

After eight globe-trotting years there, changes in the firm forced her out, and she had to decide what to do next. On the verge of accepting a job offer elsewhere in New England at a similar financial services firm, Chang recalls being in a room full of male colleagues who had interviewed her and having a sort of out-of-body experience, which she described as being "Tinkerbell on the wall looking down." She suddenly knew that she did not want to continue working and traveling constantly for the benefit of a big company, especially in such a male-dominated industry, and she turned down the job—with no plan B. With one grown son and one in grade school, Chang wanted to make a lifestyle change that would allow her to see more of her children, yet still be able to pay the bills. The glamour of her old career had worn off.

After a few months of considering her options, Chang concluded that she wanted to be in business for herself, without partners, and she engaged a franchise consultant to help select a business. In her mind, the challenges of owning one's own business could be divided into "hard" ones (product, equipment and fixed assets, location, anything that required capital investment) and "soft" ones (sales, people management). She knew she could handle the "soft" side but was very wary of planning the "hard" parts of a new business on her own, so she decided that joining forces with a franchisor was the right fit for her. After a lengthy personal evaluation and search, she was matched up with FastFrame and opened her store on a busy corner of Beacon Street in Brookline.

Chang holds the record among all FastFrame franchisees for highest first month sales, and she won the "Rookie of the Year" award from FastFrame and the International Franchising Association in early 2006. After about a year and a half in business, her shop is bustling and attracting many high-end framing clients. To her delight, Hsiu-Lan finds framing to be a superb outlet for the creative, aesthetic part of her personality, and she's found that owning this business gives her a degree of autonomy and balance in her life that she never experienced in the past. She has talented artists working as her framers, and they are fully capable of running the store when she's not there. Importantly, Chang has also found her franchisor to be a helpful, arm's-length business partner.

But one of the biggest adjustments she has gone through has been dealing with the reaction of her friends and former colleagues to her phase two career choice. "I found out who my real friends were, and I lost some friends" in the process, she admits. Many of her former colleagues in financial services were incredulous and disdainful that Chang was now running a small framing business in the suburbs. Their snobby and unsupportive reaction made Chang realize that the work they formerly shared was all they really had in common. Since then, she counts many local people as new friends, ones who respect, praise, and understand her choice to go into small business. In many ways, they seem more sophisticated than her worldly former colleagues.

The fact is, Chang herself may have felt incredulous and disdainful as her younger self if she'd been able to observe her future career choice back then, before her own paradigm about successful careers had changed. Yet Chang may have been inclined to step off the career track even sooner if not for the financial pressures of being a single mom. There's no magical age or stage in life when one is capable of making this shift. It comes at a time when a certain amount of humility gleaned from one's life experiences combines with a growing self-knowledge and self-confidence to help one redefine priorities without worrying about peers' expectations.

Redefine What a Great Career Means

It's time to rethink your definition of a great career, get over any hang-ups about prestige, and work through any misconceptions you may have about small business.

It's easy to see how a bias against (or ignorance of) small business as a career choice develops among young, ambitious women. When you heard the words "small business," you thought of neighborhood businesses. Once in the corporate world, you may have had an even harder time thinking small. In recent years, when you heard "start-up" or "small company," what came to mind was a high-tech business, full of workaholics, vying to be the next Amazon.com. You may have known that small businesses were a backbone of sorts to the American economy, but you did not easily associate your career or business opportunity with them.

Hopefully you are beginning to see why this chapter is titled "A New Way to Work Smart." It will not sound very prestigious, nor nearly as concise, to say "I own a small baked goods company," "I work on commission for a small computer consulting firm," "I spent the last year evaluating retail businesses I might like to buy," "I'm considering opening a fitness or tutoring franchise," or "I help out with finance at a small fashion company."

But don't dwell on explaining yourself to peers. (If you're hung up on this, inspire yourself by imagining saying to your friends in the future, "I own my own business.") Instead, focus on the very good, very smart reasons that you have chosen to explore a new career in small business. You want to pursue a passion. You want control over your life. You want to be involved in building a business rather than being an employee working for the benefit of a large company and its shareholders. You desire a flexible schedule. And you don't feel that you must have a high guaranteed salary and benefits at all costs.

It may be helpful to try to type yourself at the beginning of your search. Which of these eight types sounds most like you at this point in time?

1. You've always been business oriented and know enough about financial management to keep a company on track and help it plan some growth strategies. You have some preferences for what you'd like to do but you're open to good opportunities that may present themselves. *Action:* Consider buying a small business (see Chapters 3 and 4).

2. You've always wanted to own your own business, but you want some outside structure and guidance. You need a relatively low risk way of earning a good income, and you've got some money to invest. You don't want a business partner—that's too complicated. *Action:* Consider acquiring a franchise (see Chapter 5).

3. You want to do something you love part-time, on the side. The idea of turning a passion or hobby into a business (clothes, cooking, scrapbooking) appeals to you. You enjoy working with people. *Action:* Consider becoming a representative for an innovative direct sales company (see Chapter 5).

4. You have skills that you're convinced you can charge for. You're looking for a way to do what you do best as a free agent, not a corporate employee. *Action:* Consider consulting for small businesses (see Chapter 6).

5. You know someone who might need a business partner or may one day want to sell her company. You'd like to try out working with her and get the inside scoop on the company before you consider negotiating any deal. *Action:* Consider signing on as a consultant for a finite period of time, then making an offer to buy in (see Chapters 6 and 10).

6. You aren't ready for business ownership, but you like the idea of working in a small company. You may not be the owner, but you'd still expect to have a lot of control over when and how you work. *Action:* Look for a job or commission-based position in a small business (see Chapter 6).

7. You aren't happy with where your career is going and want to step off the treadmill. A close relative owns a business and is a few years away from retirement. You never thought you'd want to be in the family business, but your relative keeps reminding you that it's a good lifestyle and decent money. *Action:* Evaluate joining the family business in the same professional manner in which you'd examine other opportunities (see Chapters 7 and 10).

8. None of these choices sound quite right to you. You really crave to start a business of your own, and you've got a great idea. You are willing to go without an income while you get it started. *Action:* Start your own business (see Chapter 8).

Small Business Definitions

It's time to define a few businesses types and terms that we will be talking about in this book before we get confused by terminology.

For the purpose of this book, we're defining *small businesses* as those worth less than $1 million (that is, a selling price of under $1 million) and typically managed by one or two individuals, no matter how many total employees. The revenue level of companies this size is usually under $2 million but can vary widely; what's more important is the level of profits and cash flow, which determine market worth. In this broad category, it is common to stratify small businesses in terms of earnings or discretionary cash flow to the business owner; for example, $100K or less, $100 to $250K, and $250K and up. Owner's discretionary cash flow numbers are usually inclusive of noncash benefits like automobiles and health insurance.

Income-replacement, personal income and *lifestyle businesses* refer to small businesses that have as their minimum goal to earn a decent living for an owner, to in effect replace what she may have earned working for someone else.

Midmarket companies generally are described as businesses with sales in the $2 million to $50 million range. It becomes harder for businesses of this size to be owned by an individual; often, owners are comprised of a group of partners, family members, and/or private investors. Professional managers are often employed to run these businesses when they get to a certain size. When bought or sold, midmarket companies are represented by intermediaries who call themselves "investment bankers" rather than "business brokers."

High-growth, high-potential, venture-backed businesses—these buzzwords define companies that pursue an ambitious, risky business model and need considerable amounts of capital to break even. Their business goal is wealth creation as opposed to income or lifestyle. Founders of companies like these are usually unable to get bank loans (*debt financing*) since their companies may not become profitable for a long time, and banks worry that loans won't be paid back. Instead, they get working capital by getting investors to buy shares in their company (*equity financing*). This money doesn't need to be paid back, because investors get stock in the company in exchange for their cash. Founders, therefore, do not maintain control for long.

Reasons to Love the Small Business World

Here are some other ways to describe small businesses that will hopefully put a more personal face on their advantages:

- Small businesses are less rigid, bureaucratic, and formal than big companies.
- Small businesses can be located anywhere—far from big cities, or even at home.

- Small businesses offer owners and employees alike the ability to work flexible hours.
- In small businesses, results matter; face time doesn't.
- Small businesses must be profitable to survive (by the way, being profitable is more fun!).
- Small businesses don't have to worry about fluctuations in their stock price.
- Small businesses can make decisions that are in the owners' self-interests.
- Small businesses don't have to conquer an entire market category—just a niche.
- Small business owners can set their own pace of growth.
- Small businesses offer the quintessential general management experience.
- Small businesses don't require advanced degrees or credentials as a prerequisite to entry.

AUTHOR INSIGHT
Take a Consulting Gig to Figure Out If Small Biz Is for You

I'd spent three years trying in vain to buy a business with a partner and had evaluated several possible acquisition candidates. A potential partner and I came close to buying one of them with the help of an SBA bank loan, when the owner decided not to sell. Time to revert to plan B. I took a little time off and went back to a part-time research job at Harvard Business School.

As I searched through my Rolodex for unexplored leads, I arranged a lunch with a woman I'd met before who owned an importing business. We shared an interest in importing from China, and I was impressed at what she'd built and how it suited her lifestyle needs. As we talked that day, it dawned on both of us

(Continued)

AUTHOR INSIGHT *(Continued)*

that we might be a good fit for each other. She had grown the six-year-old business as much as she could on her own and was even considering starting another project on the side. But she knew she couldn't handle her current day-to-day responsibilities, expand her business, start something new, and keep it all together at home, too. By the end of the lunch we had formed an agreement for me to consult for her. Less explicit—but understood—was the possibility that if it went well, I might go into business with her. In a few weeks, we'd signed a simple consulting agreement and I got started on a three-month, half-time project to help her map out the future of her company.

Because she was very open with me about her business, and because I had agreed to the consulting project with no strings or expectations attached, the arrangement worked out very well. The key to this dynamic was that she was willing to trust me and let me help her, and I was willing to perform at a professional level for her for a modest fee (my hourly rate worked out to about $35). The chemistry was great, and the pressure and politics were absolutely minimal. In addition to completing the business plan and other financial analysis that I contracted to do, I also assisted her in other areas where I could see that my help would add great value.

My business and financial skills were a good contrast to the owner's product development and sales abilities. In a short time, I had provided valuable help to the company while simultaneously getting a very close look inside the business before deciding how to proceed. This was a win-win situation for both parties, and it gave me confidence to contemplate what I'd do next.

About Money

We can only avoid thinking about our personal financial situation for so long. Ask yourself not only how much money you have to invest in an entrepreneurial venture, but what kind of money you are looking to make. If you're considering entrepreneurial pursuits purely to make as much money as possible, or if you need or desire a steady high income, say $150,000 or more in year one, then this book may not be for you— *unless* you have a considerable sum to invest in a business right off the bat. If you have the means to acquire a business worth $1 million, then $100,000 to $150,000 (or more) in owner's discretionary cash flow may not be unrealistic. If you start smaller than that, it may be several years before you achieve that kind of income (but by growing, you may meet or exceed that level relatively quickly).

To a certain extent, I subscribe to the philosophy that if you do what you love, the money will follow. However, I also believe that if you are considering joining the small business world for lifestyle reasons in addition to financial ones, you need to start with modest expectations, for two reasons. One, you will need some start-up capital to start, buy, or buy into a business. Unless you are up for a very risky, very leveraged business venture with outside investors or considerable loans, it's best to start fairly small, which means that you can only draw a modest amount out of the business once you're running it (think: enough to live on). Second, to achieve significant financial gain in the long run as a business owner, you must grow the business steadily and reinvest as much as you can in the short run. You may draw only a small salary but be building equity value in a company that you could sell someday, or which may ultimately generate the six-figure income you desire.

Some women who are reading this book are fortunate to have a spouse who provides a primary or secondary income for the household. If you've left your job and taken time off to raise children, you know how your family can temporarily live on only one income. My advice to you is this: Don't treat your entrepreneurial venture as merely gravy to your household income. Set your sights higher, whether by necessity or in the name of ambition. Remember that the most basic goal of running a viable business is to make a profit; this is a worthy goal and not to be equated with greed. Create a healthy income stream for yourself as quickly as possible, even if what you'll be earning in your phase two career in small business is supplemental to your partner's income.

Here's the way to think about your income goals: What do you need to bring home to make your efforts worthwhile? Maybe it's different this year than it will be next year. Be honest, but don't fixate on earning a salary on par with what you used to make as a full-time employee. Finally, be the smartest businesswoman you can be so that by running a successful business, you can create something that has intrinsic value over and above your modest *draw* (a business owner's take-home pay).

If you're the sole breadwinner in your family, don't despair. Perhaps you don't have the luxury of being able to approach this process with lifestyle goals in mind, but that probably means you'll be a better financial manager! In fact, I've found that it's often the *less* affluent women who offer the best examples of small business entrepreneurship, probably because their financial needs are very real and thus the stakes are higher. Know that plenty of regular people with limited financial means have either worked happily in small business to make ends meet *or* have bought companies with a nest egg for a down payment, then paid off any loans with cash flow from the business.

The key is being *smart* in choosing your path in the small business world—choosing the company or industry that is the right fit for you and has potential to grow, and managing that business smartly and efficiently. Throughout this book, you will encounter women who have been generous in sharing financial details about what they've done so that you can compare and do some numbers for yourself.

What You Have Going for You

The big differences between you at the beginning of phase one of your career and you at the beginning of phase two of your career are *your prior work experience* and *your inner confidence and instincts*. You may no longer have the mobility or the willingness to sacrifice everything for a career that you did when you were 22 or 28, but you have something now that you didn't have then, and that is your experience and maturity as a businessperson (not to mention excellent juggling skills if you've been running a household at the same time).

Change the way you think about business careers, and put those skills and that maturity to work for you in the small business world. There are millions of small businesses out there that have survived the initial start-up phase, and they need experienced, seasoned, versatile, open-minded people to help them grow to the next level. They need to tap into the largest skilled (but underutilized) workforce in America: women like you. And you need the flexibility that they offer that big corporate America does not.

CHAPTER THREE

Why Start from Scratch If Someone's Done It for You?

*W*hat if you could remove some of the uncertainty of being an entre-preneur, come up with an idea that has been proven to work, and fast-forward to the future of running that business, rather than starting it? It's truly hard for anyone to convert a passion for a new product or service into the reality of a well-run, well-financed business that could outlast its founder. The millions of existing small businesses that have survived that start-up period and are already contributing to the economy have a lot going for them from a risk profile point of view. If this is an appealing idea, and if you have previous business experience and skills, buying a business may be a much more suitable alternative and match for your skill set than starting from scratch.

Business brokers, serial business owners, and even bankers and attor-neys can tell you: The advantages to beginning with an existing business are numerous. It's also the fastest way to become a business owner. The advantages are equally applicable to both men and women, though I feel women should take special note (but don't expect to hear that from the mostly male world of business brokers, bankers, and attorneys). Buying a business can be more predictable, less risky, and less intense than starting one, all of which can make this form of entrepreneurship more palatable to midcareer women who are balancing other responsibilities at home.

When you buy a successful going concern instead of founding your own, you can end up with a viable product or service, a trained staff, and an existing clientele. Most attractive of all, if you buy a cash-flow-positive business, you've got immediate income. If you do your homework and find a business with good potential for sales growth, you can often increase revenue by about 20 percent or more within the first 12 to 18 months of buying a business.

Buying a business is not for everyone, but if you're savvy enough to evaluate existing businesses properly, and if you have some money to invest, you can skip the awkward risky years and get on with the business of running a business.

Statistical Food for Thought[1]

A majority of U.S. business owners of firms with revenues of $1 million or more started their businesses themselves, according to the Center for Women's Business Research (CWBR), which analyzed 2004 Census Bureau data. However, women business owners were much more likely than men to have started (rather than purchased, inherited, or acquired in some other way) their companies (73 percent of women owners started from scratch versus 60 percent of men).[2]

In almost every article or book about women entrepreneurs, it's usually proudly remarked that the number of women-owned businesses is growing at twice the rate of all privately owned U.S. firms, a statistic routinely reported by the CWBR and cited by the Small Business Administration (SBA), the National Women's Business Council, and others. Women are starting businesses at a faster rate than men. Of course, this is a good thing—or is it? Starting a business is inherently risky, and although data on failure rates is open to interpretation, some researchers estimate that 70 to 90 percent of all small businesses fail within the first 10 years. Yet many women dream of breaking away from corporate life (or home life) to start a business. Consequently, there are quite a few books that encourage women to start entrepreneurial ventures, and especially to start them from home.

The tendency of many, perhaps a majority, of women starting new companies is to go it alone. Most women start their businesses with a small nest egg, or they borrow from friends and family, use their personal credit cards, or tap into their home equity loans. They are less likely to get investor financing; on average, 95 percent of all investor financing goes to men.[3] Typically, women-owned small businesses stay small, the classic cottage industries, and all too often women shut down their businesses when they need to move on in life rather than planning ahead for a sale or transition to a new owner.

A woman I spoke to who recently made a personal decision to stop accepting orders for her home-based stationery business (which I'd categorize as cottage industry) reflected modestly, "When women ask me about my business and say they'd like to do something like it, I always tell them to be honest with themselves about whether they're starting a business for what I call 'mental health reasons,' or whether they really want or need to create a financially viable business. The two are very different." Whatever women's personal motivations, those who don't concern themselves with growth or income may find that they're branded as nonserious or unambitious by the outside business world.

This book embraces the notion that there is an optimal business size for every individual business owner. Too small, and it's not really worth the opportunity cost of your time, nor is it saleable. Too large, and it can end up controlling you rather than the other way around. Yes, growth is important, but what size company would really be perfect for you or for me, from a financial, daily management, or lifestyle point of view? For most women, finding that happy medium is difficult. I'd like to challenge women to be smarter about the way they become business owners. The quality and sustainability of women-owned businesses, as well as the personal satisfaction level of the owners, are even more important than their sheer prevalence.

Downsides to Starting from Scratch

One thing this book won't do is sugarcoat the experience of starting a business, although you'll find some inspiring examples of start-from-scratch entrepreneurs in Chapter 8. You can look to popular media to find amazing and happy stories of entrepreneurs who beat the odds. But you need to know the facts. Starting a business is intense, lonely, financially humbling, and time consuming. A start-up will probably require your full focus. Although some founders successfully start a business on the side while holding down a regular job, many women will not have the time to devote to both a regular job *and* a start-up. You must soberly consider whether you have that great business *idea*, whether you know exactly what business you'll be in, and whether you have the time and energy to develop your concept properly.

If you're lucky enough to have the idea and the ability to create a product or service, remember that until you can afford to hire employees, you must be the jack (or Jill!) of all trades: sales, operations, finance, receptionist, IT support, and so on. You'll be alone and overwhelmed at first. And if you have children at home, you may find it very hard to carve out quiet time to start your business in your study, guest room, or garage. If you already feel torn between career ambitions and family, starting a business from scratch may intensify rather than ease those feelings of conflict.

Founders of brand-new companies often feel that they have nothing to lose when they start a company on a shoestring. But what about the loss of income they otherwise could have earned? It might take five or six years to get your company to the stage where it produces a decent income for you and a small group of employees or independent contractors. It's also possible that your business idea won't fly, despite your best efforts. There are so many unknowns. Even with your great planning and forecasting skills, it's hard to know for certain exactly how much capital will be required, how long it'll be before you can hire employees, and how long it'll take for the business to break even.

There are also many nonfinancial distractions when starting a business from scratch (ironically, this may be one reason that nonfinancial types prefer starting to buying). You must choose a name, incorporate the company, find office space and equipment, hire employees, develop your product or service, plan your rollout strategy, come up with marketing materials, and so forth. Above all, you must inspire customers about your product or service, and you must serve them well. Profitability is theoretical until your business is well established. Many small business owners continue to focus on the products and the infrastructure when they really should shift their focus to include the bottom line. Women whose businesses are still small and who don't depend on their business to support the whole family are especially vulnerable to neglecting the financial viability of their businesses.

Contrast that situation to taking over an *existing* small business. It already has a name, a product, an office location, marketing materials, and employees. If you come in as a new owner or even as a consultant or employee, you must first analyze how the business is doing. You often start by evaluating its finances. How much revenue? What are the margins? Where can cost savings be achieved? What are the expensive projects the company should consider undertaking in order to grow? In short, your focus is on the bottom line from the very beginning. This may be a helpful mandate for women who don't naturally gravitate toward financial matters.

Review Your Goals and Compare Starting to Buying

Always go back to your goals. What is it that you're really looking for? If you identified with the list of career goals in Chapter 2, review them again here and consider them in the context of buying versus starting a business.

- *Your goal:* Control over your work life and schedule. *How to achieve it:* Predict what your daily life would be like if you owned a particular business. Choose a business that gives you the control you want. Find a going concern that doesn't shut down just because you take the afternoon off.
- *Your goal:* Pride and self-esteem about what you do. *How to achieve it:* Associate yourself with an established company, and you've got an established reputation! Plus, you have worked smarter, not harder, to get there. That's an ego boost.

- *Your goal:* Decent compensation. *How to achieve it:* When you buy an existing business, you buy an existing cash flow stream. If the company is healthy enough, you have in effect bought yourself a decent living wage. Distinguish between the outlay of cash to buy the business (an investment) and the outlay of cash to cover a modest salary as a working owner (an expense of running the company).

- *You want:* Female role models who excel in business and in life. *How to find them:* A thorough business search is likely to offer you opportunities to meet interesting women. When you buy into an existing business, you will also be instantly connected with suppliers, customers, and other industry contacts.

Not Invented Here — How Will This Make You Feel?

Buyer, beware: Buying rather than starting offers you less freedom to design your dream product or service, and it definitely requires a certain amount of business savvy. Are you able to take someone else's business idea, accept it as your own, and do what it takes to make it thrive? I think this may be harder for women than men. Women entrepreneurs are often inspired by a dream of doing something "worthwhile." It's harder for them to feel that someone else's business will be meaningful to them.

Remember that once you buy someone else's company, you can make it your own. Let go of your ideal business profile and focus on gradually shaping an existing company to be more in your image. By doing so, you should be able to grow much more quickly and achieve financial success much sooner than by starting from scratch.

Here are some examples:

- *Erin Hanlon,* whom you'll read about again in Chapter 9, bought a landscaping and nursery business on Long Island, and she promptly turned it into a gathering place for her community by selling coffee and hot cider, starting a Kids Club, and holding an Octoberfest.

- *Wendy Pease,* whose story is also featured in Chapter 9, bought a small language interpretation company that had no online presence. In her first year in business, she set up an impressive web site and positioned the company as a leader in web site localization and translation. Meanwhile, she retained all the old owner's clients and can say that the company has been in business for 18 years.
- *Joanne Giudicelli,* who didn't found a company but partnered with another woman who had invented cool tennis racquet overgrips called "HipGrips," found a clever way to direct a portion of the company's proceeds to the nonprofit Tennis and Education Foundation, which awards college scholarships to deserving inner-city student athletes. Read more in Chapter 10.
- *Geoff Smith* (yes, a man!) bought a company after devoting 12 years to a start-up that he eventually shut down. Geoff bought an ailing business and turned it around. He says: "My creativity is channeled through creative sales strategies, new product implementation, operations efficiencies, and personnel retention. I do not have to worry about a new technology, political change, or a power player in the industry pulling the rug out from under me. . . . The point, if not obvious, is that being on the cutting edge feels great and can provide a long-shot opportunity for the big financial win, but there are many low-tech opportunities that are far less risky and provide equity growth and good income. However, they may provide less of an ego boost when comparing careers at reunions."

Only you will be able to judge which path is most appropriate for your individual personality, background, and interests, but the chances are good that you can get excited about a business opportunity that wasn't your idea.

AUTHOR INSIGHT
Are You an Idea Woman or a Businesswoman?

When I was a sophomore in college, I really wanted to run a lit-tle business on the side, and I tried to think of a good entrepre-neurial idea. At my school, any student-run business operating on campus had to be run under the auspices of the Student Agency system. You were required to turn over about 11 percent of your revenues to a professionally administered office that helped you with accounting, billing, collections, and supplier payments, and filled key needs such as storage and office space, a van pool, and other general business help. Students had to get approval to start a new business; less well publicized was the fact that graduating seniors transitioned their agencies to underclass-men (you could not sell your agency when you graduated).

I had observed the success of the Student Refrigerator Agency, the Student Tuxedo Rental Agency, and others, and tried to come up with an idea of my own. My idea was to sell preapproved small appliances permitted by the school's fire code (if it wasn't on the list, it wasn't allowed in the dorms). Let's face it, mine wasn't a par-ticularly exciting idea. I myself had trouble getting passionate about it when I went one day to present the idea to the head of Student Agencies, a guy named Bart. Bart said to me, "I'm not so sure about your idea, but would you be at all interested in looking at the Student Flower Agency instead? It was started by a woman named Annie who's graduating in June, and we need to find some-one to take it over."

Yes! Lights went on in my head. I loved flowers! It had never occurred to me that I could take over an existing business, but I knew right away that this was going to be so much more fun—and more profitable—than selling small appliances! And it was. I ended up taking over the agency with another sophomore as my partner, Anastasia Vrachnos, who has a style totally different from mine and is to this day a great friend. Annie trained the two of us in the art of flower arranging, introduced us to her wholesalers, and worked with us for a whole semester before she graduated.

In the next two years, we took the basic model that Annie had developed—selling and arranging flowers for special occasions like Valentine's Day, house parties, and reunions—and we increased the sales for those occasions while at the same time adding all sorts of new categories. We sold house plants at the beginning of the school year for students to decorate their dorm rooms; we sold wreaths, greenery, and poinsettias at Christmas; we sold flowers at graduation; and we offered gift packages with balloons at certain times of the year. We more than doubled Annie's sales and split about $22,000 in profits over the course of our junior and senior years. Not bad for a part-time business run by 20-year-olds in the late 1980s. But even better was the pride we felt at what we had accomplished; we even won an award at the end of the first year for the highest increase in sales among the 20-odd agencies.

I sometimes wonder what might have happened to the small appliance business. No one ever started it, to my knowledge, and while it could have been successful as a sort of monopoly for a while, it would have been hard to compete on price with CVS and other stores close to campus. Not only was it smart to pick something I loved doing (working with flowers), but I also chose a proven business model, I had a partner with whom to share the challenge of growing the business, and we got considerable help and training from the departing owner. I know now that those four factors stacked the odds for success in our favor. This valuable early experience also taught me that it was totally okay, even preferable (for me), to be the entrepreneur who grew the business rather than the idea person who started it.

Assess Your Strengths

As you review your career goals and try to determine how you can succeed in the small business world, you should assess your strengths and proceed accordingly. Ask yourself whether you are more of a passionate idea/product person, or whether you're the strong and nimble business type—the general manager. I believe that both types are capable of small business leadership, but the latter will do especially well buying, rather than starting, a business. Although there are always shades of gray, it's helpful to assess where you fall in the spectrum before you begin searching for a business. Businesses need both kinds of women.

You're more of a business type if:

- Business for business's sake is intellectually stimulating to you.
- You enjoy making businesses more profitable and efficient.
- You're good at planning and organization.
- You're more analytical than emotional about business matters.

You're more of an idea type if:

- You don't think of yourself as a businessperson.
- You believe that if you focus on serving your customers well, the rest will follow.
- You feel driven to express your personal creativity through business.
- You refuse to work with or do business with anyone you don't like or respect.

If you're open to the idea of partnering with others, remember that the two types may complement each other well, as my Flower Agency partner Anastasia and I did. If you prefer to be the sole owner, and tend to fall into the passionate category, you can compensate by taking business classes, reading business books, and hiring good bookkeepers, accountants, and advisers. On the flip side, if you're the analytical type, you must search extra hard for a business that awakens a passion in you.

Great Concept, But Can I Afford to Do It?

Many people have a misconception that they could never afford to buy a company. Women who have been in the corporate world or exposed to big mergers and acquisitions or venture capital-backed start-ups may be especially guilty of this misconception. You may assume that acquiring an existing company requires a huge amount of cash and that you'll be in debt forever or will have to give up equity to outside investors.

It's true that the acquisitions you read about in the press require large sums of money and legions of professionals, and are all-consuming. But the world of small business is not an institutional world. It's owned and run by private individuals who depend on their businesses to earn a living. Whereas a large company with many shareholders can afford to employ necessary managerial talent, most small private business owners *are* the management in their companies. When they want to make a transition in their lives, they usually sell the company to another individual, someone who also wants the business to support his or her family and does not have vast resources to buy the company outright or pay a high premium.

In an odd way, many women for whom this book was written will find that they are primed for the financial reality of buying a small business because they've already lowered their expectations for a guaranteed, high income. Some will have left the working world for a while to raise children or to reassess their careers and future; others may have been laid off in a corporate restructuring and experienced the loss of income that resulted while they were between jobs. Many women have persisted with their careers but are working reduced hours, and they are used to more modest salaries. Still others remain in their high-paying jobs but have decided they're willing to make financial sacrifices in order to achieve independence, control, and a better quality of life. Another financial experience many of these women have in common is purchasing a home; the large down payment and monthly mortgage payments on a house are not dissimilar to how most small business purchases are structured. All-cash deals are rare.

Have you ever heard the expression *buying a job*? That's what a lot of people who buy businesses think they're doing. It may sound crazy to pay money to get a job when you could just go out and get hired! But we're living in a world where layoffs and restructurings are common, and many smart people who are tired of being at the mercy of fickle companies decide that they'd be better off paying up-front for an opportunity to earn a decent amount of money, especially if, through their own efforts and business smarts, earnings have unlimited upside. My local Motophoto franchise owner probably fits into that category—I'd bet good money that he used to be a corporate type earning good money. Since I'm a regular customer, I see that he's now running a prosperous business that provides a quality service. I also see that he's not always around; he has the flexibility to come and go because he's hired good store managers.

If you're not aiming to be the next Microsoft, but you still want to shoot high, think of buying a business in this way: You're paying a small premium to obtain a permanent job with a modest salary, albeit one that you have total responsibility for and can grow large if you choose. How high a premium, you ask? Well, the key question is this: What was the down payment? That's how much cash you're really putting in, because the rest ought to come out of the business's cash flow, not your bank account. If you choose a healthy company and structure your deal properly, the business should be able to pay you a modest salary *and* pay back any loans you took out to purchase it. The ability of a business to both service its debt and pay you a salary is key to the calculation of a small business's worth (in contrast, high-potential start-ups are usually valued on the basis of future earnings projections, not past performance). If structured correctly *and* run well, a business you purchase should pay for itself over a number of years, plus offer you the chance to recover or increase your equity investment if/when you sell it.

Darren Mize, co-founder of Gulf Coast Financial, a Tampa-based business valuations firm, says that the average down payment, even on a business worth $1 million, is 15 to 20 percent. Let's say you bought a business for $400,000 and put down $60,000 in cash. It's quite possible that that business has a discretionary cash flow of $150,000 and is able to

pay you $75,000 per year in salary as well as $75,000 to the bank to service your debt. If you can live on $45,000 per year and save $30K of that
$75K salary, you can make up your initial investment in two years! Com-
pare that to spending two years on a start-up and drawing no salary. You'd
be out $150K in lost salary, and you still may not have $150K in cash
flow by year two. Which is more affordable?

Valuing Businesses for Sale

A little knowledge is a dangerous thing, but since this book aims to give
you a realistic sense of what's involved in buying a business, it must include references to valuing them. If you buy a private business, you don't
want to be at the mercy of the seller or the broker; you want to be able to
do some homework yourself on what is a reasonable price to pay for a
solid business in a certain category.

I recommend two excellent sources of data for the layperson who
needs to estimate the value of a company for sale: (1) the BIZCOMPS
database (www.bizcomps.com), which reflects actual data from the
sale of thousands of private companies, as reported by business brokers,
and is available on a subscription or per-data-request basis (Pratt's Stats
is another similar, excellent data source); and (2) the annual *Business
Reference Guide* written by Tom West (a founder and past president of
the International Business Brokers Association, the IBBA). West's guide
is used by business brokers as well as business buyers and sellers, and
starting in 2006 is comprised almost exclusively of "Rules of Thumb,"
hundreds of pages that give the reader specific examples and research
about the usual price at which small businesses in certain industries
change hands. (Business valuation and industry background information found in West's earlier editions is now packaged in separately published books.)

To give you a general flavor of what you might have to pay for a business, I've excerpted on the following page some overall rules of thumb
from West's 2004 *Business Reference Guide*.[4] To calculate affordability to
you, remember that the money out of your pocket is whatever your down

payment is (the rest will be seller or bank financed, and business proceeds should fund payback—see Chapter 9 for more details on financing).

- Selling price as a multiple of gross sales:
    Average: 44 percent
    Mean: 37 percent
- Selling price as a multiple of seller's discretionary earnings (SDE):
    Average: 2.42
    Mean: 2.03

Here are some specific industry rule of thumb valuation examples, from West's 2006 *Business Reference Guide*:

- Antique shops/dealers: 20 percent of annual sales, plus inventory (p. 32).
- Clothing stores: 2.4 to 2.8 times SDE plus inventory (p. 188).
- Day care centers: Depends on enrollment. If fewer than 40 children, valuation equals SDE; 40 to 85 children, 2 to 3 times SDE; more than 100 children, 3 to 4 times SDE (p. 241).
- Sign manufacturing: 50 percent of annual sales; 2.5 times SDE (p. 472).
- Wholesale distributors of durable goods: 2 to 2.5 times SDE, plus inventory; 5 times EBITDA (p. 725).

For a more detailed valuation example, please see Appendix F.

BUSINESS BUYER PROFILES
Reality Check—Can I Swing This Financially?

Nina Gomez's last and highest salary in the corporate world was $120,000/year, when her employer went out of business. She decided to stay home for a while, and for five years worked part-time in various roles for a much reduced annual income, equating to $20,000 to $50,000 per year, while at the same time conducting a business search.

Eventually, Nina found a small printing business she wanted to buy into. The business had revenues of just under $1 million but discretionary cash flow of less than $30K per year (down from years past and much lower than it should be for a business of that size). Nina struck an agreement with the owner to value the business at $160,000. She first bought a 25 percent stake in the business for $40,000 in cash, with an option to buy up to a maximum of 50 percent in the future. The business could afford to pay her a salary of $45,000 per year, plus auto expenses; therefore, she would be able to recover her initial investment and begin paying for additional equity after one year's time.

With Nina's help the company's gross and net profit margins began to improve significantly, and Nina hoped to receive some profit distributions in addition to her salary if both owners agreed that the company could distribute some cash. She could foresee such distributions being as high as her salary each year, or higher (thus she could possibly receive $90,000 or more per year). As the company's performance improved, Nina's equity stake also became more valuable. Nina felt that, compared to the alternative of starting a business from scratch with her $40,000 nest egg, but foregoing a salary for a year, she had come out ahead financially—she now owned 25 percent of a company with $1 million in sales (the equivalent of $250,000 in revenue), which would have been hard to duplicate in a single year on her own.

* * *

Lauren Belliveau was not in the market to buy a business, but her neighbor Addie Tarbell had been looking into it for a while, and Lauren occasionally helped Addie evaluate potential acquisition targets. The two women happened to use the same Merrill Lynch financial adviser, and one day, that adviser (a woman) mentioned that a third client of hers was interested in selling her business. Addie was intrigued, and this time so was Lauren.

The business, a home party pottery painting and firing company called Pottery at Your Place, was still in a nascent stage of development, but the idea had big potential (it follows a direct selling model; see the latter part of Chapter 5). The founder, Peg Gaillard, had spent more than five years developing the concept, learning the art of painting and firing pottery, recruiting 25 sales reps, and fine-tuning the direct sales business model. Her vision was big, but she got to the point where she didn't want to be the one to execute and grow it, so she decided to sell.

What Lauren and Addie and one other woman, Lee Arthur, jointly agreed to buy was not much more than a great head start, a well-developed idea. They paid Peg a total of $25,000 for the business. Tangible and intangible assets included two kilns, a small amount of inventory, a nicely done web site, a sales force of 26 independent reps, a revenue base of less than $100,000 per year (with negligible profits), and the all-encompassing "good will."

The three new owners decided to pool their money and time to buy and run the business, but because it isn't yet self-sustaining, all three of them work at it part-time and continue to hold down other jobs. Their partnership model is unusual and somewhat complicated, including a formula for dividing profits based on the contribution each makes to the business. But no matter how imperfect, it's working. The business they bought may not be generating lots of income, but it's well beyond the idea stage.

Why Small Businesses Are for Sale

So why is that seemingly perfect small business for sale? Is there something wrong with it? Well, there are as many reasons for businesses being on the market as for houses; you have to investigate a little. Many sellers are selling for human, rather than economic, reasons: marriage, divorce, health problems, retirement, relocation, lack of a family succession plan, or just plain burnout or desire for a new challenge.

When you read a glowing "Offering Memorandum" for a small business, you'll naturally wonder why the owner is selling if the business is as great as it purports to be. Often the selling memorandum will boast that the owner has been able to draw a healthy amount of cash but work only part-time. Should you believe these claims?

Yes and no. Be discriminating and be prepared to do your due diligence, but don't come across as suspicious. Realize that many small businesses truly are set up to provide an owner income and flexibility. Small businesses with this profile are generally not aiming to become the next Fortune 500 corporation; if they were, the owners would be working 80-hour weeks, reinvesting all profits into the company, and seeking expansion capital from outside investors. In contrast, the lifestyle business owner is content to run a steady business and grow it organically, and usually to draw out the maximum amount of cash rather than reinvest it.

One reason commonly given for selling is simply "a desire to do something else." The seller may be older or just plain tired; possibly the owner doesn't have the skills or energy to take a business to the next stage. Many business owners do the minimum they have to do in order to create a certain amount of income for themselves. Usually there are some low-hanging fruits, or areas where a new owner could make an impact right away (for more on this subject, see Chapter 6). Often there are also hidden problems that the owner may try to conceal from prospective buyers.

The thing to remember is that a Main Street business is owned by a regular person, or perhaps two or more people, but not by a large group of nonworking shareholders. You yourself know from having made job changes over the years that you don't want to do the same thing forever; sometimes you want or need to move on. Small business owners are the same, but they don't have an easy way of making a change. Ironically, the flexibility they enjoyed while running their own company doesn't translate into an ability to sell it quickly—this is one downside to being a business owner. Business owners enjoy much less job mobility than the general population. When they want to make a change, they usually need to take at least a year to prepare a business for sale and find a willing buyer.

The market for small businesses is small and highly subjective. Because there's no public market for small companies, and because most businesses are local and not easily relocatable, they must market themselves to an audience of prospective buyers and hope that the right buyer will show up and that the timing and terms will be right. The most attractive businesses will attract the interest of multiple prospective purchasers, but not always at the same time. To a business broker, closing the sale of a private business is like being a matchmaker—not only must the price and terms be acceptable but the people involved must like each other and be willing to work together during a transition.

Some businesses for sale either aren't valuable enough to buy or won't ever find the right buyer. One of the most interesting parts of Tom West's book reveals just how hard it can be to sell a "Main Street business." These are companies that will sell for under $1 million, often have less than $1 million in sales, and have fewer than nine employees (76 percent of all businesses with one or more employees fall in this category). West estimates that 20 percent of such businesses are for sale at any one time, but only one out of five will ultimately change hands.[5] The lesson for you: The market for the sale of small private businesses is imperfect, as are the businesses themselves. A sale depends on the fortuitous match of a willing seller and willing buyer. Still, good opportunities abound.

Considerations When Beginning Your Search

Once you have decided that you are going to search for a business to buy, there are many questions you should be asking yourself. To name just a few:

- What kind of business would I like to own and run? Can or should it be located at home? (See Chapter 4.)
- How much money do I have to invest, and how much should I reveal about my finances to brokers? (See Chapter 4.)
- Should I do it with a partner? (See Chapter 10.)
- Might I start by consulting for a small business owner rather than taking the big step of buying a company? (See Chapter 6.)
- Does anyone in my extended family own a small business that I should consider joining? (See Chapter 7.)
- Do I know where to find good advisers, including small business attorneys, accountants, bankers, business brokers, and even insurance or HR specialists? Should I seek out mentors? (See Chapter 4, the end of Chapter 8, and Chapter 9.)

Talk to Other Women Who Have Done It

This book is filled with stories of women who have started second careers in the world of small business, many by buying a company and making it their own. While it's inspiring to read their stories, don't neglect to use your own network of contacts to find women closer to home who have done these things and are willing to talk to you about it face-to-face.

People enjoy talking about themselves and their work experiences if the person asking is truly interested. Women will usually be glad to share their stories with other women and perhaps inspire them to follow in their footsteps (or help them avoid some of the mistakes they made).

Begin by thinking about friends, and friends of friends, who may have run small businesses, no matter how small. Then look around your community (or search on the Internet) for the types of businesses you might be interested in; some of them will be run by women. Ask them if you can buy them coffee or lunch and hear their story. Ask them if you can spend a day at their place of business to see if it might be right for you. Before you get too far along, read all of Chapter 4, because it will give you the skinny on what the process of searching for a business will really be like.

CHAPTER FOUR

Finding the Right Business for You

*I*t's one thing to decide you're interested in the concept of buying or joining a small business, and quite another to actually find that perfect business that is available and interested in your advances. Aside from commission-based consultants who will help you choose among franchise opportunities, business brokers who will act as a buyer's broker for a very specific search, and a few nascent ventures that match skilled independent professionals with interim project work,[1] there's no formulaic matching or counseling service that will match women with the small businesses that need them. (But maybe there should be—entrepreneurs, take note!)

Are you self-directed? Small business opportunities won't just fall in your lap, unless you're extremely well connected (usually a result of having bought and sold several businesses before). You must approach your business search methodically, like a job search. Yet finding the right business is only the beginning. Before you can dive into improving the business that you're so excited to have found, you face a long process of discovery, negotiations, due diligence, lining up financing, closing, and transitioning. You may even have to go through this more than once.

You'll experience less frustration and enjoy your search more if you not only mentally prepare yourself for the process but are realistic about timing. When you're midcareer, job searches can take many months, often more than a year. Business searches can take just as long or longer. If your aim is to buy a business, allow at least a year for the process, and consider keeping your day job if you can't go that long without an income. The amount of time it will take to find the right business will vary depending on whether you intend to conduct a full-time or part-time search. Meetings with business brokers and possible acquisition targets, not to mention research and due diligence, take time.

Here are three keys to a successful business search:

1. Know *what type* of business or job suits you—consider your personality, skills, experience, interests, geographic preferences, lifestyle concerns, colleague and customer preferences, and so on. Try to visualize yourself in various scenarios, and be true to your instincts.
2. Know *where* to look for it.
3. Know *how* to approach the business, evaluate the business, and close the deal.

This chapter walks you through all three key challenges. Although the information is geared toward buying a company, it's also relevant to the woman who wants to work or consult for small businesses. If that's your aim, you'll be able to move more quickly to seize good opportunities because you're making less of a commitment. Either way, once you're in the frame of mind to look for an existing business, the only thing to do is to get started. Educate yourself. Begin networking.

That's what Madelyn Yucht did. Her story will put a personal face on this process, and then you'll be ready for some practical information and advice.

BUSINESS BUYER PROFILE

Firm Criteria plus Research Lead to the Purchase of a Staffing Company

When Madelyn Yucht and her partner and boyfriend Ravi began their search to buy an existing business in the Boston area, they had no fixed ideas about what industry they wanted to be in, but they were firm about certain other criteria. Madelyn was giving up her consulting practice, and they both planned to work full-time in the business, so they first determined that the company must already be generating around $100,000 per year. Second, they wanted a business that allowed them to work somewhat flexible hours. Third, they wanted to be in a market where there was growing demand for their product, rather than having to create demand for something brand-new. Finally, they wanted to be able to perform critical functions at the company themselves if they were short on staff. Madelyn and Ravi had put aside about $50,000 each, or $100,000 total, to use for a down payment. Their plan was to find a business together, grow it as fast as possible, and sell it again in three to five years.

Since they were interested in both retail and service businesses, they took a close look at a few companies for sale to see if that would help them narrow the field and rule out certain business or industry categories. The first business they seriously considered was a day spa in Quincy, Massachusetts. Interestingly, it combined retail hours with a service offering, and this particular business offered excellent income. "It was a cash cow, really a thriving business," Madelyn recalled, so it seemed to meet their financial and market demand criteria. But after one day observing what the business was like, Madelyn told Ravi it was all wrong. They'd be at the mercy of their employees, since the two of them didn't do nails, massage, or hair. Plus, the business was open nights and weekends, and Madelyn just didn't find it appealing.

Before ruling out retail altogether, they looked at a clothing store in Cambridge. But Madelyn soon realized she hated what she described as "religious retail": sitting in a store and praying that customers would come. In addition to her anxiety about walk-in customer traffic, retail hours seemed very limiting from a lifestyle perspective. From that point on, they decided to stick to service businesses.

After several months of searching, they found a staffing company that was a close fit with all of their criteria, McKenzie Staffing. The business was grossing $300,000, with earnings of $90,000 per year. The business focused on human services staffing and specialized in placing mental health workers, but Madelyn and Ravi could easily see expanding into (or acquiring) other staffing categories such as child care and legal staffing. They were also confident in their ability to recruit and schedule mental health workers if they had internal staff turnover problems.

Madelyn and Ravi were determined not to pay more than two times earnings, and they were able to negotiate a valuation of $180,000 for the business. They initially bought only two-thirds of the company (each put in $60,000 in cash for a one-third share) and became partners with the founder, but within a year they bought him out. Ravi put up most of the cash for the other third, so he and Madelyn ended up with a 60-40 ownership split.

Their first three years at the company, which they'd renamed CareWorks, were amazing. Early on, they brought in an aggressive salesperson, and after a year and a half, they expanded into child care staffing. Revenues soared to $2.2 million, and annual earnings plus fringe benefits like automobiles and health insurance reached $250,000 to $300,000.

Unfortunately, the upward trend didn't continue forever. The prospects for the company were excellent; the limiting factor was the deteriorating personal and working relationship between the partners. Madelyn wanted to sell the company when their partnership faltered, but Ravi wasn't willing to sell. As the two of them faded somewhat from day-to-day management, the business shrank. A few years later, they finally reached an agreement to sell the business to a key employee who had started the child care staffing division. The deal, which involved a four-year, seller-financed payout, represented a decent, though not spectacular, gain over what they had originally paid.

Madelyn shared some tips for buying a business:

- Determine your criteria up front to streamline the search and find a good fit.

- Beware of buying an owner-operated business that is very dependent on the departing owner's expertise. If you do buy an owner-operated business but are planning to hire someone else to run it, be sure that there is enough money to pay that person and you, too.
- Determine whether the business is in a period of ascendancy, descendancy, or stabilization, and analyze *why*. You can often negotiate a good deal when divorce, sickness, retirement, or another external factor has caused a decline in a business, but don't buy a business that has declined so much it can't recover.

Which Business Type Suits You?

When you're in the initial exploratory phase, find a way to narrow your search so that you're not blindly pursuing every opportunity out there. You'll have a chance to change your parameters later, but for now, try to figure out which type of small business is most attractive to you. Most small businesses fall into one of the basic categories in the following list. Bear in mind that there are franchises available in most of those categories as well (see Chapter 5 if you're inclined to go with an established firm or brand, yet do your own thing).

- Service
- Manufacturing
- Distribution
- Retail
- Restaurant or food-related
- Internet
- Direct sales, home market
- Franchises
- Vending, coin-operated, route-based

What follows is a description of each main business type, with basic rules of thumb about running that type of business, including hours, location, travel, employees, and other lifestyle considerations. When evaluating different business categories, consider what kind of people you want to work with and which type of customer you'd enjoy serving.

SERVICE COMPANIES

Service companies provide a service to customers, and such services run the gamut from computer networking to storage and transportation to space planning, personnel agencies, landscaping, dry cleaning, health services, travel services, money management, marketing services, all types of consulting, construction, and just about any other work you can imagine. Real estate agencies, a classic midcareer choice for self-starting women, are service businesses. The mature U.S. economy is truly a service economy above all else, and many jobs, professions, and small businesses fall into this category. Your own skills and talents from a previous career can be turned into a service business. Likewise, an existing service business, with its current talent pool and customer base, can be a takeover target.

Knowledge-intense service businesses offer a low barrier to entry. If you have specialized talent or knowledge that someone else needs, you can hang your shingle on the door and begin accepting customers. Finding and keeping clients, however, is another story, and often a full-time endeavor.

- *Hours:* Some service businesses absolutely must observe retail or at least regular business hours. Others are completely flexible. Although you can sometimes control your time commitment based on how much work you take on (a positive), you are in the business of serving customers and must attend to their needs and requests even at inconvenient times (a negative for women seeking predictability). In fact, you must be open and ready to receive phone calls during regular hours and even after hours in some cases, because this is how you either get new clients or provide the service.

- *Location:* Service businesses can be located almost anywhere, which is a plus for lifestyle concerns. However, take note that businesses that employ a lot of people need to be in convenient, desirable locations to attract good staff.
- *Travel:* The amount of travel varies widely based on the business. Check this out before you buy a service company.
- *Other insights:* Service businesses are people businesses. Expect to spend a lot of time dealing with employees—recruiting, training, managing. Enjoying this aspect of the job, as well as being outgoing, is helpful in managing both employees and customers. But note that it's harder to get financing for service companies, because they tend to have less collateral.

MANUFACTURING COMPANIES

Manufacturing companies make products to sell to distributors and/or retailers. They range from producers of heavy or industrial products, such as equipment and chemicals, to light industrial manufacturers of things like furniture, toys, or consumer products. Other categories include printing and publishing, food products, metal or stone fabrication, and many others.

Domestic manufacturing concerns are on the decline in the American economy, as production moves to countries with lower labor costs, like China, but you can still find small specialty manufacturers on the block, and they are often in need of business modernization or cost cutting. (In fact, you may want to convert them into importers by helping them to outsource overseas.) In addition to traditional manufacturers, there are handicraft companies that make handmade items like specialty clothing, kitchen cabinets, jewelry, pottery . . . you name it.

- *Hours:* Because you don't need to deal directly with the public, hours can be flexible and are usually shorter than service or retail. However, you have ultimate responsibility for both making and selling a product, which can be quite challenging unless you have the background or have learned all you need to know about your product. Don't underestimate the necessity of mastering details and knowledge of the actual manufacturing process, even if you have employees to do that work.

- *Location:* Manufacturing companies are often located in an industrial area outside of town, where it's cheaper to own or rent a large facility. This can be a downside because of potential long commutes.
- *Travel:* The amount of travel required depends on the actual business. Some travel can be at predictable times, such as going to annual trade shows.
- *Employees:* Manufacturing companies usually have a large number of employees, and possibly an aging or unionized workforce.
- *Other insights:* Manufacturing businesses often need specialized training or highly skilled staff; carefully assess whether you will be able to carry on running the business when the seller—often the craftsperson or creative force—leaves the company. Likewise, although less industrial or high-tech manufactured products tend to be more appealing to the nonengineer, seriously consider the competitive landscape. If you're passionate about keeping manufacturing jobs in the United States from going overseas, you'd better be sure that it's economically viable for a particular company to maintain that business model, before you buy it.

WHOLESALE/DISTRIBUTION COMPANIES

Wholesalers, or buyers and sellers of goods, act as intermediaries between manufacturers and retailers and deal in either durable or nondurable goods. Their functions can range from mainly warehousing and inventory control to value-added operations like designing and outsourcing production of goods. Distributors are often the marketing and sales arms for the actual manufacturers. For example, prepared food companies rely on distributors to sell their products to grocery stores. A distributor of electronic products for homes and autos will promote branded products for which it is an authorized dealer. However, a distributor of refurbished medical equipment may operate more like a service provider, offering repair services as well to hospitals and physicians. A product sourcing company may provide components of a product, like packaging, but not be responsible in the least for helping to market the final packaged merchandise.

- *Hours:* Hours tend to be more flexible than retail or service businesses, as you don't have to deal directly with the public, and instead can make appointments with suppliers and customers. Depending on the pace of growth of the company, it is probably feasible to adjust your time commitment to the amount of business you want to handle. Just be aware that the company's revenue and profits will reflect your choice.

- *Location:* Depending on what product is being distributed, some companies can get away with keeping minimal warehousing facilities, or locating their warehouses apart from their offices. This means that you may be able to work closer to home or in more convenient locations than if you need large industrial spaces. If the product being distributed isn't bulky or is drop-shipped to customers from manufacturing facilities, it is even conceivable for your office to be in your home.

- *Travel:* Depending on the actual business, many established distributors can keep travel to a minimum since they know their suppliers well and can do business remotely. Some travel, such as going to annual trade shows, can be at predictable times.

- *Other insights:* Distributors' key assets tend to be their customer bases and, to a lesser extent, their supplier relationships. They don't typically have as much in the way of valuable assets as do manufacturers (i.e., equipment, proprietary products, trade secrets, technology), although many carry high levels of inventory. Distribution companies worry less about U.S. manufacturing competitiveness than do actual manufacturers, as they don't assume responsibility for actually making the goods, only for finding and selling them.

RETAIL BUSINESSES

Retail businesses are consumer-facing and open to the public during regular scheduled hours. Retail businesses sell products produced by manufacturers, and it is retail businesses we are perhaps most familiar with when we think of small businesses. Flower shops, clothing stores, gift shops, bakeries, and bookstores are all retail businesses (and it's easy to find all these types of retail businesses for sale). Some retail businesses are service businesses, too, such as a framer or a packaging facility.

- *Hours:* By and large, your working hours are spent at the store, perhaps 10:00 A.M. to 6:00 P.M., Monday through Saturday—a long week! To maximize your profitability, you may want to be there personally most of the time instead of hiring more sales people, which limits your flexibility as well as your ability to go on vacations. On the positive side, hours are at least predictable.
- *Location:* Successful retail businesses must be located in high-traffic (or high-need) destinations that draw in customers, and parking is usually very important. Existing, thriving retail businesses have already succeeded in conquering the biggest challenge in retail: location. Don't be naïve about how easy it will be to open a retail business in a location that is convenient to your home. If proximity is a requirement, give a thought to Internet businesses that don't have to worry about a brick-and-mortar location.
- *Travel:* In a retail business, travel is usually minimal, except for regularly scheduled buying trips (the exception to this might be if you own stores in more than one geographic location).
- *Employees:* You'll have to deal with mostly unskilled employees. Expect a lot of turnover, and be prepared to spend time on training and customer service expectations.
- *Other insights:* Don't romance the retail lifestyle. Many women romance the notion of owning a shop that contains

items they'd personally like to own or consume. Such inspiration can be very dangerous in business, and may give you all the more reason to buy a store with a proven formula rather than starting from scratch and finding that not everybody wants to buy what you like. The reality of running a retail business is often different from the dream; you must deal with frequent rejection by a fickle public, not to mention rejection by your friends, whom you may have incorrectly assumed will become loyal customers. (An alternative for women who like the idea of retail but want to sidestep the risks and long hours is direct selling; see Chapter 5.)

RESTAURANT AND FOOD-RELATED BUSINESSES

Restaurants and food outlets are businesses with which we're all familiar because we patronize them. Most restaurants specialize in breakfast, lunch, and/or dinner, evening lounge/bar business, or special occasions. Restaurants and food-related businesses require you to deal directly with the public and to prepare and serve food. The challenges to successfully operating a restaurant or food business are unique.

- *Hours:* Most restaurant businesses require pretty grueling hours that usually include either early mornings or late nights, whether you are the manager or chef or both. This is probably the least family-friendly of all business categories, but many bakeries, catering businesses, and prepared-food delivery businesses offer either early morning hours or great flexibility. Operating a bed-and-breakfast may also be a more family-friendly choice, although you're living with your business 24 hours a day.
- *Location:* Location is extremely important unless you're a caterer or primarily deliver food.
- *Travel:* There is no travel required, as a general rule. Personal travel can be difficult to schedule.

- *Employees:* Restaurant owners must spend a lot of time hiring, training, and managing employees. Other than chefs, employees are not usually highly skilled and tend to be transient. Turnover is high.

INTERNET BUSINESSES

Most small businesses enjoying the label of "Internet business" can also be placed in a standard category like retail (e-commerce) or service (for example, subscription services), but some defy traditional description. Many sites offer news, information, or research tools for free, and are supported by advertising revenues; others are set up as a marketing tool to drive business to another revenue center.

One of the most prevalent examples of small business on the Internet today is the eBay business. The eBay auction site (www.ebay.com) has become a huge conglomeration of individual online retailers, most of them operating as virtual small businesses without a storefront. EBay is the tool these business owners are using to reach their customers, and millions of people now earn a living this way.

For someone who is geographically challenged, an online business may be a good solution. If you don't want to start one from scratch, you can find established Internet businesses for sale. Checking them out may require a little extra due diligence and business savvy.

DIRECT SALES, HOME PARTIES, MULTILEVEL MARKETING

In brief, in these businesses you bring products directly to consumers, often through home parties. Sales representatives operate as independent small retail businesses but without the brick-and-mortar retail location. They can work part-time, flexible hours, which is why these types of business have traditionally attracted women looking for supplemental income. Part of the direct selling business model involves recruiting other people to be reps in other territories, then getting a commission on their sales. But a word of caution: You must choose a reputable company, since pyramid schemes and false promises abound. See Chapter 5 for more details.

FRANCHISES

A franchise is basically an authorization to sell a company's goods or services, or to use its name in selling similar services, in a particular territory. Many of the business types mentioned previously can be found in established franchises that are available for purchase. In addition to the opportunity to set up new franchises, existing franchises are bought and sold every day. See Chapter 5 for a detailed discussion of franchises.

COIN-OPERATED, VENDING, OR ROUTE-BASED BUSINESSES

Coin-operated businesses include retail service or entertainment establishments such as laundromats and game rooms in malls or bars. Vending or route-based distribution businesses usually involve coin-operated machines dispensing food, drinks, or common drug store supplies. Some are classier than others: One business I followed up on a few years ago involved placing high-end self-dispensing espresso coffee machines in hospitals, doctors' offices, auto show rooms, and so on.

While this type of business may not be immediately appealing to the readers of this book, it is worth mentioning for two reasons. First, you will see many ads for these types of businesses in the classified ads, so you should be able to spot them (and skim over them if not interested). Second, vending route businesses offer the ultimate in flexibility and control, although they may be low-brow and not hugely lucrative.

Where to Look

There are established markets for the straightforward sale of independent private businesses. Even if you're not sure whether you want or can afford to buy a company, these are good places to start familiarizing your-self with what's out there.

CLASSIFIED ADS

You can find businesses advertised for sale in local and national newspa-pers and trade periodicals. In most city newspapers, usually on Sundays, there is a full page or more in the classified section entitled "Franchise and Business Opportunities" or something similar. Start reading these on a weekly basis. The first week you read them, circle all that sound inter-esting and follow up by phone. In ensuing weeks, you will find that many ads are repeats and you'll be able to spot the new listings easily. The listings are alphabetical, and the sellers and brokers try to draw at-tention to their listings by first word choice, which may or may not get at the heart of what the business is.

WEB SITES

Businesses for sale may be listed at several web sites, including www .bizbuysell.com and www.mergernetwork.com. Over the past few years, these web sites have become increasingly comprehensive and useful, to the point that you can't conduct a proper business search without them. In contrast to printed classified listings, these listings are searchable by business type (service, retail, manufacturing, distribution, and so on), size, and geographic location. Many businesses that claim to be relocat-able will come up regardless of the location you specify. If you use these sites regularly, you'll be able to spot new listings easily; some also show you how old a listing is. Don't disregard old listings; remember that the market for small businesses is small and imperfect and that it can take a long time to find the right match between buyer and seller.

BUSINESS BROKER WEB SITES AND NEWSLETTERS

Business brokers are intermediaries between sellers and buyers of busi-nesses. They almost always represent the seller, although you can hire a buyer's broker when you have in mind a very specific type of business you want to buy. Most brokers advertise their listings on their company web sites, on major online hubs like BizBuySell, and in newspaper classified ads. In newspaper and magazine ads you'll find URLs for independent local business broker offices as well as national, franchised business brokerage companies.

One nationwide business brokerage with over 300 franchised offices in the United States and worldwide is Sunbelt Business Advisors Network (www.sunbeltnetwork.com). Sunbelt calls businesses with $1 million or less in revenues and up to 20 employees "Main Street businesses." About 95 percent of U.S. businesses fall into this category. Another nationwide business brokerage is VR Business Brokers (www.vrbusinessbrokers.com); their offices are also franchises. VR claims to have "sold more businesses in North America than anyone else."[2] Four years after the company's 1979 founding, the original principals of the company helped found the International Business Brokers Association (IBBA),[3] now the organizing force in the brokerage industry.

LAWYERS, ACCOUNTANTS, FRIENDS, AND REFERRALS

After you've invested some time in the search process, you will have built a network of contacts that could potentially refer you to business owners who are thinking of selling but haven't formally listed their companies with a broker. Once you've begun to network with professional advisers, they may think of you when they hear about potential opportunities, retiring business owners, and other leads.

Some businesspeople make a career out of purchasing companies; the first one they buy is a stepping-stone to the next, and the next. They are in a much better position than the first-time buyer to utilize their network to find acquisition candidates.

Realistically, you shouldn't expect many referrals from these relationships if you are brand-new to buying businesses. However, it's never too early to start networking.

Working with Business Brokers

As is true in most industries, brokerage firms are diverse in their range of expertise and services. A few large, consolidated firms make up a significant proportion of the world of brokers; the remainder are independent brokerage firms or sole practitioners.

If you like a particular person or firm's approach, take a close look at both their listings and the services they provide to help you successfully navigate the acquisition process. But unless you've specifically hired a broker to represent you, remember that *the broker represents and is commissioned by the seller.* (Brokers typically get paid commissions of 8 to 10 percent on the sales price of a business, and the commissions are paid at closing by the seller.) Moreover, brokers are duty-bound to protect the confidentiality of the seller so that the company's customers, employees, and vendors aren't aware of the sale. However, these obligations don't prevent them from assisting the buyer in the offer process, negotiations, due diligence, or financing. A good broker will also have a system in place to involve the right accounting, legal, and other professionals who serve as your advisers at the right times.

Keep in mind that brokers will mainly show you the listings they have in queue, in addition to any others that may be listed with a proprietary network of which they're a member. But you aren't limited to reviewing listings with a single broker; in fact, it's only natural that you'll meet many brokers while searching for the right business. You have a chance to comparison shop not only for businesses but also for brokers; you may decide that you trust a particular broker and therefore want to give his listings special consideration.

The best brokers are seasoned professionals who understand the point of view of both the seller and the buyer; many have owned small businesses themselves. Interacting with business brokers can be very educational. Still, you can't rely solely on the offering memorandums they prepare. Due diligence is your responsibility. By the time you're ready to close on the sale of a business, you should know at least as much as, if not more than, the listing broker knows about it.

A word about gender: The business brokerage industry is 93 percent male,[4] and since the industry is set up to represent sellers, you don't get to choose a broker who is especially in tune with the needs of women. However, the ironic twist is that what male business brokers have forever been pitching to mostly male buyers is exactly what women are looking for: independence, flexibility, self-sufficiency, and lifestyle.

BUSINESS BROKER INSIGHTS
A Prominent Female Broker Shares Her Tips

Deborah Moore is one of the founders and charter board members of Sunbelt Business Advisors Network (SBAN), the largest business brokerage firm in the world, with 340 locations. She shared her thoughts about women and small business with me during a series of meetings.

- *It's a male world, but it's made for women, too.* "One of my biggest disappointments is not seeing more women involved in buying businesses. In my experience, less than 4 percent of businesses transacted through intermediaries are acquired by women. The percentage of women business brokers is just about as dismal. Yet I feel that women are very well suited to small business ownership. They just need to know going into it that most of the professionals they'll be working with—brokers, accountants, lawyers, bankers—as well as other business owners, will be men. Despite that, women should use their strong relationship and communication skills to win over not only these advisers but also their employees, suppliers, customers, and local community members."

(Continued)

BUSINESS BROKER INSIGHTS *(Continued)*

- *Be self-confident.* "Women have to believe in themselves. They should have faith in their talents, skills, and capabilities for owning a business and leading it to greatness. Education alone doesn't give you the internal drive and confidence that you need to succeed in business. There are a lot of women who have the experience and street smarts necessary to run a business, large or small."

- *Don't be a prima donna.* "You have to be willing to get your hands dirty to succeed in small business, even doing something you find humbling. We've represented scores of service businesses over the years. One particular listing was a cleaning service with great potential for expansion. The owner historically took about $100,000 per year in personal income out of the business and worked about 40 hours a week. The asking price, at $130,000, was excellent—a very favorable multiple—but most prospective buyers snub their noses at a cleaning service because they identify it with being a maid. Another example is a man we represented who started by flipping hamburgers at one of the top three burger chains. He worked his way up to manager and, after the owner died, approached the franchisor to support him in the purchase of the business. Twenty years later, he and his wife own 25 franchises. Don't be afraid to start *somewhere.*"

Sample Ads for Businesses on the Block

To give you a feel for how businesses for sale are advertised, I spent an hour searching BizBuySell (www.bizbuysell.com) to select a few interesting listings. These ads have been edited and fictionalized, so you can't pursue them, but they give you an idea of what to expect.

Specialty Sporting Goods Manufacturer. *Asking $450,000 / Gross sales $625,000 / Cash flow $110,000. An opportunity for energetic new ownership to take an established, profitable business to the next level. We make products for windsurfing and kayaking enthusiasts, selling to retail shops and distributors worldwide. Owners selling in order to pursue other interests. Company located in a growing "quality of life" destination in the Southeast. Owner financing and training negotiable. Price includes $45K in inventory.*

Community Newspaper and Printing Business. *Asking $180,000 / Gross sales $235,000 / Cash flow $55,000. Great opportunity to own a long-established community newspaper, control what you do, and make an impact on the community in a suburb of Los Angeles just 30 minutes from downtown. Side printing and office supply business can be expanded to add income. Reason for selling: divorce. Offering 90 days consulting; owner financing negotiable.*

Executive Search and Recruiting Firm. *Asking $675,000 / Gross sales $495,000 / Cash flow $315,000. A first-rate search firm focused on middle to senior level executives in the financial services and health care industries. The five-year-old firm has exclusive contract fee agreements with several top banks and hospitals. Owner will stay on as long as needed for a smooth transition. Located in Boston area. Reason for selling: other interests.*

Wholesale Hobby Supplies. *Asking $400,000 / Gross sales $320,000 / Cash flow $110,000. This business manufactures and distributes specialty arts and crafts products to a niche market. No prior experience necessary to successfully operate this business. Based in the Midwest, but relocatable, since customers place orders by phone, web, and fax. This is a complete turnkey operation with processes so systemized it could be run absentee. Accounting recently modernized; clean books and records. Will consider limited seller financing.*

Playground Equipment Sales and Service. *Asking $500,000 / Gross sales $1,980,000 / Cash flow $170,000. Bring joy to children by running a playground equipment sales and service company. This company has 10 employees and services the state of New Jersey. We work with government agencies, schools, military, and other customers in designing their playgrounds and outsourcing the construction. A great company for someone with sales and marketing talents. Seller financing and training available. Reason selling: pursuing other venture.*

EBay Store for $30K Down. *Asking $65,000 / Gross sales $490,000 / Cash flow $79,000. A resale of a top franchise that helps people sell items on eBay. Located in a busy mall in Miami, Florida. Many of the store's customers have multiple items to sell and want us to facilitate the process; we take from 25 to 35 percent of every sale. Reason selling: owner relocating. Over $50,000 of furniture/fixtures/equipment included in sale price.*

Day Spa and Spray Tanning Salon. *Asking $199,000 / Gross sales $185,000 / Cash flow $65,000. This chic facility in Atlanta, Georgia, is well located, has many repeat customers, and can be expanded depending on the new owner's interest. New management could expand massage offerings, nail services, and/or private parties for groups of women.*

If these listings piqued your interest, log on and start searching for yourself!

Evaluating the Industry and the Target Company's Niche

One of the potential advantages to being a small company rather than a large player is that, simply by defining your niche and doing what you do well, you may be able to succeed in an otherwise competitive industry. For example, if you sell rare botanical prints and offer supreme customer service, you probably can worry less about competing with mail-order catalogs like Horchow or retailers like Pottery Barn that sell framed pictures. If you manufacture a certain kind of widget that is similar to one that a larger company makes but not one of its high-priority products, you might be able to avoid serious competitive scrutiny and coexist happily in the market. That said, industry dynamics can change quickly, and you cannot be complacent.

If you are going to buy a small company, you have to go beyond asking what type of business suits you. You must also evaluate the attractiveness of the industry and the target company's prospects within that industry. Here's a short list of questions to ask yourself.

Four-Step Process to Analyze Your Chosen Industry and Company

1. How attractive is this industry? Is the market growing or declining?

2. How well is the company doing relative to industry norms and averages (research this at a business library[5])?

3. Is this company overly dependent on one customer or supplier? If one or the other becomes more price sensitive, are margins healthy enough to absorb it?

4. Does the company have a competitive advantage, and can I maintain it? Are barriers to entry too low? (For example, is great customer service enough? Do I need proprietary technology, bigger economies of scale, a more innovative product, or a new sales person to succeed in the future?)

The first two steps in the process may cause you to weed out a target company altogether. (I once looked at a men's neckwear company but ruled it out because it was in a declining industry category.) Conversely, the latter two steps, if you can see a way around the challenges, may help you understand what you're getting into and how you could make improvements.

The Process of Shopping for a Company

How does the process work once you have responded to an ad? Let's go through the typical sequence of events that you will follow when evaluating acquisition candidates. (This section glosses over a process that can get quite complicated; for more detailed information and advice on buying businesses, consult your broker, attorney, banker, or some of the more comprehensive titles listed in Appendix J.)

STEP 1: FOLLOW UP ON ADS WITH PHONE CALLS OR E-MAILS

Usually this contact will be through an intermediary/business broker. I recommend that you use a fill-in-the-blank fact sheet to ask questions about the business, so that you don't forget to ask for key information (see Appendix E for an example). In addition to keeping track of where you saw the ad, who the broker is, and where the business is located, ask questions such as these:

- What is the reason for selling? Are there any problems the business is facing?
- How many years has the business been in the hands of this owner?
- What is the owner's day-to-day involvement?
- What were gross sales each of the last four years?
- What was the owner's discretionary cash flow each of the last four years?
- What is the asking price for the business?
- How did you arrive at the asking price?
- Is the seller willing to finance the purchase ("take paper," "carry money")?
- Is the seller willing to stay on for a transition period?
- What are the ways that a new owner could grow and improve this business?

STEP 2: SIGN NONDISCLOSURE AGREEMENT

Signing a nondisclosure agreement (NDA), also known as a confidentiality agreement, is generally required before you'll be given a written summary of the business for sale. One promise you'll usually have to make is not to contact the company principals directly; you must go through the intermediary. Although one can get paranoid about the legality of signing NDAs, my advice is to sign them unless they appear terribly onerous.

Learn to spot problem clauses on your own, so that you don't waste lots of valuable legal dollars on reviewing NDAs for companies you look at but don't buy. For example, be wary of unreasonably restrictive noncompetition clauses that say you cannot use any information you've learned from the subject company in a similar business in the future (make sure the language only prevents you from using specific proprietary information about the company itself, rather than intelligence about the industry). If you're genuinely concerned that particular language in the NDA is too onerous as written, write in language to protect yourself, then initial it (you can often get away with this without further discussion).

STEP 3: RECEIVE OFFERING MEMORANDUM

Offering/selling memorandums usually contain an executive summary with the company's history, a list of key personnel, a description of the business model, and very high-level financial statements (occasionally tax returns are included). They'll also suggest a purchase price and purchase terms and will usually give a rationale for the purchase price. Given that most small businesses try to minimize paper profits for tax return purposes, the broker typically tries to restate the company's financials to demonstrate that many of the expenses listed on the tax returns should be "add-backs" to seller's discretionary earnings (SDE)—for example, owner's salary, benefits, automobile expenses, rental expense if the seller also owns the business premises, and so on.

For those used to working in very professional, well-staffed business environments, let me warn you how disappointing these memorandums can be, especially when the company profiled is very small. Many are poorly written, poorly researched, and incomplete, partly because brokers cannot justify the effort required to produce thorough documentation when the subject company itself keeps poor records and doesn't have a written business plan. But remember: This is not reason enough not to look at the company!

STEP 4: SUBMIT A LIST OF QUESTIONS TO DEMONSTRATE SERIOUSNESS

Most brokers try to screen potential buyers, and they want to know how interested and knowledgeable you are before they introduce you to the company. They'll also often want a personal financial statement from you to prove that you have the resources to buy a company. Be brief and reserved when filling out these forms—better yet, have a standard form that you're willing to share, and don't reveal more (until serious negotiations begin). If you're seriously interested in an opportunity, draw up and pass on to the broker a thoughtful list of questions and requests for data. In addition to drilling down for more financial information, ask key questions about the industry, business model, competition, and current staff. The goal should be to get the broker to obtain the information from the owner and, if appropriate, to arrange a time when you can ask the owner some of your questions in person.

STEP 5: MEET THE COMPANY IF INTERESTED

This is when it really gets fun. You'll know from this first meeting whether you're interested or not. Never forget that you'll be partnering with the seller of a company for a while, until the transition is complete and you've paid the seller in full. Establish an atmosphere of trust and respect; this will set the stage for civil and pleasant negotiations later. It helps to like the seller and think you could work with him or her (but not forever, obviously). If you possibly can, spend a full day at the business so you can observe what working there will really be like. (This may have to wait until the due diligence stage.)

STEP 6: REQUEST TAX RETURNS AND OTHER INFORMATION

Some companies may want to hold back detailed statements until you make an initial offer, but the more you can learn about the financial state of the company before you make an offer, the better. If you aren't a numbers person, you'll definitely need an accountant or savvy financial adviser to help you evaluate the company before you buy. If you're good with numbers, you may be able to postpone professional involvement until after a term sheet is signed and due diligence begins.

STEP 7: CREATE A VALUATION MODEL WITH THE FINANCIALS AVAILABLE

As a general rule, most small businesses (under about $1 million in value) sell for between 1.5 and 3.0 times SDE.[6] It's important to come up with your own SDE or EBITDA number (invariably lower) through a close analysis of the financial information given to you by the broker, then determine a fair multiple.

Don't be surprised if the seller thinks the business is worth a lot more than you do, but be prepared to justify why your assessment is less. If you think the multiples used in the offering memorandum are unrealistic, suggest other numbers and cite your sources or reasons. If the business isn't being run the way you think it needs to be, be sure to subtract those additional costs from the SDE number before you apply an appropriate industry multiple. (For example, if the previous owner was working 60 hours a week but you think it's more reasonable to assume 40 hours a week from the owner and to delegate the remainder of the work to paid staff, adjust the numbers accordingly so that the cost of staff time isn't incorrectly lumped in with the owner's compensation.)

Deciding which valuation models to use and what the right multiples are for businesses in different industries is beyond the scope of this book, but you can peruse a sample valuation and expert advice in Appendix F. I also recommend Tom West's *Business Reference Guide*, published annually.

STEP 8: MAKE AN INITIAL, NONBINDING OFFER

At this point, you'll have to put a stake in the ground as to how much the business is worth, how much money you personally will put down, how you'll come up with the rest of the money (bank financing, seller financing, or some combination), on what schedule, and so on. An average down payment ranges from 15 to 30 percent, although the seller may expect to get 50 percent or more by combining your down payment with the amount a bank is loaning to you.

Never begin with your best offer, although you'd better figure out the best and highest you'd go from the get-go (and don't stray from it; don't get swayed by emotion, as hard as that is!). Although the offer is nonbinding, it should be made in good faith. If you can't or don't expect to follow through, don't say otherwise.

STEP 9: NEGOTIATE TERMS WITH SELLER

Sellers will always want to get most of the money up front, and buyers will always want to minimize the amount they pay up front, so expect some back-and-forth. This will happen while you're shaping a draft business plan and exploring financing. Meanwhile, remember that you're not committed to buying until you've done your due diligence and signed a purchase and sale agreement. Also remember that, if you've bid way under the asking price, the seller may feel offended by your offer and dismiss it out of hand, especially if he or she has spent many years building and nurturing the company. Unless you are in a competitive bid situation, you'll do well to back up your offer with research, market comparables, and an analysis of what the business and you yourself can actually afford.

STEP 10: DRAFT A BUSINESS PLAN

If you're serious about the opportunity, and it looks like you might be able to strike a deal, start drafting a business plan as if you owned the company today. See Appendix A for a sample business plan and Appendix B for an excellent outline. Make sure your business plan answers the questions any financiers will ask about the business: How will you run it? What will you change? Where are the growth opportunities? What does the competitive landscape look like? Why are *you* the person to own and run it?

STEP 11: SEEK BANK FINANCING

As early as you can, develop relationships with banks or other lenders, discuss hypothetical purchase terms with them, and comparison shop. If you have confidence that you can get outside financing for a portion of the business purchase, this will increase your negotiating power with the seller. Think about how you'll divvy up the full purchase price into component parts: down payment, seller note, and bank financing. (Before you even get to this point, you should have cleaned up any credit issues, paid any back taxes, and otherwise established yourself as a good credit risk). See Chapter 9 for more advice on financing the purchase of a business.

STEP 12: BEGIN DUE DILIGENCE AND DISCOVERY

Get a lawyer and accountant to help you if you haven't done so already. Allow several days or even several weeks for due diligence. It can be awkward if the company's employees don't know the company is being sold, but don't let this stop you from learning as much as you need to know to make a good decision. Review financial records, contracts, leases, inventory, customer and supplier relationships, and so on.

STEP 13: GET SELLER TO COMMIT TO A TRANSITION

Don't go through with a deal until you are comfortable that the seller will work with you for a fixed amount of time to show you the ropes, introduce you to his customers and contacts, and answer any questions you may have. If at all possible, your agreement should also state that the seller will not be able to directly compete with you after the sale goes through. In the best of all worlds, the seller will be selling in order to do something completely different, will be willing to work with you for a few months, and will still be owed money through seller financing (that way your interests will be aligned, and he/she will have a vested interest in seeing you succeed).

STEP 14: FINALIZE ANY OUTSIDE FINANCING

Usually an offer to purchase that includes bank financing will be made contingent on actually getting the financing approved. At the point when you are finished with due diligence and have satisfied yourself that you want to go ahead with a negotiated deal, you must finalize your loan application and get approval from the bank.

STEP 15: CLOSE THE DEAL

When outside financing is involved, closing the deal usually takes about 60 to 90 days. In addition to the obvious need for savvy legal representation, think carefully about timing of the takeover, employee transition issues, your own tax issues, and so forth. I also strongly recommend that you allow yourself enough time to finish a cogent long-term business plan *before* you close on the company. Once you sign on the dotted line, you will be thrust into the day-to-day of running the business and putting out fires.

Hmm . . . This Still Doesn't Feel Right

If you have read this far but have a gut feeling that buying a business isn't for you, it's good that you recognize that early. Here are seven warning signs that may indicate you'd be better suited to starting a company instead (see Chapter 8):

1. You don't have sufficient capital to invest.
2. You still can't imagine running a business created by someone else; creating it from scratch offers a type of satisfaction you don't want to miss.

3. You have your heart set on selling a unique product or service all your own.
4. You feel the need to develop your own name as a brand name.
5. You don't want the stress of dealing with preexisting problems.
6. You can't achieve the company culture you desire in your acquisition target because of existing employees or company image.
7. You can't stand working with employees you didn't hire yourself.

Not everyone is suited to taking over an existing business, and there are good reasons for certain people and certain business models to go the start-up route. But do be honest with yourself, and recognize that some of the reasons for wanting to create it yourself instead of capitalizing on someone else's good business idea relate to *ego*. Peg Gaillard, who started a company from scratch and later sold it, admitted: "I always wanted my own business, and I really wanted to prove myself, and do it my way. Now I've got my ego in check. I've learned enough about business to admit that I can't do everything myself."

CHAPTER FIVE

Franchises and
Direct Selling Companies

*I*f you are now convinced of the advantages of starting with an established business, but the market for small companies seems disorganized, potluck, or disparate to you, you might like the order, guidance, and potential financial upside afforded by franchises and direct selling companies. In fact, many former corporate managers who want to go out on their own gravitate toward the structure, proven concepts, and brand recognition of franchises or direct selling organizations (*note:* direct "selling" rather than "sales" is the preferred industry term). This is true today more than ever, as the range of opportunities has grown and become more innovative—the iconic fast food chains are only the tip of the iceberg.

Simplistically speaking, in exchange for an initial up-front investment (considerable for franchises, very minimal for direct selling companies) plus your own smarts and hard work, you get the chance to do business under an established brand name, according to a combination of mandates and voluntary guidelines from the parent company, and you become part of a larger community of business owner colleagues. Because the model is so prescriptive, it's tempting to think you're buying a "business in a box," with all instructions included. But although franchises and direct selling opportunities take some of the guesswork out of small business ownership, they certainly aren't devoid of risk and in fact pose unique risks of their own.

You may have already come to a foregone conclusion about franchises and direct selling that has little to do with an analysis of risk or financial opportunity. You just *know* on a visceral level that franchises and home-based selling aren't right for you.

Nevertheless, *keep an open mind, and don't skip this chapter!* There's probably a lot you don't know about the opportunities that exist and the women who enjoy pursuing them. Did you know, for example, that franchising opportunities exist in a wide range of industries, including advertising/direct mail, eBay auction selling and shipping services, home inspection and renovation, business consulting, art education programs for children, telecommunications, and even business brokerage? Did you know that 74 percent of the American public have purchased goods through direct selling, which is a $97 billion worldwide industry?[1] Or that the proportion of direct sales entrepreneurs who are women has grown to nearly 80 percent?[2] Did you ever consider looking at either a franchise or direct sales as a starter business, after which you'd move on to open or buy an independent company?

This chapter provides a framework for evaluating the various categories of franchises—including new and resale franchises—and direct selling opportunities. It also includes some upbeat stories of real women who have chosen these small business paths and thrived.

Franchising Basics

Let's begin by examining some of the basic elements that make up the diverse business of franchising.

- *Definition.* If there's so much variety, how do we actually define franchising? According to the web site of the International Franchising Association (IFA), "Franchising is a method of distributing products or services. At least two levels of people are involved in a franchise system: (1) the franchisor, who lends his trademark or trade name and a business system; and (2) the franchisee, who pays a royalty and often an initial fee for the right to do business under the franchisor's name and system."

- *Forms of franchising.* There are two primary forms of franchising: product/trade name franchising and business format franchising. The former is simpler and involves the sale of the rights to use a name or trademark in order to distribute products (examples: General Motors distributorships, Exxon stations, Coca-Cola bottling and distribution), while the latter involves a deeper business relationship between the franchisor and franchisee (examples: Krispy Kreme Donuts, Century 21 Real Estate, MaidPro, H&R Block, Children's Orchard secondhand children's clothing shops, Décor and You interior decorating businesses). This chapter is concerned mainly with business format franchises.
- *Industry categories.* You can quickly browse the types of opportunities available on the IFA's web site (www.franchise.org), an industry membership organization. Over 1,000 franchisors in more than 75 business categories are members of the IFA, and among them are most of the names that dominate the American retail landscape. Many other franchisors (an estimated additional 2,000) are not IFA members but may be working toward that goal. "Franchised small businesses today provide jobs for more than 18 million Americans," IFA President Matthew Shay said in a September 14, 2005, press release.[3] The IFA online categories are as follows:

Accounting/Tax Services	Chemicals & Related Products
Advertising/Direct Mail	Children's Services
Auto & Truck Rentals	Clothing
Automotive Products and Services	Computers
Batteries	Construction: Materials, Services
Beverages	Consumer Buying Services
Business Brokers	Convenience Stores
Business Services	Cosmetics
Business/Management Consulting	Dating Services
Campgrounds	Dental Centers
Check Cashing/Financial Services	Drugstores

(Continued)

Educational Products & Services
Employment Services
Environmental Services
Financial Services
Fireworks
Fitness
Florists Shops
Food: Baked Goods/Donuts/
    Pastries
Food: Candy/Popcorn/Snacks
Food: Caribbean
Food: Ice Cream/Yogurt
Food: Pizza
Food: Restaurants
Food: Specialty
Franchise Consulting
Golf Equipment
Greeting Cards
Hair Salons & Services
Handyman
Health Aids & Services
Home Furnishings
Home Inspection/Radon Detection
Hotels & Motels
Insurance
Janitorial Services
Jewelry
Laundry & Dry Cleaning
Lawn, Garden & Agriculture
Maid & Personal Services
Maintenance, Cleaning &
    Sanitation
Marine Services
MedSpa
Metal

Online Auctions
Optical Aids
Other
Package Preparation/Shipment
Painting Services
Paralegal Services
Payroll Services
Pest Control Services
Pet Sales
Photography
Pre-employment Screening
Pressure Washing & Restoration
Printing/Photocopying Services
Publications
Real Estate Services
Recreation: Equipment &
    Supplies
Recreation: Exercise/Sports
Rental: Equipment & Supplies
Retail Stores: Specialty
Security Systems
Senior Care
Senior Living Communities
Sign Products & Services
Tanning Centers
Telecommunication Services
Tools & Hardware
Transportation Services
Travel Agents
Vending
Video/Audio
Vitamin & Mineral
Water Conditioning
Weight Control
Wildlife Management Control

- *Up-front cash investment.* Initial franchise fees typically range from $15,000 to $75,000, but can be as low as $3,000 and as high as $500,000. Newer franchises may occasionally lower or waive their franchise fees, often in exchange for a longer time commitment. The franchise fee is by no means the only up-front investment you will make; a typical franchise opportunity may cost $150,000 to $250,000 in all,[4] including build-out of physical location; purchase of equipment, vehicles, supplies, or inventory; and a couple of months of working capital. The purchase of many franchises can be financed with SBA-guaranteed loans requiring 15 to 25 percent down, and some lenders specialize in loans for specific franchisors.[5]
- *Revenue split.* A percentage of gross or net revenues, often within the range of 4 to 10 percent, is typically paid as a royalty to the franchisor, either monthly or quarterly. It is critical to realize that you must pay the royalty *even if your business isn't profitable.* Theoretically, the marketing help from a well-known brand name and the economies of scale offered by a larger outfit will allow you to afford this extra business expense, but it doesn't always work out this way.
- *Advertising fees.* In many cases, franchisees also contribute an advertising fee (often 1 to 3 percent of revenues) to reimburse the franchisor for expenses incurred in maintaining national or regional advertising campaigns.
- *Training.* It is common for many franchisors to provide initial training in aspects of running the franchise, as well as an operations manual and ongoing support and assistance, but the amount and nature of training vary widely. Franchisors may also provide marketing and promotional materials, area site selection assistance, and insurance coverage to franchisees.
- *Government oversight.* Franchising is not heavily regulated, although a Federal Trade Commission (FTC) regulation requires franchisors to disclose certain information to prospective franchisees before they consummate a deal. Some state governments

regulate franchising: Between 14 and 20 states (depending on how you look at them) require some sort of registration or other formalities before a franchisor is allowed to do business in the state, but some are stricter than others, and not all of them actually review the franchisor's documents. (Those 20 states, according to one expert, are California, Florida, Hawaii, Illinois, Indiana, Kentucky, Maryland, Michigan, Minnesota, Nebraska, New York, North Carolina, North Dakota, Rhode Island, South Dakota, Texas, Utah, Virginia, Washington, and Wisconsin.[6]) For more on the legal aspects of franchising, see the "Researching Franchise Opportunities" section later in this chapter.

Women in Franchising

The lack of recent statistics on women in franchising is deplorable, especially considering how eager the industry purports to be to recruit them, but the latest data available is still very interesting. A study conducted by Women in Franchising, Inc. in 1997 with the help of federal grant money reported that of the more than 320,000 franchise units then existing in the United States, only 10 percent were solely owned by women, while another 20 percent were owned by male-female partners. Franchise Solutions cites that the average annual income for female franchisees in 1998 was $68,140.[7] A 1999 SBA study showed that nearly 50 percent of women-owned franchises cost less than $75,000, versus 21 percent of male-led franchises, indicating that women either prefer smaller franchises or lack access to capital for larger ones.[8] These figures are old, and I suspect that some newer, more appealing franchise concepts have subsequently lured a lot more women to the industry. Two examples mentioned to me as having a higher-than-average proportion of female franchisees were a dating franchise called It's Just Lunch and a wine retailer called Wine Styles.

Kathy Tito, director of product development for franchise referral site Franchise Solutions, Inc., is on a mission to get the word out to women about franchises. She conceived and helped set up a web site called Franchise Solutions for Women (www.franchisesolutionsfor women.com). Tito remarks, "The variety is what surprises folks as they begin their research. Most people just think of food. But informed women do thorough investigations of different industries and what it will mean from a lifestyle perspective before they buy."

While I was writing this chapter, through referrals and personal connections, I located about eight or nine female franchisees to interview for the book. They all had positive stories to tell about their franchising experiences. These women described their experiences with phrases like "great quality of life," "enables me to give back to my community," "ended up really enjoying it," "a much better fit than I imagined," "so much easier to succeed with a known brand name," and "the hand-holding is amazing."

After those interviews, however, I contacted an outspoken critic of the franchising business model, Susan P. Kezios, who heads both the American Franchisee Association (AFA) and Women in Franchising, Inc., and I read a book that she recommended, *Franchising Dreams,* by Peter Birkeland. Both Susan and the book reminded me that for every eight or so success stories, there are probably twice as many or more disillusioned franchisees or downright failures. Susan gave me names of three unhappy women who owned a fitness center franchise, a vitamin supplement retail franchise, and a sandwich outlet franchise, respectively. Having never owned a franchise myself, I wanted to be extra cautious about playing up the positive aspects of owning one.

The dark side of franchising, I came to see, had a lot to do with inaccurate perception or assessment of risk in a particular franchise opportunity. While a poor assessment of risk can doom any business venture, the complexity of the franchising business model and the way it is marketed to potential franchisees suggest that gullibility is particularly dangerous, and research is paramount. Since giving women the tools to evaluate business risk is a recurring theme of this book, I was eager to glean some insights from franchising experts.

Risk Profiles of Franchisees and Franchisors

One expert I interviewed, Scott Evert, director of franchise sales and resales at Sunbelt Business Advisors Network and a serial business and franchise owner himself, noted that in his own experience, he'd found that women were slightly more likely to buy franchises than to purchase independent businesses (perhaps 25 percent versus 10 percent, respectively, of the sales he'd brokered). Could it be that some of these women believed they were taking more calculated risks, and less risk overall, by choosing franchising over other small business opportunities?

In his book *Franchising Dreams*, Peter Birkeland defined the social profile of three categories of franchisees: "neo-franchisees," "disillusioned franchisees," and "sideliners." You must read it for yourself to get all the nuances, but suffice it to say that smart, educated women with prior work experience and some capital reserves (coincidentally, the exact profile of the satisfied women franchisees I'd interviewed) fit right into the "neo-franchisee" category, the most successful of Birkeland's three profiles. According to him, one of the defining characteristics of this group is "the realization that they are but a small part of a system, that their business—no matter how big—is relatively unimportant to the franchisor. . . . Neo-franchisees realize that their profitability is up to them to achieve."[9] This, plus their education, experience, and financial capital, makes them more sophisticated and confident than other franchisees.

Birkeland also quoted a franchise consultant as saying this: "I've found that women and corporate dropouts make the best franchisees. Women make outstanding franchisees because they do what they're told, plus they're well organized, more motivated, and better at supervising and training. Corporate dropouts share many of these same characteristics." However, the consultant added, "these are not the risk takers."[10]

These last remarks may strike you as inflammatory, even sexist. But they do reveal how women are perceived in the industry, as well as how some women (and former corporate types) tend to perceive the risk involved in franchising. What's ironic is that the non–risk-taker who shuns the idea of buying an established independent business in order to buy a brand-name franchise may be taking on *more* risk. As Chapters 3 and 4 try to show, making a brand-new business a financial success is usually harder than maintaining the financial success of an existing one, and even the best brand name and turnkey solution cannot guarantee success.

Scott Evert ranks the risk in acquiring various types of businesses on a spectrum like the one below. His scale is "primarily for novices who want to mitigate risk," and he notes that the riskier opportunities are not necessarily bad ones and could yield higher returns.

- *Least risky*: Buying an existing franchise with cash flow adequate to service the debt and pay the owner a salary commensurate with a highly paid general manager in an absentee situation, with money left over for upside, growth, or a rainy day.
- *Less risky*: Buying an existing, nonfranchised business in a nondeclining industry with all of the above attributes.
- *Fairly risky*: Buying a new franchise from an established brand with 300 to 500 franchisees.
- *More risky*: Buying a new franchise from a franchisor with an emerging brand and 50 to 300 franchisees.
- *Even more risky*: Buying a new franchise from a franchisor with only 10 to 50 franchisees.
- *Most risky*: Buying a new franchise from a franchisor who's just starting out.

Scott also counseled strongly against investing in a franchise that had not gone through the disclosure process in at least one of the states that require registration, unless the investor is a very experienced former franchisee. But he agreed that it's impossible to generalize about risks without examining the industry dynamics, market size, saturation points, prospects of a particular location, and strategic direction (and ethics) of the franchisor organization. To prove this point, he reminded me that "I can find you unhappy and happy franchisees in *every* large organization." As I mentioned before, I encountered mostly happy franchisees. What follows are two stories of women who weren't initially interested in franchising, but have been happy with their choices.

FRANCHISEE PROFILES

"Not Interested"—Stories of Women Who Changed Their Minds about Franchising

New Franchisee

Louise van Osten's worst career nightmare—being downsized and having to go through the humbling experience of meeting with an outplacement consultant—came true. Formerly a vice president in a high-tech software company, Louise feared that any new position she might find would require her to commute into New York City from her home in New Jersey and travel the country, neither of which she wanted to do with two young kids at home. Even so, "They had to drag me kicking and screaming to meet with the outplacement consultant."

It turns out that this wasn't such a bad idea after all, since outplacement consultants offer what most of us lament we don't have access to: midcareer counseling services. Louise was pleasantly surprised by what happened next. The consultant steered her into an entrepreneurial workshop, where she met a franchise broker who helped convince her that buying a franchise not only was not beyond her reach but could help her to meet her lifestyle and income goals. Thus the corporate refugee found a safe haven in franchising. Louise became the 28th franchisee and the first in New Jersey of Foot Solutions, a shoe chain that sells comfort shoes and makes special insoles.

Four years later, the parent company has over 170 franchisees and van Osten's store, based in Ramsey, NJ, is in the top 10 to 15 percent in sales. She chose Foot Solutions in part because it was a newer company and she could help it grow—she actually offers consulting services to the franchisor, who pays her to help other franchisees with retail and business challenges.

* * *

Resale Franchisee

Cindy Canzano had always dreamed of owning a bridal shop. After a 15-year career in the modular home manufacturing business (she began as an accountant and rose to the position of president in a large New Hampshire company), Cindy decided to take the money she'd made over the years and invest it into a business of her own. She was going through a divorce and needed a good income right away. When she found a bridal shop for sale she hoped she'd found both a lucrative business and the answer to her entrepreneurial dream. While looking for a business valuation firm to help her price it, however, Canzano encountered Brace Carpenter of the brokerage firm Carpenter Hawke & Co. in Boston, Massachusetts, who counseled her that the numbers didn't look so good.

To her surprise, he suggested she look instead at a Mail Boxes Etc. (MBE) franchise resale he'd listed in Waltham, Massachusetts, urging her to "look at the numbers!" Cindy flatly refused, wasn't interested. Weeks later, however, when she wandered into the Waltham store, she was impressed with its cleanliness, location, and bustling business, and agreed to review the deal. She bought it for $160,000, mostly in cash up front, and ran the business for nine years, generating an income for herself of about $135,000 per year. Nine years later, when UPS bought out the MBE stores, Cindy had grown the annual revenues of the business by 1.5 times and was able to sell it privately for $350,000.

Today she marvels at how much she enjoyed running that "social, relationship-oriented business," which she declared a "much better fit" than the bridal shop. She also enjoyed the "wonderful income," and laughs that she couldn't have found a job that would have paid as well.

Cindy is now co-owner of an independent consumer electronic business that she bought before she sold her MBE franchise. In 10 years' time, annual revenue at Easy Access Distribution has increased 25 times, from $200,000 to over $5 million. She advises women considering entrepreneurship to "look for a franchise or an existing business, because it takes a good five years to build a business and make any money."

Researching Franchise Opportunities

In general, it's much easier to research franchises than to research independent business opportunities. Yet, because the business model must work for both you and the franchisor, they're complicated, and there's a lot to learn. Your research should encompass both the formal and legal aspects of particular franchise opportunities, as well as financial modeling and the informal research that helps you to assess "fit." Here are a few places to get started:

- *"Franchising Basics: The Official IFA Course."* This online course is offered for free by the IFA on its web site. You can link to it from www.franchise.org or find it directly at www.ifa-university.com. It is comprehensive and helpful, but remember that it is presented by the franchisors' trade association, the IFA.
- *Web sites of franchise consultants, brokers, and franchisors.* After you become generally familiar with franchising, begin shopping around for specific concepts that appeal to you on web sites with databases, listings of franchise opportunities, and testimonials from franchisees. Today, you can do extensive research on companies before ever contacting them. (See more about franchise consultants and brokers later in this chapter.)
- *The franchisors themselves.* If a franchisor knows that you're seriously interested in evaluating its franchise, you can get right down to business. Each party assesses the other—the franchisor

must evaluate you and decide whether to offer you the chance to purchase a franchise, and you must consider whether you will act on the opportunity if it is offered. However, the first contact between franchisors and franchisees isn't always direct—many franchisors outsource some marketing and sales to referral sites and brokers.

- *Franchisor disclosure documents.* The FTC rule requires franchisors to provide prospective buyers with a comprehensive disclosure document called a Uniform Franchise Offering Circular (UFOC), a copy of their standard franchise agreement, the franchisor's audited financial statements, a list of the names and addresses of all franchisees of the franchisor, and any other agreements the franchisee is required to sign with the franchisor. This disclosure package must be given no later than two weeks before agreements are signed or money changes hands.[11] While most franchisors won't share these with you until you've filled out a very detailed questionnaire, you should not hesitate to fill out the questionnaire for a franchise you're seriously considering. (You can also browse documents filed in the state of California without anyone's permission—see www.corp.ca.gov/caleasi/caleasi.htm.)
  - *The UFOC.* Once you've honed in on an interesting opportunity, do not neglect to read the entire offering circular, which is intended to disclose all material information a prospective franchisee might need to make her decision about whether to invest. Too many potential franchisees are put off by the length and legalistic nature of the UFOC and don't read it carefully. You'll probably be surprised by some things you find; one UFOC I read committed the franchisee to "devote substantially all of your effort and time to the on-premises supervision of the Center" (so much for a lifestyle business!). While reviewing a UFOC may feel like a burden, having that much information about a company is truly an advantage. Contrast this to the poor quality or even lack of information you'll get when buying an independent small business, where

conducting due diligence is up to the buyer, and the seller provides relatively little documentation.

- ○ *The franchise contract.* You're expected to sign a contract for anywhere between 5 and 20 years. These contracts are not only long-term, they are simply *long,* and almost entirely in the franchisor's favor. Some feel that locking in negotiated terms for a long period, say 20 years, is in their best interests. On the flip side, some franchisees want to get out of their contracts early. Read them carefully, as some terms may shock you, and they may not be negotiable.

- • *Web sites of franchisee advocacy organizations.* After you've seen the pro-franchisor IFA educational resources, don't forget to check out the web sites set up by groups of franchisees, including the American Association of Franchisees and Distributors (AAFD, at www.aafd.org) and the American Franchisee Association (AFA, at www.franchisee.org). At the AAFD web site you can find the "Franchisee Bill of Rights," "Eight Things to Look for in a Franchise," and the "AAFD Franchisee LegaLine," a network of franchise attorneys who offer special programs for AAFD members. See www.franchisee.org for "The Twelve Worst Franchise Agreement Provisions" and "The Problems Franchisees Face."

- • *Franchise attorneys.* You will need to hire an attorney specializing in franchise law if you intend to go through with a purchase. It's best to wait to do so until you yourself are fairly well educated about franchises; otherwise, you'll be paying top dollar for an education you could get mostly for free. Use your franchise attorney to rigorously evaluate the UFOC and franchise contract of the franchise you ultimately decide to purchase. (In addition to hiring a good attorney to review these documents, you can retain Kezios, Evert, or other industry experts to conduct a business review of the UFOC for about $1,500; they are willing to consult by the hour as well.) A short list of AFA-recommended attorneys can be found at www.franchisee.org/legalresource.htm, and there are links to franchise attorneys on the IFA's web site (do a "Supplier Search" for attorneys on www.franchise.org) and the AAFD's web site.

- *Ratings.* You can find annual ratings of franchises in *Entrepreneur* and *Success* magazines (and on their web sites). These are somewhat subjective and depend on the particular methodology used by the magazines in their surveys.

- *Books.* Many books in libraries and bookstores can provide insight and education about franchises. Some good ones are noted in this chapter and listed in Appendix J.

- *Expos and trade shows.* Many franchisors recruit potential franchisees at annual expositions such as the International Franchise Expo held in Washington, D.C., which typically attracts more than 200 franchisor exhibitors and 20,000 prospective franchisees.[12]

- *Personal interviews.* Another excellent way to research buying a particular franchise is to ask other franchise owners questions such as the ones that follow, some of which are suggested in the free IFA course. Be sure to consider at least two or three different franchisors so that you have some basis for comparison. If you make the effort to call or visit 15 to 20 franchisees from each of the franchisors you are considering, you'll learn a great deal.
  - If you had a chance to do it again, would you buy another franchise from this franchisor?
  - Are you making as much money with this franchise business as you expected you would make?
  - Are the people who run the franchise company honest and fair?
  - Do you feel that the franchisor cares more about (1) selling products and services or (2) selling franchises?
  - What are the principal challenges confronting your franchise organization and what is the franchisor doing to address them? Do you believe these tactics will work? Why?
  - What is the *second* best franchise in this industry, and why?

FRANCHISING SUCCESS STORY
Cash Flow Relief, Bulk Discounts, and Flexibility

It took Julie Marcus by surprise when she realized that she could continue running her home-based small business and solve her biggest business problems by becoming a franchisee to a company called Proforma. (It had been even more surprising, and atypical, when she'd placed her resume on Monster.com and Proforma came knocking on her door, actually recruiting her to do just that!)

Julie's background was in advertising and "incentive premiums," promotional logoed merchandise that companies special order for events and employee perks. Julie had done this work for an advertising agency and later for a promotional product/corporate gift company, but she'd been laid off while pregnant and therefore had limited options. Eventually, Julie struck out on her own as a distributor of promotional merchandise.

However, doing this solo meant that she had to front the manufacturing cost of the products well before she'd get paid by her customers. Establishing credit with multiple suppliers was very hard, and Julie was using a personal credit card to finance the orders. Pretty soon, Julie had maxed out the amount of business she could take on simply due to lack of funds.

At that point, a couple of friends in the business mentioned to her a franchise company called Proforma that not only sold promotional merchandise but also printed business forms and supplies. Julie looked into the opportunity and was favorably impressed. The parent company paid for her to travel to their headquarters to check them out, and provided her with one week of intense training once she signed on. Because of her background in the industry, she was able to negotiate a good deal with Proforma and keep her start-up costs to a minimum.

Six months after Julie had gone out on her own, in March 2004, she was in business again—the *same* business, essentially—as a Proforma franchisee. Julie is remarkably independent in her business. She works from her house. She decides her pricing and chooses her suppliers. The difference is that she has an infrastructure to fall back on. For that, she hands over 9 percent of gross revenues. But best of all, with the new setup came an end to her cash flow worries. Proforma pays all her vendor bills for her up front, and provides her the buying power of a large company. Julie can (but doesn't have to) buy from Proforma's preferred suppliers, who offer prices that can be much less than the wholesale prices she was able to negotiate as a new, independent business. She is responsible for sales, but Proforma helps out a lot with promotional campaigns. Proforma will also prescreen multiple potential clients to set up sales appointments for her, at a cost of $50 each.

In her second full year of business, Julie booked $615,000 in revenue (a little more than double what she did in her first year) and achieved profit margins of more than 10 percent, and her income surpassed her most recent corporate salary. Julie's goal for year three is $750K in sales, and then $1 million the year after. As for her working hours, she currently puts in about 30 to 40 hours per week, whenever she wants to (she's an early morning person). She recently brought on a former colleague to work with her as a sales rep; by adding staff, she aims to both grow the business and keep it humming if she takes time off occasionally for vacation or personal responsibilities.

Julie, who "loves independence," resisted the concept of a franchise initially, and that held her back. But her husband, who took an undergraduate course in franchising while they were both students at Babson College, helped convince her that franchises offer a proven business model. Reflecting on her choices, Julie says: "It's funny, I didn't think my story was that big a deal—I just did what I had to do in order to make things work and in order to survive. So it's nice to see that others do think that I've done something pretty cool."

Franchise Consultants, Brokers, and Referral Sites

If you're comparing franchising to buying an existing independent business, you'll find that the industry is well set up to attract and educate newcomers (whereas the world of independent business buying can seem lonely and intimidating). Industry experts are divided as to whether this is a good thing. In my humble opinion, one of the best things that the industry has to offer savvy potential buyers is the wide availability of free, no-strings-attached counseling services to prospective franchisees—so long as you don't rely on them to make your decision for you.

Among the players are *franchise referral sites*. Their business model is to collect advertising revenue from franchisors and to provide online research resources and information. They claim to be impartial, but often they're operated by or affiliated with franchise brokers, who are paid on commission. Still, they can be great sources of knowledge. Examples of referral sites include:

- Franchise Solutions (www.franchisesolutions.com).
- Franchise Solutions' related site, www.FranchiseSolutions forWomen.com (their parent company also owns broker site FranchiseBuyer.com).
- Franchise Gator (www.franchisegator.com).
- Be The Boss (www.betheboss.com).
- Your Franchise Consultant (www.yourfranchiseconsultant.com).

Franchise brokers, whether they call themselves consultants or brokers, and whether they represent sellers or buyers, are paid a commission by the franchisor if and when you buy a franchise. The organized, one-on-one counseling that's available to serious purchasers typically includes a phone interview; a questionnaire about your experience, interests, financial resources, and personality; analysis of the questionnaire; creation of a profile of you as a potential franchisee and a discussion of that profile with you; and finally, a short list of franchises you should consider contacting.

One of the big advantages of using these services is that you can narrow down your prospects and be more efficient with your time, but one disadvantage is that they only market the franchises they've agreed to represent (according to Evert, Sunbelt represents about 85). Often, the consultants will help you contact the franchisors, evaluate any offers, and walk you through the purchase process. The following companies are franchise brokers:

- FranChoice (www.franchoice.com).
- FranchiseBuyer (www.franchisebuyer.com).

- FranNet (www.frannet.com).
- The Entrepreneur's Source (www.theesource.com).
- Sunbelt Business Advisors Network (www.sunbeltnetwork.com)—a worldwide, franchised business brokerage that sells both independent businesses and new or resale franchises.
- VR Business Brokers (www.vrbusinessbrokers.com)—a worldwide, franchised business brokerage that sells both independent businesses and new or resale franchises.
- BizBuySell (www.bizbuysell.com)—a listing service for brokers, as well as an advertising service for franchisors. This service partners with FranChoice for one-on-one consultations.

You can also check the web sites of independent business brokers, many of whom represent franchise resales.

Once you spend time working with a consultant or broker, you should remember that *you're not obligated to follow through*. Brokers realistically expect a certain portion of the people they counsel to just walk away, or to postpone a decision. "The buyer owes the broker nothing except courtesy, frankly," says Kathy Tito of Franchise Solutions, Inc. "Women tend not to hesitate to speak with consultants and ask for help, so you should publicize the fact that this is free." Women looking for midcareer guidance and options, take note!

Warning Signs

However, do be careful! Smart women can be swayed by their hearts rather than their heads, especially when a slick group of professionals exists to woo them. Michael Seid, the author of *Franchising for Dummies*, said in a July 2001 article in *Entrepreneur* magazine, "Many prospective franchisees take brokers' recommendations as gospel, deferring to the brokers' experience. Don't let this be you."[13] Seid, who owns a franchise advisory firm, is most wary of your missing the right opportunity just because it's not on a broker's client list. Scott Evert of Sunbelt also suggests "avoiding any brokers that begin hawking franchises without inquiring about your needs, monetary and otherwise."

Susan Kezios concurs that potential franchisees must be wary of the slick sales pitch. As an advocate for franchisees (not franchisors), she has testified as an expert witness in Congress many times. Her goal is not only to help women (and men) avoid bad contractual deals, but also to introduce pro-franchisee changes to state and federal legislation governing franchising. She herself is a former franchisee and former employee of a franchisor. As you read the positive, happy stories about women franchisees in this book, counterbalance them with the following warnings and frank talk:

- *The goal of franchisors is low-risk expansion on your nickel.* "Companies franchise in order to use other people's money and energy to grow their business idea," reminds Susan. The business model is designed to shift investment risk from the parent company to the franchisees, although, to be fair, the parent company still must deal with the daunting challenges of competition, product differentiation, and quality control. Franchising may be a good growth strategy because of the faster speed to market. Still, "A franchisor's definition of success and your definition of success are very different," says Susan.
- *Owning a franchise is like renting an income stream for a fixed period of time.* While it may provide a good income while you're running it, you cannot count on being able to sell it for what you think is a fair price (though you can't guarantee such an exit with an independent business, either). When franchises are renewed, the terms may change. Your unit's royalty rate may go up to 8 percent from 5 percent, and you or a new owner may have to pay another franchise fee. You can't sell based on a multiple of your own historical cash flows unless you secure certainty on the new rate from the franchisor. Plus, you'll need permission from the franchisor to sell to a particular buyer. Susan advises: "Never think beyond the term of the contract. You must be able to leave at the end of the term with finances and emotions intact."

- *Don't expect the franchisor or the broker to help you estimate your earnings potential.* Only the earnings claims that are made in the UFOC can legally be shared by franchisors and brokers to indicate future earnings, and many UFOCs share only sales information, not profits. Franchisors are afraid of sharing the unaudited financials from their franchisees because of the risk of lawsuits from unsuccessful franchisees who may claim that they were "promised" to make a certain amount of money. Disclosing historical financial results of their franchisees is at their sole discretion, and most don't do it. Susan believes that "this is a glaring omission in the laws governing franchising," and she is lobbying to change that. (By contrast, Scott Evert thinks that there are good reasons for those laws, and he recommends that you create cash flow projections for yourself after interviewing other franchisees and lenders.) To get an idea of what you might expect in a food, retail, or service franchise, check out *How Much Can I Make? Actual Sales, Expenses, and Profits on 137 Franchise Opportunities* by Robert Bond. Bond says on his book cover, "The single most important task for a prospective investor is to prepare a realistic cash flow statement that accurately reflects the economic potential of that business."

Despite these warnings, many female franchisees I've talked to have raved that consultants help ensure a good fit between franchisors and franchisees. Hsiu-Lan Chang (mentioned in Chapter 2), who bought a FastFrame franchise and is thriving, had great things to say about FranChoice's services. Cindy Canzano appreciated that her broker steered her away from a lackluster independent business and toward a franchise that he knew was making good money.

Perhaps the best advice is to avoid the sales pitch cycle until you've explored and researched many of the opportunities available to you. If you find you're interested in a newer, seemingly innovative franchise concept, be especially diligent in reviewing the history of the franchisor company before you let anyone pressure you to buy it. The bottom line: Do your homework, negotiate the best deal possible, and go into franchising with your eyes open, and you will hopefully have a great experience.

Is Franchising Right for You?

This is a complicated, personal question, but here's a way to start answering it: Rather than focusing on the odds, *focus on the fit*. Consider that franchising or direct selling might fit you. Ask why you may have ruled out these categories and whether you should reconsider. Is it the "not invented here" syndrome? Maybe it's a resistance to the idea of what seems like (or blatantly is) a greedy money-making machine. Perhaps the merchant mentality feels pedestrian. Some people are deterred by the high start-up costs. Being skeptical is a healthy business habit; in fact, women are experts at using their gut instincts and intuition to support or rule out jobs or businesses. But if you're dismissive without doing any research, you're not doing yourself any favors.

Before you take the plunge, you need to ask yourself why you'd invest in a franchise rather than buying an independent business or starting one yourself. There are pros and cons, and you may be more suited to one or the other. Ask yourself some key questions: Will you be comfortable abiding by the franchisor's rules of doing business? Or are you too independent-minded? You'll never have complete creative control over the business. Some people actually find that to be a relief, but some don't. Realize that you'll have to share your revenues with the franchisor; consequently, being frugal and watching your margins is very important. Because you've paid an initial franchise fee and are committed to paying an ongoing royalty stream, you may have more capital at risk than do entrepreneurs who start from scratch or buy independent businesses. Aside from that, your franchisor may not survive today's competitive economy if it doesn't continue to innovate.

However, the advantages are compelling: not having to reinvent the wheel, not being completely alone in your business, starting out with a brand name that has clout. For example, a Snappy Auctions franchisor told me that the eBay sellers who work through him get 20 to 30 percent more for their goods because buyers know that they're buying through a nationwide, trustworthy outfit. You may also find it easier to get financing—or the franchisor may provide some financing to your business. Whether franchising is right for you also boils down to what you want to do every day, and whether you can find a business category and opportunity that lights your fire.

Direct Selling: Franchising's Poor Cousin

Okay, so maybe you like the franchise model but aren't ready to commit the money or the time. You'd like a "business in a box" but you don't have tens of thousands of dollars to invest, nor can you imagine keeping full-time retail or office hours. Let me introduce you to what I consider franchising's "rich little poor cousin": the clever, respectable direct selling industry of today. Right off the bat, I will tell you that yes, I *am* talking about the Tupperware model—I am, but I'm not. A lot has changed since the days of the traveling salesman, the original Avon lady, and the Tupperware parties of the past century.

Direct selling basically means the marketing of products and services to consumers face-to-face, away from fixed retail locations. It's promoted as being cost effective and offering more personal service and more detailed information about the promoted products to consumers. Signing on to be a sales consultant for a known brand name in a particular territory is a very accessible way to enter the world of small business.

Do you have modest expectations for your business? Direct sellers are essentially independent business owners who take on relatively little risk and enjoy a lot of flexibility in how they run and grow their businesses. In contrast to franchises, start-up costs and legal commitments are minimal, and evaluation and approval of new sales reps is pretty easy and uncentralized. In fact, you'll be asked to recruit new sales reps, and their sales will contribute to your compensation. You can contemplate doing direct selling on the side while holding down a 9-to-5 job or being a stay-at-home parent (and many people do, most of them women). However, because you're encouraged not only to sell as much as you can but to recruit others to sell the same products, the sky's the limit when it comes to what you can earn. That said, for most people it's a modest return, a personal-income business that may be only supplemental.

Similar to the way that franchising has certain negative connotations for some people, so has the concept of direct sales or home parties earned a bit of a negative stigma. Unflattering associations that come to mind include pyramid schemes and multilevel marketing scams. Yes, scams do exist. But before you rush to judgment and dismiss all direct sales opportunities, take the time to read about some of the innovative, appealing ones that exist today.

Don't forget to pay attention to the word *sales*, because selling is what it's all about. Whether you're selling kitchen implements, software, scrapbooks, or clothing, it helps to be extroverted and sales-oriented, and a passion for the products is a must. In fact, passion for the products can turn an otherwise shy or administrative type into a very effective, non-pushy sales consultant.

Clara Bitter of Asheville, North Carolina, who is now a representative for a direct selling company, is a former franchise owner and was once a start-from-scratch entrepreneur. From 1986 to 2000 she opened or purchased a total of six TCBY franchises in western North Carolina. She sold four of them in 1999 and the other two in 2000, and is positive about her experience and the financial returns. She is now a seller of Worth clothing, a line of luxury women's apparel sold by appointment (see more about Worth below in the section about trunk shows).

When asked to compare her experience owning franchises to that of building a business as a direct sales consultant, Clara says, "The big difference between the two is the time factor. I worked so hard during those years with TCBY, and then wanted to slow down. For women who want to start on a shoestring and build something part-time, selling from home is a great option."

Direct Selling Industry Resources

The Direct Selling Association (DSA, at www.dsa.org) is the leading national trade association of firms that manufacture and sell goods and services directly to consumers. The DSA has just under 200 active members, all of whom have to apply for membership, undergo a rigorous approval process that involves complying with the DSA's Code of Ethics, and share financial details with the industry body. The DSA's "2004 Direct Selling Growth & Outlook Survey" reveals that direct selling industry sales in the United States exceeded $29.5 billion in 2003 (a sizeable fraction of the world total), with more than 13.5 million direct sellers nationwide. The biggest sales regions are the South (36 percent of annual U.S. sales) and the West (24.8 percent). Today, 79.9 percent of all U.S. direct sales people are women, and 85.1 percent of all U.S. direct sales people work fewer than 30 hours per week.[14] There must be something appealing about this choice, if *10 million* American women are doing it.

The Direct Selling Women's Association (DSWA, at www.dswa.org) is a fairly new international association that works to unite women in direct selling around a shared vision of personal and financial success. The site offers online teleclasses (for example, on recruiting and team coaching), educational articles (for example, "The Art of Bookings"), and selling tips, all designed to help members with their network marketing, party plan, or other home-based businesses.

Another industry referral site and online resource is Direct Selling Opportunities (DSO, at www.directsellingopportunities.com), which, along with its companion site Direct Sales Women (DSW, at www.direct saleswomen.com), represents 80 home-based selling opportunities.

Party Plan Sales Model Examples

Each direct sales company follows one of the two basic types of sales strategies, person-to-person or party plan; occasionally they do both. The traditional direct selling model is person-to-person (for example, someone who sells CUTCO knives or encyclopedias), and this still accounts for about 69 percent of all direct-to-consumer sales.[15]

The advent of home party sales in the 1950s (e.g., Tupperware) gave direct sellers the opportunity to demonstrate products in a home setting and socialize at the same time. Whereas selling Tupperware used to be one of the few socially acceptable ways that women could pursue a career in business, today party plan selling is a deliberate choice for many women who want to be stay-at-home moms with a part-time job on the side—as well as for some who want to pursue it full-time.

Most direct selling companies operating on a party plan model require that you buy a start-up kit (for as little as $150 to $200) that contains a sampling of products and marketing materials. As the sales consultant, you're responsible for coming up with names of people to invite to events or shows for the products, and you schedule and host such events. When you sell the products, you're entitled to keep a certain percentage of the revenues (typically 25 to 40 percent—it varies by company). There are two types of compensation plans: single-level and multilevel. With multilevel compensation, you are rewarded for finding new sales consultants for the company. Not only do you receive a portion of their subsequent sales as a commission for recruiting them, but you also rise in the hierarchy of sales people as you do so, and you take on some management responsibility for your team.

Some innovative party plan direct selling companies today include:

- **Creative Memories**—offers hands-on workshops and scrapbooking products for organizing and presenting photos, memorabilia, and stories in photo-safe albums (www.creativememories.com). See the feature article about rep Dianne Eib later in this chapter.
- **The Pampered Chef**—sells high-quality kitchen products through in-home shows (www.pamperedchef.com). See also Doris Christopher's autobiography, *The Pampered Chef: The Story Behind the Creation of One of Today's Most Beloved Companies*. Her company was bought by Warren Buffett.
- **Tastefully Simple**—a direct seller of convenience-driven gourmet food mixes and kits through home parties, catalog sales, corporate gift accounts, and web site sales (www.tastefullysimple.com). Tastefully Simple's primary line consists of items that can be prepared with just one or two additional ingredients.
- **Discovery Toys**—offers educational books, developmental toys, software/computers, toys, games, and videos for children (www.discoverytoys.com).
- **Longaberger Baskets**—one of the largest direct selling companies, Longaberger offers baskets, pottery, wrought iron accessories, handbags, and prepared foods through home shows (www.longaberger.com). Tami Longaberger runs this family busi-

ness, started by her father in 1973. She was named head of the National Women's Business Council in May 2005.

- **WineShop at Home**—consultants help others host easy and fun at-home wine tastings and represent an exclusive line of custom labels, wine gifts, and accessories for both consumers and corporate clients (www.1800wineshop.com).
- **The Furnished Garden**—sells gardening accessories and decorations (www.thefurnishedgarden.com).
- **The Happy Gardener**—sells products encouraging environmentally conscious gardening (www.thehappygardener.com).
- **Pottery at Your Place**—onsite pottery decorating parties and workshops (www.potteryatyourplace.com). This early-stage company was mentioned in Chapter 3.
- **High-end women's clothing lines:** The Carlisle Collection (www.carlislecollection.com), The Worth Collection (www.worthny.com), Etcetera clothing (www.etcetera.com), and Juliana Collezione (www.julianaonline.com).

DIRECT SELLING BUSINESS PROFILE
Do What You Love, and Get Others to Do It, Too

There's no doubt about it: Dianne Eib loves what she does. At a very basic level, Dianne's business is about asking women in her community, "Are you caught up with your pictures, ladies?" She then urges them to attend a "Get Together" or "Ladies Day Out" workshop to get their photo albums, scrapbooks, and baby books organized. As a Kingston, New Hampshire–based consultant to fast-growing direct sales company Creative Memories, Dianne gets paid to facilitate these gatherings, to teach women how to preserve and organize their photos and mementos, and to sell them the supplies they need to do it. Dianne has created her own small business within a big business, and she's passionate about what she does.

She remarked that seeing the devastation of Hurricane Katrina and other big storms in 2005 reminded her of how valuable her workshops and products are to people: "The loss of one's house and possessions is completely devastating, but the survivors must feel a particularly keen loss over their ruined photographs and scrapbooks, which aren't usually replaceable."

A former field sales rep for Hallmark, Dianne spent 14 years servicing both specialty card stores and mass market retailers. She left Hallmark to become a sales consultant with Creative Memories in 1993, around the same time she had a new baby. She invested just $165 in a kit of supplies. Twelve years into it, she still works part-time (an average of 20 hours a week, 46 weeks per year) and is among the top 1,500 sales consultants among 90,000 worldwide at Creative Memories. Her current annual earnings contribute significantly to family income and are close to the same pay she got at Hallmark, but unlike her job there, she's able to work part-time and from home. However, direct selling does not offer a guaranteed salary, and consultants at Dianne's level must also be prepared to front a few thousand dollars at a time for inventory.

A good portion of what Dianne earns comes from multilevel commissions rather than her own first-level sales. Dianne says a full two-thirds (around $18,000 annually) of what she makes is in the form of commissions from women she's recruited to be consultants for Creative Memories. Dianne, who's reached the "senior unit leader" level, is responsible directly or indirectly for 75 sales reps joining Creative Memories (14 of whom she recruited herself and the rest of whom were recruited by the other 14). That said, the company does offer bonuses to consultants who order regularly every month, and Dianne says that consistency is one of the keys to success in direct sales. In other words, it may be tempting to take the busy summer months off, but it's better for business to keep on plugging year-round.

As a "senior unit level leader," Dianne gets several opportunities per year to travel to meetings and conferences where she can network with other consultants—not to mention the fun she has with the groups of women who regularly join her get-togethers. She thrives on the relationship and networking aspect of direct selling.

So, who is best suited to run this kind of small business? Dianne says anyone can do it, but that many successful consultants are smart women who need to contribute to family income and "want great things for their kids but want to be there for their kids too."

Trunk Shows: Highbrow Direct Selling

Earlier in this chapter, I mentioned that direct selling and home parties have a bit of a negative stigma. Well, there's a subindustry in direct selling that recoils from using the word home party because it might turn off its highbrow customers, not to mention its own salespeople. In fact, most of the companies operating in this subindustry are not members of the DSA (one exception is Tanner Companies, which owns the Doncaster line). I'm talking about the world of fashion trunk shows. Although the vocabulary is different (*private* or *semiprivate appointments* instead of *home parties*, and *agency* as a synonym for *sales consultant*), the idea is substantially the same.

There's a big business in selling designer fashions privately, in women's homes, especially in smaller cities and suburbs lacking many high-end shopping outlets. High-end women's clothing lines, for which an average price per piece might be $150 to $400, include the Carlisle Collection (www.carlislecollection.com); The Worth Collection (www.worthny.com); Etcetera clothing (www.etcetera.com); and Juliana Collezione (www.julianaonline.com). Customarily, sales consultants or "agencies" send invitations four times a year to quarterly showings of their collections. They book private or semiprivate appointments for the week or two that they have the line's sample set displayed in their homes. They then order, take delivery of, and personally hand-deliver the clothing to their customers. Customer profiles include working women who appreciate the convenience of one-stop shopping for their business wardrobe, hard-to-fit affluent women who love personal shopping attention, and anyone particularly fashion conscious with money to spend.

Sales consultants are encouraged to buy and wear the clothing themselves to help promote it; typically, they themselves are part of the social strata from which they're recruiting potential customers. Clara Bitter, a Worth consultant, states matter-of-factly, "There's a good bit of pressure from the company to sell, sell, sell, but if you can stand the heat, it's a darn good business to be in." On the "Career Opportunities" section of the The Worth Collection web site, the pitch goes like this: "You've spent years building relationships; friends, other women who admire your taste, your style and your integrity. Isn't it about time you began to profit financially from all that effort?"

And profit they do, especially if they work at it as a full-time job. Here's a hypothetical example of a hard-working, relative newcomer, based on insight from some industry experts. Let's call her Yvonne Adams. Yvonne becomes a consultant for Luxury Designs. She holds four shows per year in her home, setting up 60 appointments each time based on 200 invitations sent, yielding 30 actual buyers. She manages to sell 100 pieces per show (an average of 3.3 per paying customer), or 400 pieces per year, at an average sale price of $300 per piece. (These numbers aren't far off; brand-new consultants are reportedly encouraged to sell 75 pieces per show). That's $120,000 in gross revenue. Yvonne gets to keep 25 percent of gross revenues; that's $30,000 per year, before expenses of $1,500 per year on advertising and mailing supplies and another $1,500 per year for Luxury Designs' seasonal collection materials (binders with design, fabric, and other information, and other supplies from the home office). So a net of $27,000 is her take-home profit, plus a perk of steep discounts on clothes for herself. Yvonne hires "committee helpers" who assist her with private appointments, but they're compensated by getting a discount on the clothing, not by the hour.

How much is Yvonne working for her $27,000 per year? By my account, probably no more than 100 total work days per year, or about 40 percent of a full-time workload. On a quarterly basis, I estimate 2 days to develop the mailing list, 2 days to mail and stamp the invitations, about two weeks (10 days) to call customers to set up appointments, one week (5 days) to show the clothes basically full-time, and about two weeks half-time (5 days) to receive and deliver the clothes. Add a day for administrative tasks and cleanup, and that's 25 days per quarter, or 100 per year.

Thus, on an annualized, full-time basis, this is like earning close to $70,000 per year, at the entry level. Not bad, especially considering that she works in concentrated periods four times per year, which can be scheduled whenever she wants to work, except for the designated four weeks of private showings. As Yvonne builds up her network or puts more time into it, it's conceivable that she could become one of those superstars who sell many hundreds or even thousands of pieces per year and enjoy six-figure incomes. Yvonne is in business for herself, but she's virtually guaranteed not to lose money if she can sell at least 40 pieces per year. Her one-time start-up costs were minimal—maybe $2,000 to buy display equipment and racks if new (see one vendor at www.robertham.com), much less if she found them used.

If you're one of those women who's always wanted to own a retail clothing store for women, take note. Contrast Yvonne's experience to setting up a retail boutique from scratch. Ann Hunter, who for over 18 years has run the popular store Lucy Ann's in Asheville, North Carolina, with partner Lucy Stella, cautions that setting up a high-end boutique today could easily cost $100,000 up front for physical build-out, inventory purchase, and marketing. The two owners elaborate, "Then you've got your monthly rent, your travel expenses to go to 'market' to buy your inventory, and all the other costs of doing business." Not only that, but you yourself have to make all the buying decisions; you don't have a home office in New York picking out designer collections for you to carry in your shop. You may need to get outside financing to make it work. And then, what if your store can't make it? What do you do with unsold inventory? We've all seen and felt sorry for merchants who open up with a bang and close down a few months later when they can't make a go of it. I'm not trying to discourage you—only to open your eyes and suggest that you compare your dream of selling clothes at your own store to selling clothes from your own home.

The trunk show model is not a get-rich-quick scheme, by any means, unless you're the parent company (and even then, it's a business with risks, like any other). In fact, if you're not selling the highest of high-end merchandise in your trunk shows, you can't make very much money doing it. Take as an example children's clothing sold through trunk shows. I know a woman who makes just $800 per year doing it; her real motivation is getting a discount on clothes for her own children.

Final Thoughts on Businesses in a Box

If you're highly entrepreneurial and fiercely independent, you should question whether franchises and direct selling opportunities provide the right fit for you. They tend to be best for women who like and appreciate a certain amount of outside guidance and assistance. However, if you don't want a day-to-day business partner, yet don't want to start and run a business all by yourself, a franchise may be a good idea. The corporate structure is like an arm's-length business partner, without the interpersonal relationship challenges. Does either description hit home? If so, and if you really need income (maybe you lost your job or got divorced), take a good look at franchising, and be sure you've done a good cash flow analysis. If you're just looking for a way to get back into the fray and build a business with minimal investment and flexible hours, consider direct selling.

Whether you're looking at big-time, medium-time, or small-time opportunities, be prepared to wade through a lot of sales pitches before you determine what you really want to spend your time doing. The advantage to having so much information at your fingertips is also a disadvantage—it's easy to become overwhelmed with options and to end up doing nothing.

CHAPTER SIX

A Piece of the Pie—Working for, Consulting for, or Partnering with Existing Business Owners

"*I* don't know what I would've done without you." This phrase, a pleasure to hear if directed toward you, is an indication that your work is appreciated and valued, perhaps even unexpectedly so. In the small business world, after a business owner finally reaches out to hire an employee, engage a consultant, or bring on a partner, she often realizes that filling that gap in the company's capabilities was absolutely necessary and should have been done a long time ago. Small businesses are notoriously short-staffed, and business owners tend to shoulder all the responsibility for longer than is really healthy. What this spells for you: *opportunity*.

If you're not ready to buy or start a business, don't have the funds, or just want to test-drive the small business world before you buy into it, consider becoming that indispensable employee or consultant first. Small businesses, especially those owned and run by one or two individuals, almost inevitably need improvement, modernization, financial reorganization, sales efforts, better corporate record keeping, or other specialized help. Owners often don't feel up to doing it themselves, preferring to maintain the status quo as long as possible. They may not be recruiting or asking for help (the biggest obstacle for you), but if you can identify those in need and find a mutually appealing way to help, you may be surprised at what you get in return—a good job, a great experience, maybe even a chance to buy into the company at some later date.

You'll find that most small businesses have never written a strategic business plan, because it's hard for the founder/owner to rise above the everyday challenges to think about, let alone write about, the long term. This is where your fresh perspective and skills come in. A business plan can galvanize even the sleepiest of small businesses into purposeful action and growth. So can new sales opportunities—are you willing to work on commission? You may also face fertile ground if you're a former corporate attorney—many small businesses need to update their corporate minute books, review their forms and contracts, find ways to protect their intellectual property, create employee handbooks, and so on. The ways to improve small businesses are often very obvious, and you can use the professional business savvy that you've developed during your stints in the more mature corporate world to help transform and grow them.

Compared to being a business owner, working for a small business as an employee or consultant requires less of your time and money and carries less responsibility, so it may be less daunting and more achievable to you. Be aware, however, that compensation may be capped and may never be as lucrative as an owner's, and you won't have complete independence to run the company the way you wish. If you really enjoy consulting, and you also want that financial upside and owner's independence, you can also consider using the ideas in this chapter to establish yourself as a professional consulting firm—a small business unto itself. But whichever way you look at it, working with existing business owners is a collegial way to join the small business economy—you'll never be alone.

PROFILES OF JOBS IN SMALL BUSINESS

Temporary Placement Turns into 13-Year Career

When Cindy Barrett went back to work as a single mom when her kids were ages 8 and 10, she went to a temp agency looking for part-time employment, despite the fact that "everyone told me I couldn't get satisfactory intellectual stimulation from a part-time job." Determined to find something interesting that also paid the bills and allowed her to work 20 hours per week (she later increased that to 40), Cindy took a job doing data entry at a family-owned oriental rug and carpeting business in Massachusetts.

Two weeks after she began entering data in the company's new computer system, one of the four owners asked her, "Can you handle business management?" and her real career there began. She became the director of marketing soon after and has stayed more than 13 years with the company, which has grown from nine people and $1 million-plus in sales to 45 people and over $7 million while she's been there.

Cindy points out that small business owners seem to have better luck with temporary employment agencies than they do recruiting through web sites like Monster.com, which can lead to an overwhelming flood of resumes. Says Cindy, "Some of the company's longest-lasting employees came from temp agencies, and they were all women."

Cindy, who once owned a small landscape design business, loved the small business world but at the end of the day wanted a paycheck and preferred being an employee to an owner—at least while her children were still at home. She found that her job provided tremendous flexibility to allow her to manage her nonwork responsibilities. Cindy's still an integral part of the team at her company, but she may decide to go back to business ownership in the future, possibly by starting a consulting or importing business.

* * *

A Cool Small Company Finds Huge Demand for a Temporary Position

HELP WANTED

Part-time (15–20 hours/week) administrative and marketing opportunity in a five-year-old family vineyard and winery business. Fill in for the founder during her maternity leave. No promise of permanent employment. No benefits. No dedicated office space. Prefer elite college graduates and MBAs. $20/hour.

Is this job for real? This employer wants to hire an experienced advanced degree holder on a temporary, half-time basis with no benefits and perks for the equivalent of less than $20,000 per year? The average total first year compensation for graduates of the top 30 MBA schools was $136,569.[1] Do you think there will be many takers?

In fact, Courtney Kingston of Kingston Family Vineyards (based in Portola Valley, California, and Casablanca Valley, Chile), interviewed over 40 candidates who applied for a job of this description, although her ad was a little less blunt. To seek possible candidates, Courtney went straight to the places where bright, underemployed women lurked: the Stanford Business School Alumni Association's Women's Directory and the Palo Alto/Menlo Park Mothers' Club. Courtney ended up hiring a UCLA MBA, Stanford undergrad mother of two who wanted to reenter the workforce in a manageable way now that her youngest is in kindergarten. I interviewed Courtney about a week before she started contacting applicants, and she subsequently told me that almost all of the candidates were "professional women/mothers seeking flexible, challenging, interesting work that fits with their parenting lifestyle."

It's too early to say whether the woman Courtney hired will have a permanent place in the company (or will get a raise), but it seems like a good fit in the short term. Courtney found a very qualified candidate to fill a gap in the company at minimal cost, and the woman she hired got her foot in the door in an interesting industry, with an opportunity to renegotiate terms after a few months of proving herself. (Read more about how Courtney started her business in Chapter 7.)

Does it make you uncomfortable that small businesses pay just what they must to get good people to sign on? that they may not offer health insurance? that they pay for certain types of work by the hour, or on commission only? If so, try to get over your hang-ups, or go back to the corporate world, where compensation and benefits are more predictable. The small business world is not necessarily less generous (in fact, it can pay better), but rather more meritocratic and market-driven. Try to think of this as being business oriented, not unfair or discriminatory. When you evaluate opportunities to work or consult for small businesses, especially on a short-term basis, be prepared to be paid for specific work and results rather than to be put on payroll with a steady salary and benefits.

Put yourself in the place of a working business owner, and you'll probably see that she's shouldering a lot of risk personally and can't afford to make big hiring mistakes. Being asked to prove yourself is only natural in a small, growing business. Personally, I don't think the women in the two previous examples felt taken advantage of in the least. But they did make a conscious decision to take a risk, betting that the initially low-paying job would lead to something more.

If there was a well-known, organized way for women to find rewarding part-time or temporary jobs in small businesses, demand for it would surely be high. During the course of researching this book, I came across a few innovative matching services and temporary job databases for skilled female (and male) professionals who aren't interested in full-time corporate employment, including Mom Corps, Aquent, and The Hired Guns (see note 1 for Chapter 4). While I enthusiastically support all of these efforts, they are more likely to fill project and skill gaps in corporate America than in the small business world, which needs the services of this talented and underutilized labor pool just as urgently. I'd like to see small businesses compete for this talent (you), too; there's certainly enough talent to go around.

Common Consulting Opportunities

Consulting opportunities in small businesses often parallel what the owners are already doing (but don't have enough time for) or should be doing (but aren't good at), such as business management and planning, financial management and planning, aspects of administration that relate to a company's growth, and sales. Other sure areas of opportunity relate to modernization and use of new technology. As previously stated, the ways to improve a small business are often obvious.

But business owners who actively seek out consultants to help them are a rare breed; more typical is the busy business owner who is continually saying and thinking, "I really should focus on that one of these days." Whether the business owner takes the initiative to hire help or you take the initiative to offer it, the following ideas are a typical shopping list of what many small businesses need (or need *more* of). As you read the list, do you recognize any of your own core competencies?

Business Management

- A written business plan.
- Facilitation of strategic planning sessions with company owners and managers.
- Help setting up an advisory board.
- Business worth evaluation.

Financial Management

- Financial projections and modeling; goal setting.
- Accounting systems design or customization (e.g., setting up an intuitively useful chart of accounts, tracking project profitability, better management of accounts receivable and payables).
- Outsourcing payroll.
- Analysis of working or expansion capital options; assistance with bank negotiations or application preparation.
- Analysis of pricing strategies.

Administration

- Personnel benefits analysis (i.e., best practices in similar small companies).
- Recruiting help (especially salespeople).
- Business insurance issues.
- Relocation to a more suitable office location.

Sales and Marketing

- Sales and new business development (including recruiting, hiring, and training).
- Competitive market research.
- Creating or improving the company's web site.
- Trade show strategies.

Legal Counsel

- Corporate record keeping—minute book, stock ledger, state filings.
- Employee handbook.
- Review of contracts and business forms.
- Filing for trademark or patent protection.
- Documentation of verbal understandings between partners.
- Preparation for due diligence by outsiders.

You may choose to offer a wide breadth of these services if you have the know-how, in which case you can keep yourself very busy in just one business at a time, or you may want to drill down in a particular area, making your services available to several clients at once.

The biggest challenge will probably be landing your first consulting clients. The very best place to start looking for work is through your own connections and networks of friends, family, and former colleagues and business associates. As long as you present yourself well and offer a low-risk, results-oriented product at a competitive price, it should be relatively easy to get your foot in the door somewhere. Unsure if someone will pay you what you think you're worth? Just ask—you may be surprised! Many small businesses will be willing to part with $5,000 or $10,000 (or more) to get a better big picture of their company's business health or to tackle some business tasks they've been procrastinating doing. If you can explain how your expertise can contribute to the bottom line, chances are good that they'll be receptive. Beyond that, learning how to make a good living as a consultant is an individual art that you will have to fine-tune for yourself; luckily, there's a low barrier to entry. See Appendix J for two books that can help you develop a consulting action plan and research the relevant legal and tax issues.

CONSULTANT PROFILE
Setting up a Professional Practice to Consult for Small Enterprises

In contrast to the modestly compensated temp job, the work that Meave O'Marah provides as a part-time CFO and management consultant garners about $150 per hour. Five years ago, Meave left her job as vice president of strategic planning and director of finance at Advantage Schools, Inc., a national charter school developer and operator, to start The Owner's Representative, a one-woman consulting firm in Dedham, Massachusetts, "dedicated to providing management expertise to small and mid-sized businesses and non-profit organizations that are experiencing or planning for growth." Meave is now working a 40-hour work week in four days, and most of her clients book regular time with her on designated days, so her schedule is quite manageable. Her clients haven't yet outgrown her and are very happy with the arrangement, and Meave hasn't had to do any marketing to get new clients since 2000.

Although Meave's first plan was to consult for venture-backed, high-growth start-ups, she realized early on that the biggest, steadiest demand would come from smaller, self-financed or debt-financed companies, where control remained in-house rather than with a large board. What The Owner's Representative does for its clients ranges from accounting system customization, budgeting, and financial projections, to strategic business planning, best practices contracting, and benefits recommendations. In addition to the expertise provided by Meave on a weekly basis, her clients typically have someone on staff to handle the day-to-day bookkeeping, an outside accounting firm to do just the year-end taxes and audit, and an outsourced payroll service. They can get along quite well like this for years, up until the point when they must hire a full-time, experienced CFO (estimated by Meave to be when they are at about $5 million in revenues). And although Meave gets paid well for her big-picture financial contributions, the small businesses get a good deal as well.

"What people don't realize is that working for small businesses can be very lucrative. You can make decent money because businesses can pay you more per hour than they can pay a full-time hired hand. They get the equivalent of a very experienced person, but it costs them less because they just pay for the time they really need," Meave explains. Of course, it took her a few years to reach this level of business and financial success, and she relies on her domestic partner for health insurance, but by now she has built a very successful career wholly on her own terms. She has surpassed her salary at her previous job, works nearby, travels considerably less, and has in the same period of time enjoyed starting a family.

Why did Meave leave her old job to go out on her own as a consultant? There were many reasons. She had always wanted to start something on her own. She was tired of working 50 hours or more per week, plus travel. The glamour of dealing with big boards filled with multiple stakeholders had worn off.

But perhaps the tipping point was when her father died unexpectedly and she wanted to take some time off. "People at work were stunned that I would take three weeks' leave," she complained. That's when she decided she had had enough of the grueling pace of venture-backed start-ups. She took two months off to rest and regroup, and then started her company, trying out various consulting concepts before seizing on her successful formula. She is now about to hire another consultant to work with her, and she hopes to offer him a buy-in agreement after two to three years if it goes well.

Consulting as a Stepping-Stone to Business Ownership

Have you been considering joining a friend or acquaintance in his or her existing business? Why not consult for the business for a while to see whether it is a good fit? If, like me, you view a business consulting opportunity as a possible stepping-stone to business ownership, you'll want to approach opportunities selectively and analytically. It's all right (and even preferable) to be up front with potential consulting clients about your interest in possibly buying or buying into their business. If that's your end goal, you may not want to waste your time working for a company that has no intention of allowing someone to buy in. Conversely, if you are approached by a business owner to possibly join forces, you can buy yourself some time to evaluate that opportunity and help the business owner by agreeing to a consulting project on professional, arm's-length terms. The business owner should be able to hire you for a short-term project with no further obligations, and vice versa. While neither of you have anything to hide in such an up-front relationship, both of you stand to gain a lot by getting to know each other better before contemplating being business partners.

How do you find a situation like this, if one hasn't presented itself already? Maybe you have a friend, cousin, or former classmate who started a business and is looking for a business partner or just for some help. Perhaps you've been looking at companies for sale through intermediaries, and after finding a good fit, you negotiate an option to buy in after you've worked with the company for a certain period of time. Occasionally, people who set themselves up as professional consultants become so captivated by a particular business that they want to consider working there or buying a stake. There is no typical way to find a consulting project that could turn into an ownership opportunity, but the advantages to this approach are obvious.

Prospective business buyers often find themselves wondering: Wouldn't it be great if I could just work here for a while to see what it's really like? This might be possible; even though most business owners are looking to sell 100 percent of their companies and exit the business within a fixed period of time, some businesses use brokers to find new partners or investors.

That said, in a typical buy-sell situation, you're given a chance to read a prospectus on a company, visit the business, meet with the owners a few times, and then—*if* you've made an offer to buy and it has been accepted—perform due diligence on the subject company before going through with the purchase. Time is usually tight, and invariably you don't learn the full story of the company until after you take it over. This formal purchase process is an arm's-length one, and it assumes that you will be taking complete control of the company and can subsequently change it however you see fit. Having the control to make changes when the business becomes your own makes up for the lack of earlier insight about the way the business was being run.

Although brokers will usually counsel sellers that it's not in their best interests to display their dirty laundry to a potential purchaser, if you can talk the seller into an inexpensive consulting deal, it can be good for both of you. Maybe the company has been on the market for a while, and maybe the broker and the owner are both willing to look at creative alternatives, like allowing a new owner a trial period or selling only part of the company.

In a recent pay-to-join telephone conference organized by Business Valuation Resources,[2] Jeffrey Jones, of Certified Business Brokers in Houston, Texas, told the audience, "If most brokers would admit their true success rate of selling the micro to small size businesses . . . [they'd tell you that] only about 25 to maybe 30 percent of those businesses actually sell." Jones also revealed that most businesses his firm sells have been on the market for 7 to 10 months, and that his firm "walks away from three out of four businesses that we talk to about selling their business for the very reason [that] either they've got nothing to sell at all, or the seller thinks [they're] worth a lot more money than we do."[3]

While this may be surprising to you, even depressing, think of it as *an area of opportunity*. Some of those businesses that seem to have nothing to sell, and those that are under delusions about how valuable they really are, can be built into viable businesses over time with outside help in the form of consulting.

Take, for example, the case of a talented tote bag manufacturer I once met who wanted to sell her business and move on to something else. Her business was not worth much because (1) it was wholly dependent on her as the only product designer, and so the company's biggest asset was about to walk out the door; (2) she was selling door-to-door to little boutiques, which was time-consuming and kept sales volume very low; and (3) she was having the bags sewn by local seamstresses rather than overseas, and therefore her costs weren't competitive. As it was, she had nothing much to sell. But imagine if a savvy businesswoman had helped her out for a few months, creating and implementing a business plan that called for outsourcing aspects of product design, finding a large corporate client who would place repeat orders in larger quantities, and trying out an overseas manufacturer. At that point the company would have a future as a stand-alone entity, and if you'd been the consultant who helped it get to that point, you could have either received cash fees for your services or a chance to buy in at a rate that reflected the value of your contributions, or both.

Many older business owners care so much about their companies that they want to transition out of them very slowly, even over a period of years. This can work to your benefit. No matter how good your business ideas are for modernizing a company and improving its business prospects, the person who really knows the industry and the customers is the existing owner. If she is willing to entertain an agreement with you that begins with consulting and perhaps morphs into a chance to take over the company one day, you may have the best of both worlds: an owner willing to open the books and show you the ropes, and a long period of time in which to use your modern business smarts to evaluate and improve the business in question. Just make sure that you're being paid fairly for your consulting or employment contributions so that buying in is an entirely separate transaction.

Buying a 50–50 or Minority Stake in a Business

If you decide to buy into a company and continue operating it together with its existing owners, some words of advice are in order. Avoid partnering with very controlling personalities. Learn how to diagnose the company's business health in order to carefully define how you will participate in its future growth, and articulate your respective roles with the other owner(s). Realize that the transition from consultant to part-owner will significantly change the dynamic with the other owner(s), and do everything that you can to ensure a good start to your new partnership (see Chapter 10 for more on partnering). Be fully cognizant of the risks and liabilities you are taking on. And on a positive note, realize how fortunate you are to be able to lean on and learn from the other owner(s) in the first few months or even years.

It may sound like an oxymoron to become a business co-owner in order to gain control over your work and life, when you really don't have control over the company because you're not the majority owner. But there's a difference between having voting control and being controlling. Likewise, if partners are able to respect each other's roles, responsibilities, and job titles, someone who does not own a majority of shares can have a strong influence over a company's day-to-day business operations.

Knowing what sort of business situation you're walking into is critical to both making a good first impression and making a valuable impact. There's a good chance that the Main Street business you want to consult for or buy into needs to make some fairly significant changes to thrive and grow to the next stage, but the owner is in the dark (or in denial) about what needs to be done. Michael Watkins, a professor at Harvard Business School and the author of *The First 90 Days: Critical Success Strategies for New Leaders at All Levels*, would call such situations "realignments" (as opposed to start-ups, turnarounds, or "sustaining success").

Rather than being in dire straits, which would force small businesses to close down or declare bankruptcy, the small business is more likely to be ignoring some subtle problems that, if left untreated, could bring the company down. Watkins would say that "success consists of avoiding disaster."[4] Usually the basic business model is strong, but the business is being run too casually. For example, inventory levels might be way too high or the inventory overvalued. Financial records may be sloppy or nonexistent. There may be a high level of uncollected receivables, and the company may not stand a good chance of being paid back. The company could be facing a legal liability or insurance-related threat that has largely been ignored up until this point. A company may be unknowingly plagued by a dishonest employee, or perhaps there is a poor fit between employees' skills and the jobs they are performing. It may be out of compliance with the terms of a loan or credit line without anyone realizing it.

Small business owners are a naturally defensive lot, and their employees tend to be as well. They are used to operating with very little oversight. So, while businesses that are in need of realignment present good opportunities to business-minded women looking to make a large impact on a small company, making that impact without stepping on anyone's toes is a delicate dance. But the rewards you can expect as a successful new business partner or executive for hire are not only recognition and gratitude, but solid financial results, and either more money in your pocket or a growing equity position.

AUTHOR INSIGHT
Jumping into a New Role at an Existing Company

Although you may have left larger businesses to avoid big-company politics, don't expect your new career in small business to be devoid of them. This is especially true if you decide to consult for or partner with an existing business owner. You'll be the new kid on the block for a while, and the quicker you can sort out the political landscape, the better. I learned this lesson myself when I not only consulted for a small business but, seven months later, bought a stake in it and became its president.

As a consultant, I'd been in the comfortable position of being hired to analyze the company and plan for its future. I presented the company with my advice and even helped implement many of my recommendations, including upgrading the accounting system, introducing pricing reform, tweaking the sales commission structure, and so on. During this period, the final control over how to proceed rested with the current owner, but she agreed with nearly all my suggestions.

Around the time that I invested in the company and became its president, I led the relocation to a new office, and I chaired a team meeting with all employees to share and discuss the business plan I'd written with the owner's input. It was an exciting meeting and a great day, and we all knew that the company was successfully poised to enter a new phase of growth. I'd been hired to be the new leader in charge of that management transition, but my business partner was still firmly in charge of product development and sales.

By quantitative measurements, the business continued to improve tremendously in many areas—revenues, profits, and gross margins were all much healthier than before I'd begun working with the company. In addition, we'd expanded our sales staff, and we were beginning to develop new business opportunities. I felt that my transition had been successful.

But there was trouble in paradise, trouble I didn't even see. In hindsight, I can see that I caused some of the trouble. For example, I continued to analyze the company and try to set it straight (like I'd done as a consultant), when my partner really would've liked me to stop analyzing and fixing and instead just go after new sales opportunities. Also, I'd been too timid to fire a poorly performing accountant, and I hadn't dared to reassign existing employees to more appropriate jobs, because everyone had been hand-picked by the founder, with whom I was still working. Therefore, when problems arose, I seemed to be complaining about them without having taken the leadership to solve them myself. In some ways I'd been too brash, and in others not nearly brash enough. But my grace period was long over, and despite the successful realignment, politics and perceptions did me in.

My significant contributions to the company basically went unappreciated, and that was painful. I'd always been the one who cared more about finances and the bottom line, but my partner was the passionate type who mainly cared about delivering high-quality products. I agreed to sell my stake back to her—for a good profit, I might add—and I left the company with a lot of mixed feelings.

In retrospect, even though I recommend that partners take a long-term view, I think that the 90-day window is a good rule of thumb. If you haven't shored up political support for yourself by the end of three months, things might all go haywire, and you might lose your job (or your stake in the business). This principle applies equally to small business consultants, midmarket business owners, and Fortune 500 CEOs.

(Continued)

123

AUTHOR INSIGHT *(Continued)*

If you're thinking of becoming a shareholder in an existing company, and especially if you're the business or financial person, heed these four warnings:

1. Recognize that a change in dynamic occurs when you become an owner instead of a consultant (or a former colleague or friend).
2. Don't be timid in making staff and outside adviser changes, so long as they fall into your designated scope of responsibility. Educate your partners and colleagues that this might occur early on, when your colleagues are willing to give you the benefit of the doubt. You'll need a coalition of supporters (both employees and advisers) who will support the organizational changes you need to make.
3. Focus much more on relationships with your partner *and* other employees than you might be inclined to do. As harsh as this sounds, do not assume that your partners and colleagues trust you. Plan on earning their trust all over again now that the dynamic has changed. Remember, you're the new one.
4. Don't make yourself expendable. You are vulnerable as a minority shareholder, and therefore you want to be perceived as a vital, needed part of the team. In my case, I had done such a good job at fixing the company's business problems that I was no longer needed as desperately as I had been at the beginning. One thing I could have done to mitigate this vulnerability would have been to go get a new high-profile customer right away—within 90 days.

In many ways, working with an existing business owner as an employee, consultant, or partner, is an ideal situation. You don't have to shoulder all the responsibility yourself, you always have someone there who knows the history of the company, and you may be able to cover for each other in terms of job hours or function, thus giving you lots of flexibility. But it is the small business choice that can be most filled with intrigue, since you are stepping into a living, breathing company and creating a role for yourself there. Be sure to read Chapter 10 for more tips on how to avoid clashing with partners and co-workers.

CHAPTER SEVEN

The Family Business Advantage (for the Lucky Few)

*T*he headline in the November 13, 2005, business section of the *St. Paul Pioneer Press* was "Not Your Typical Dream Job," and the opening of the story read like this:

> As an MBA graduate and a former management consultant, Stacy O'Reilly has achieved a career goal few people ever desire: she is the owner of a pest-control business. The allure of running Plunkett's Pest Control, a family-owned business based in Fridley, MN, has proved more attractive than pursuing a livelihood with a Fortune 500 company.

When I called Stacy with no prior introduction, she took my call immediately and launched right into the story of how she'd turned her childhood dream of taking over the family business into reality. She is now the 51 percent owner of Plunkett's, having bought the business in a complex transaction from her parents, who have bowed out completely from day-to-day management. Before finalizing the purchase two-and-a-half years ago, Stacy spent two years working in the business, first as a technician (well, yes, exterminator) and then as a supervisor. Now she's the president and owner of the company, which enjoys annual sales of $15 million and is the 38th largest pest-control business in the nation.

Stacy stressed how fortunate she felt not only to have had a family business to consider joining, but also to have avoided the internecine battles that are so common in generational transitions of businesses. Her only sibling, a brother who, sadly, passed away in early adulthood, was a great sales type but never expressed interest in running Plunkett's. No aunts or uncles were involved, either.

Aside from her luck, I was struck right away at how well Stacy fit the "smart woman" model of this book. First, she really was bright, and she'd gone about getting valuable corporate experience early in her career before thinking of working in a small business (she was a consultant for McKinsey for over four years, then worked for a couple of years each at two different mid-sized companies, one that made and sold water filters and the other in grocery delivery services). Second, it was evident that she wasn't hung up on prestige or gender roles. Her company exterminates pests, after all—not exactly a glamorous or feminine vocation. Third, and perhaps most important, Stacy had been a good planner.

Luck and Good Management

During my early business career at AT&T, I had a wonderful mentor and boss who used to smile and say, "What we need here is a combination of luck and good management." When we achieved a business success that was due in part to some outside factor, Jim would turn to me and say, "You see? Luck and good management."

I immediately thought of this maxim when I reflected on Stacy's accomplishments, because she certainly did owe them to a combination of luck and good management. Some people may feel that the expectations and complications that go along with family businesses are a burden, but just having that option in the first place is a lucky advantage that few people can even consider.

What really sets Stacy apart, however, is more good management than luck. She planned carefully for this transition, and it has paid off. In her application to Dartmouth's Tuck School of Business, she stated frankly that her aim was to use her MBA skills to buy the family business, although with her classmates she didn't exactly flaunt her intention to go into the pest-control industry. "I'm not sure that I confessed it at the time," Stacy admits. "I didn't share my ulterior motives with McKinsey, either." Yet everything she did was a building block, a nugget of experience that she planned to draw on later.

Incidentally, Stacy always wanted to make the company a little more female-friendly, too, and she's made some strides already. Five of her 130 technicians are now women (up from zero), and she's hired a female Ph.D. entomologist (who's raising a young son) on a four-day-a-week basis. Stacy, on the other hand, puts in long days and full weeks, and says she wouldn't have even thought of having kids during the two-to-three-year transition period.

The family luck and good management maxim also applies to Courtney Kingston, whom I mentioned in Chapter 6. After getting an MBA at Stanford and working in consulting and media companies, she and her brother collaborated to start a vineyard and winery business utilizing her family's agricultural land in Chile, land that had been in the family for many generations. Each generation had been charged with coming up with a way to hold on to the farm; for many years, the answer had been dairy and beef cattle.

Courtney had been exposed to the wine industry while working as a consultant at Deloitte & Touche, and when she came up with a plan to lead the family into the wine business, she had to get buy-in from other family members (capital contributions, too). Their start-up branch of the family business is now five years old, and their excellent *Wine Spectator* ratings are a sign that the young company is maturing as well as its wines. Courtney is the managing partner of the business; two brothers, a cousin, and her father are on the board. Courtney especially values her dad's help; he works with her on a day-to-day basis. On a personal note, after several travel-intensive years when she was setting up the business in Chile and California, Courtney enjoyed being grounded for a while last year when she had her first child. She values the flexibility that her business offers her.

The lesson to be drawn from the examples of these two lucky and hard-working women is this: If you have close relatives who own a business, but you've never given it a second thought, now's the time to do so. Family businesses can offer both job and business ownership opportunities. And the owners already know you, which can be a great advantage.

The fact that Stacy and Courtney's experiences were privileged may give you the impression that I'm focusing on an elite slice of the family business world, but the model applies equally well to more ordinary family companies. For example, a woman I know in South Carolina took over her family's laundry and dry cleaning business after working with her father for several years in a transition period. That business had supported her own family in her youth, and it had been owned by her grandfather and his father before that, sustaining them during the Depression and World War II. Joanne worked in the laundry in the summers as a teenager and filled in from time to time in various jobs as a young adult. After being around the business for so many years, she knew it from the ground up, and she became second-in-charge to her father in her early twenties. While her father was still alive, together they grew to seven outlets and later sold all but one. When he passed away, she inherited the remaining outlet and was able to run it almost absentee (a manager was in charge of daily operations) while pursuing other professional interests. When Joanne was in her late 50s, she sold the business to another family; they still owe her a few installment payments but have continued to modernize the business and increase revenues.

Transitions in Established Family Businesses

Most family business founders dream of passing their business down to the next generation, but few achieve that. According to Anne Francis, who runs the Family Business Resource Center in Topeka, Kansas, less than one-third of family-owned businesses survive the first generation, and only half of those make it into the third generation.[1]

Although the traditional pattern used to be that a father brought his sons into the family business, today it's just as likely to be a daughter. A 2003 Raymond Institute/MassMutual survey of American family businesses revealed that 34 percent of family firms expect the next CEO to be a woman, and that 52 percent of survey participants employ at least one female family member full-time.[2] Stacy O'Reilly says that she and her father both always knew that she would be the one to take over the business, because she had the right skill set and the desire to do so. It's not that her father was exceptionally modern when it came to gender roles, but "he was a very pragmatic businessman."

Robin Abber's parents, who in 1973 started a retail wallpaper and interior design business in Newton, Massachusetts, called The Four Walls, also came to the conclusion that their best chance for leaving the family business in good hands was to groom their daughter for the job. Robin did not set out to run the family business, but when her mother, Sheila, asked her to fill in for an employee who'd had a skiing accident, she signed on and never looked back; now she owns the company. Sheila recently passed away, and today Robin feels an even keener passion for the family company as well as an obligation to continue running it. Her father, who's still alive, retired several years ago.

Anne Francis points out in her book, *The Daughter Also Rises: How Women Overcome Obstacles and Advance in the Family-Owned Business,* that adult daughters have certain advantages when working with their fathers in the family business, in part because of their socialization. She notes that "Women have been socialized to accept authority from men, especially their fathers," and states plainly: "Daughters seem to have less need than sons to force their father out of the business." While overcompliance with authority is a negative trend, she says that some compliance is not a bad thing.

> An excellent working relationship between father and daughter can develop when she is willing to cooperate with and learn from her father rather than compete with him, to intuit and respond sensitively to his concern about losing his power and position to the next generation, and to have patience and wait for the business rather than grab for it.[3]

Daughters' talent for relating to older family members probably extends to mothers and other relatives in the family business, too.

Newly Established Family Businesses and Husband-Wife Teams

Family businesses don't start out being labeled as family businesses. In the beginning, they're just small, privately held concerns. They become "family businesses" usually by virtue of being around long enough to be inherited by or sold to others in the family who are experienced enough and of age to take them over.

Anne Francis lists five stages in the life cycle of family businesses:[4]

1. The entrepreneurial business.
2. The growing business.
3. The transitional business.
4. The mature business.
5. The dying business (obviously, one wants to avoid stage five!).

Often, when a businessperson seeks to buy a small private business on the market, she will be buying a "transitional business" owned by a retiring owner who had no family members to take it over. It thus ceases to be labeled as a "family business," unless its new owners transition to family members down the road. Deborah Moore of Sunbelt Business Advisors Network told me that "the average entrepreneur will sell or buy a business every five to seven years." Businesses that turn over that fast don't last long enough to take on the typical characteristics of family businesses.

But what about the millions of family members who manage private businesses together? For example, the mother and daughter who sell and develop real estate together; the husband and wife who buy restaurant franchises together; the sisters who start a home accessories business together. In a way, they're family businesses too, just without all the baggage and history that come with their storied cousins. What these nascent family businesses have to grapple with are run-of-the-mill partnership issues, albeit with a twist. Relatives running businesses together have even more at stake than do unrelated business partners, and they should plan as carefully (or more carefully) for a successful partnership as would unrelated parties.

Sometimes the motive for husbands and wives to be in business to-gether is to share financial burden or risk, even though just one of them may actually run the business on a daily basis. Sometimes husband and wife share ownership and management control on a 50-50 basis. Other couples decide up front that the business will employ both of them, but one of them is the chief executive. All of these models may present ad-vantages to women (and men) desiring flexibility.

I have a friend whose husband started an IT consulting firm about six years ago. They both own shares in the company, but he's the boss. The wife has worked with her husband in some capacity the whole time, but her level of responsibility and involvement has varied according to a few different factors: childbearing (she took extended periods of time off while having their three children), other professional interests (she scaled back her involvement dramatically while pursuing another busi-ness for a while), and need (she tends to drop everything else when his business goes through a crisis and needs backup). Their particular arrangement works well for their business and their family, but it's con-tingent upon her being willing to report to him.

Are Family Businesses More Family-Friendly?

One simply can't generalize about family businesses being family-friendly. Some are, and some aren't.

In family businesses that promote a culture that's welcoming to women (flexible hours, part-time arrangements, generous maternity leave, women in high-level positions), the advantages to working there can be numerous. Your family member colleagues know you, and if you've had a chance to prove yourself to them, they know what you're made of even if you encounter a day, a month, or a year when the juggling act is especially difficult. Family business colleagues may even be willing to help you jug-gle certain responsibilities by virtue of being relatives. Relatives are much more likely than colleagues to pitch in and babysit for a while, pick a child up from school, or help you through a personal crisis.

However, in larger, older family businesses, traditional gender stereotypes can be poisonous. A woman may have big ambitions for playing a role in the family business, but her presence may be viewed as temporary, and her advancement may be prevented by a glass ceiling that is particularly dated and behind the times. These situations call for an extra amount of forethought, planning, and caution before you decide to join them.

Whether the family business is established or new, family relationships certainly complicate the workplace. I agree with Anne Francis's advice: "In order to be successful, you need to be as certain as possible that your involvement in the business will be supported, not undermined, by other family members. Competitiveness, jealousy, and unresolved differences between family members have sabotaged many businesses."[5]

How to Evaluate Opportunities in Family Businesses

Your decision to join the family business or partner with a spouse or relative is one of the most important decisions you'll ever make. You should be rational and thoughtful about it. Some inadequate reasons for joining a family business are:[6]

- A belief that there will be less pressure to perform.
- A hope that you'll have more authority there than at another job simply because you're a family member.
- A desire to prove something to your parents (or whoever the owner is).
- The feeling that you're obligated or indebted to the family and must fulfill that real or perceived obligation.

The trouble with family businesses is that they usually require a pretty big commitment, and there's often no turning back once you join or take over a family company—because you've become an owner.

Francis suggests that you ask yourself a series of questions[7] to assess both your own work and career needs as well as the needs of the business. If there's a good match, that's a green light to proceed—cautiously. Ask yourself:

- What do you need most from your work (e.g., recognition, challenging work, money, satisfying and stimulating work, job security, etc.)? Can you find that in the family business?
- Have you communicated your career needs to those in charge of the business? If so, what was their reaction?
- Why are you considering employment in the family business? Are those in charge aware of your reasons?
- What job do you want? What strengths would you bring to it? What would you hope to learn and accomplish in the job?

Then try to answer these questions about the business:

- How much do you know about the family business?
- What problems does the business currently face? What will it take to address those problems?
- Why should the family business hire you? Are you the best person for the job?
- Does the business need your skills? How could you make a positive contribution to the business?

There can be several different options for getting involved in the family business. On one end of the spectrum is simply a job, and on the other end, an ownership stake (or complete ownership). Some women use a brief stint in the family business as a stepping-stone to do something else on their own. You'll have to decide what, if anything, is the right answer for you. Then, you'll have to negotiate for the role you want.

Negotiate in a Professional, Arm's-Length Manner

Just because you're related to the decision makers in the family business doesn't mean that you have to interact with them like you would at a family Christmas party. On the contrary, you'll serve your own interests (and theirs) better by conducting yourself in the professional manner you would use with unrelated parties.

Most of the advice in Chapter 4 about negotiating to buy a business and doing due diligence is applicable if you're taking over a family business, although you'll have to go about it with extra sensitivity. Although you'll be unlikely to work with a business broker in a family business purchase, you'll still need your own professional advisers (a lawyer, an accountant). You should still conduct due diligence as best you can, interview company executives, write a business plan, generate financial projections and a valuation analysis, and put your final agreements in writing in whatever contractual means are appropriate. The negotiation phase is also the time to do some worst-case scenario planning if other family members will still hold stakes in the business, while conflict and difficult situations are still theoretical (see Chapter 10 for tips). Do absolutely everything you can to ensure a professional, orderly transition of the family business, because you have a lot to lose if you don't—your treasured relationships with family members.

Further Resources

This chapter only touches on the rich subject of family businesses and succession planning. In addition to the books listed in Appendix J, some other resources to explore include the Family Firm Institute in Boston, Massachusetts (www.ffi.org). This is an institutional, professional membership organization for family business advisers, consultants, educators, and researchers. This site can point you to other helpful resources, including:

- An extensive list of family business centers and related organizations worldwide (see www.ffi.org/resAlphaDir.asp).
- An extensive list of member consultants and speakers (see www.ffi.org/otnConsSpeak.asp).

- A list of colleges, universities, and professional schools that have programs in family business. Among the many in the United States are Babson College, Baylor University, Elizabethtown College, Kellogg School of Business at Northwestern, San Francisco State University, Tulane University, University of Connecticut, and UCLA.

Two magazines you may find useful are *Family Business* magazine (www.familybusinessmagazine.com) and the *Family Business Review*, a quarterly scholarly publication.

CHAPTER EIGHT

If You're Sure You Want
to Start a Business

We are members of the same club. You can only get in if you have
founded a company from scratch and built it into something you are
proud of. The only initiation is the hell you create for yourself. And
only you know when you have finally been accepted.

—Anita Brattina, *Diary of a Small Business Owner*[1]

A t the end of Chapter 4 I gave a list of valid reasons why entrepreneurs decide they're compelled to start a business from scratch. They
boil down to a conviction that they *must* pursue a particular dream,
product, or company culture. Jumping on someone else's bandwagon
won't do. Or maybe it doesn't exist. And for many, the whole point of being an entrepreneur is experiencing the fun and pride in creating a business idea or product from scratch.

This chapter is for those women. I trust it is different from the count-
less books out there for women and men that offer an outline for a business plan along with several chapters of cheerleading and examples of
famous entrepreneurs. You know the ones I mean—they claim to be
"the only book you'll ever need" to start a successful business. I disagree
that any one book will give you all the insight you'll need, which is why I
freely recommend other books in this one.

In the early stages, what you need to know is what it will really be like to start your own business. Then, once you know what business you're in, books that offer specific industry knowledge can be especially useful. Ideally, you'd have a friend or relative who'd done it before and could tell you what to expect. However, she's probably forgotten what it was really like! The more time that has passed since someone founded a company, the less accurate her recollections will be.

For a realistic day-to-day account that doesn't airbrush the past, check out *Diary of a Small Business Owner* by Anita Brattina. It's a bona fide diary kept over 11 years by a woman who left an unsatisfactory but well-paid job in corporate America in the 1980s to start a firm in Pittsburgh called Direct Response Marketing. In this brutally honest and original diary, she tracked and shared her daily personal and business ups and downs in a way only a woman would. While the story of Direct Response Marketing is not particularly unusual, the way she tells her story is.

Like most women business founders, Brattina used very little start-up capital or outside financing. Her company grew to a respectable size, though not huge (at the end of the book it had topped $1 million in annual sales), and it was profitable. According to Brattina, she supported herself with the proceeds from her company (that is, made her mortgage and car payments, paid her bills for food and electricity). And it's a good thing that she desperately needed that income because her need provided a strong incentive to make the business work. But some years, some months, it was really dicey. Cash flow issues loomed large.

Here are Anita Brattina's words on day one: "More important than what I was going to do in my business was what I was not going to do. I was not going to work for someone I did not respect. I was not going to have my job description changed without my consent. I was not going to have to worry about corporate politics. I could finally work hard and get rewarded with a fee for my effort. Simple. Pure. I am ready."[2] Can't you hear yourself cheering for her in the background—as you write your own resignation letter?

When You Feel a Mandate to Start a Business

Many entrepreneurs feel a mandate to start a business, and in their heart of hearts they know they're not going to change their minds about starting versus buying or joining. Moreover, for many women entrepreneurs, the entrepreneurial experience is more about the journey than the destination. There's something validating about getting from point A to point B all by yourself, and point B doesn't always mean profits and financial success. It may simply be creating something that someone wants to buy. That can feel pretty great. For many women, focusing on the bottom line isn't nearly as exhilarating as proving themselves to customers and others in the outside world.

After interviewing and working with many women who have started businesses from scratch, I can honestly say that many of them, maybe even a majority, are not natural managers or business types. They are instead passionate about a particular product or service, be it a fashion industry niche, a line of baby food, yoga mats, or educational services. They become businesspeople almost accidentally, and they are more apt to take risks because they don't fully comprehend those risks. Ironically, this is sometimes the quality that allows some of them to achieve great success.

On the flip side, natural managers and women with practical business talent can fall victim to analysis paralysis. They obsess over what may go wrong, and they analyze until they're blue in the face before ever entering the marketplace. Many become too leery of the risks of starting a business from scratch to actually pull the trigger and do it themselves. Another problem that analytical types run into is that they often lack the passion and chutzpah that creative, nonbusiness types have in abundance. And obviously, the problem that passionate types run into is that they sometimes lack business sense.

One of the goals of this book is to infuse some analytical business ideas into the minds of the creative, nonbusiness types, and to infuse a little passion into the minds and hearts of the analysts. Why? Because if

141

you're going to start a business and grow it large enough to support you, you'll need both. This chapter is devoted to making sure that you get off to the right start.

Confirm That You Want to Work in the Business You Start

When you come up with your business idea, find a way to do a quick reality check to see whether you *really* want to do what you *think* you want to do. Remember Madelyn Yucht's success story in Chapter 4, buying a human services staffing company? Remember how she spent a day at a different type of business (a day spa) to help her come to the conclusion that she wanted to be in a service business instead? What I didn't mention in that chapter is that Madelyn had learned the hard way to perform a reality check early on.

Years earlier, she'd decided to start a business with her friend Judy. It was the mid-1980s, and the personal computer industry was just beginning its boom. Madelyn and Judy recognized the huge business opportunity this trend presented, and they decided they'd open a computer store to sell PCs to consumers. So for a full year, while holding down other jobs, the two of them did intense market research. They looked at possible locations. They analyzed industry profit margins. Then, at the suggestion of their husbands (businessmen both), they went out to interview 15 store owners who were just far enough away not to be competitive, to see what their keys to success were.

They quickly found out that the successful computer store owners fit one of two profiles: (1) They were computer geeks, whose expertise added significant additional value to the business; or (2) they were marketing experts, who really knew the art of selling. The store owners who were more like Madelyn and Judy ("naïve, with no added value," as Madelyn self-deprecatingly put it) were flailing. That was an eye-opener.

But the biggest eye-opener of all came when the 15th store owner they interviewed, a very successful guy, took them under his wing and said, "Before you do this, come spend an entire day in my store and see what it would be like to run it." So Madelyn and Judy spent a day there, from 8:00 A.M. until 9:00 P.M., closing time. That night, after they'd walked out of the store, they turned to each other and said, "What the hell were we thinking? With a schedule like that, we'd have no life!" After *one full year* of research, it only took *one day* to rule it out.

They were able to laugh at themselves, and they were also able to learn from and use the experience. Someone mentioned to them the adage, "The rule in small business is: Sell what you've got!" Since they'd learned so much about the computer industry, they actually went on to become computer consultants to small businesses. They worked together for six years before Madelyn decided that although she loved consulting, the computer industry was getting too sophisticated to hold her interest. Judy, on the other hand, is still going strong, more than 10 years later.

Work Smarter, Not Harder: Narrow Your Range of Products or Services

Anita Brattina came from a business background, she was passionate about her company, and she built a great business. But how long did it take her to get beyond $1 million in sales? *Eleven years.* How hard did she work? In year two, she admits she is working seven days a week and 65 hours per week.[3] Not until year seven does she vow, "The days of working 16 hours are over."[4] Did she have a family to worry about? She had a supportive husband but no children in the first 10 years of running the company, though she eventually adopted four. Basically, those first 10 years of growing her business were pretty grueling and all-encompassing.

Many of us don't feel we have 10 years to learn basic business lessons the hard way like Brattina did. And that's exactly why Brattina put 54 text boxes of "Lessons Learned" alongside her actual diary entries—to help other women learn from her mistakes, work smarter, and save valuable time in their own businesses.

Chief among Brattina's lessons learned was the importance of *narrowing her range of products and services.* She mentions how, shortly after leaving her job and setting up an office in her apartment, she took a class in writing a start-up business plan. Next to those diary entries in her book, she later reflected:

> *Even after being in business for eleven years, I look back on my first business plan and feel sure that it was a waste of time. . . . Here's what I wish the instructor had forced me to think about: What business are you in, exactly? I find that most floundering businesspeople cannot tell me exactly the business they are in without offering a long-winded explanation. . . . Instead of a business plan, I needed guidance in narrowing my range of services, narrowing the list of business categories I wanted to market, and guidance and ideas about the pricing of my service. I wish she'd shown me how many $350 sales I would have to make to earn $100,000 per year and then shown me how to earn $100,000 if I were selling a $10,000 service.*[5]

I created the following chart based on the data Brattina shares at the start of each chapter. Look at how long it took her to reach $1 million in sales, and look at how many employees her business had to support along the way. You can see it in the numbers: A lot of people worked very hard to get the work done, and they weren't getting rich. (Hmm, how long will you be willing to be overworked and underpaid? Especially when personal obligations get in the way . . .)

The Life Cycle of Direct Response Marketing,
As Told in Diary of a Small Business Owner

Year	Average Sale	Average Monthly Sales	Annual Sales	Number of Employees	Services
1	$ 350	n/a	n/a	0	M, DM, TM-C
2	$ 800	$10,000	$ 100,000	2	DM, M-C, DS
3	$ 1,000	$18,000	$ 220,000	7 (most P/T)	DM, DS, TM-C, M-C, ML
4	$ 1,000	$20,000	$ 240,000	5 (most P/T)	DM, DS, TM-C, ML, TM

The Life Cycle of Direct Response Marketing (Continued)

Year	Average Sale	Average Monthly Sales	Annual Sales	Number of Employees	Services
5	$ 2,500	$20,000	$ 260,000	12 (most P/T)	DM, TM, TM-C, DS, ML
6	$ 2,500	$20,000	$ 270,000	12 (most P/T); let 8 people go end of year	TM, DM, ML
7	$ 3,500	$30,000	$ 370,000	12 (most P/T, rehired)	TM, DM, Me, A, DS, PR
8	$ 5,000	$40,000	$ 480,000	20 (most P/T telemarketers)	TM, DM
9	$ 5,000	$45,000	$ 550,000	30	TM
10	$ 7,500	$60,000	$ 750,000	35	TM, DM
11	$10,000	$90,000	$1,100,000	40 plus 20 temp	TM, telephone research and fund-raising

Key to Abbreviations: M = marketing; DM = direct mail; TM = telemarketing; DS = design services; ML = mailing lists; C = consulting; Me = media; A = advertising; PR = public relations; P/T = part-time.

Now notice the far-right column. Note how the number of services got pared down and down until Direct Response Marketing was focusing on the one thing that it did best: telemarketing. Only then did the business really take off. Focus, focus, focus.

Could she have gotten there more quickly? In fact, Brattina mentions being at an industry meeting in year 10 when she ran into a guy named Jim to whom she'd taught telemarketing basics as a consultant 10 years prior. In that same period of time, she and Jim had each built telemarketing companies from scratch. Jim's roughly $15 million company had 1,200 employees around the country and operated in 20 states. Anita's had 40 employees and was just getting close to the $1 million mark. Jim, too, had struggled with focusing on too many services at the start, but he got past that hurdle much earlier than Anita did. Anita notes that "Jim R. figured out from his business experience that a narrow service to a narrow market is the fastest way to grow a company."[6] Now, it's fair if you don't want to be Jim, if you don't want or need a company that big, but almost no one would dispute that it would be better to get to $1 million (or better yet $2 or $3 million) *faster*.

Reduce the Company's Dependence on Its Founder

What happens when a small company simply *is* its founder and can't be defined any other way? when a company would crumble if the founder wasn't there to run it? The short answer is, it wouldn't be worth much, so avoid this situation! Depending too much on the founder is a huge negative for any small business, but it also seems to be a trap that people fall into without realizing or admitting that their company is too tied up with themselves. Why? Because it's easier, and because it flatters the ego (admit it!).

No matter how emotionally tied you are to your business idea, continue to remind yourself that your company should be an entity with a life of its own. It will never grow large or be worth much if you are the only one who has the skills to run it, or if you personally mastermind every customer relationship, or if you keep all the intelligence in your head instead of recording it in a notebook or on a computer. You do need to delegate, and you need to focus most of all on generating new sales (more on that later), which you can't do if you're busy doing everything else.

Many women are very creative and have a vision for a business that simply must be created from scratch. Some of them even brand the company's products using their own names. Great, fine—but the smart ones hire others to carry out their vision or help run day-to-day affairs when they get to the point that they can afford to do so.

START-FROM-SCRATCH PROFILE
Hadley Pollet Inc. and Its Founder, Hadley Pollet

You fashionistas out there may recognize the brand name Hadley Pollet for her signature, colorful jacquard belts with oval tortoise-shell buckles. These well-known designs have now been copied by other designers, imitation being the ultimate form of flattery (not to mention intellectual property problems!).

Not surprisingly, Hadley Pollet is a person, too. When Hadley was at Rhode Island School of Design (RISD), classmates remarked that her name was made for fashion, because of the symmetry of the six letters in her first and last names. She's developed a graphic logo to weave into her textiles, too, that subtly says to those in the know, "Oh, that's a Hadley Pollet." But Hadley was quick to tell me that the brand and the company name are distinct from her as a person, although she is the CEO of the company. Her designs, she says, change based on the "social and political climate" for fashion. In other words, she tries to figure out what designs will speak to people and sell well, rather than basing the designs solely on her own tastes.

The company grew to about $2.6 million in annual revenues in its first three full years in business, so relative to most women-owned businesses, it's been on the fast track. Hadley, who is young and hasn't yet started a family, was able to work long hours throughout the early years of her start-up, and she freely acknowledges she couldn't have built the company the way she did if she'd had young children at home. In fact, the company was run out of her home for three years (that's where her employees came to work every day) until she finally leased an office space in Cambridge, Massachusetts, at the beginning of year four.

Pollet's style and the business wisdom she shared with me reflect an interesting mix of personal philosophy and practical business lessons. Pollet attributes this mix and her success to her "combination of right brain and left brain" personality. Her background in business (marketing and PR), design (her degree from RISD and innate fashion sense), and industry knowledge (one of her biggest clients at an ad agency where she worked was a textile company with a specialty jacquard fabric division) also provided her a nice balance between the analysis and passion that I mentioned earlier. As you read some of

I47

the following convictions and business advice that she shared with me in an interview, you might see this combination, too.

- *Nurture good energy, banish bad.* Pollet believes that in a small company, energy needs to be flowing correctly; her concepts of "energy" actually draw from her own avid practice of yoga. She evaluates her employees and business partners from the perspective of how they'll impact the overall energy in the business, remarking: "When the energy is right, it's right." Her textile designs certainly also project an exotic energy and harmony.
- *Fashion is about manufacturing.* Pollet reminds us that "Although people think fashion is very glamorous, there's really no glamour at all in my business. At the end of the day, it's manufacturing." Her company's fabrics are custom-made all over the world, but traveling to visit the manufacturers is more grueling than glamorous.
- *Trade up over time to build your team.* When it comes to building a staff and a support system of managers and advisers, Pollet is tough, making changes whenever necessary. She recommends starting small based on what you can afford and then "trading up" when you can pay someone more. For example, she began with a part-time bookkeeper, now employs an experienced finance manager three days a week, and expects one day to graduate to a proper CFO. Currently, Hadley Pollet employs seven full-time and four part-time staff, almost all of them women. She comments, "You can't be in a female-oriented industry like this and have women working for you without offering part-time opportunities." I couldn't agree more (and getting these "smart women" to work for you is often a bargain).
- *Play big company politics.* Pollet doesn't believe in letting big companies walk all over you just because you're small. "You have to be very tough—don't give away discounts," she says. In the cutthroat fashion industry, gross margins are very thin. Many a famous fashion designer has had trouble paying the bills, and Hadley Pollet hopes to avoid those troubles. She insists on selling at the department store markup price to everyone, large and small, believing that this will go a long way toward avoiding customer conflicts and jealousy over pricing and

discounts. She has held firm on this point until now and only in year four began selling her products to department stores. They've finally come around to paying her standard prices.

- *Keep reinventing yourself.* Pollet acknowledges that it's hard to be first. She started a trend with her belts, and she's been copied left and right by cheaper imitators. She says that to succeed in a competitive market-place, "You have to reinvent yourself all the time, like Madonna!" This lesson is especially apt when you enter a new market or invent a new product—one day competition will rear its ugly head and you'll have to problem-solve on the spot.
- *Pull yourself away from the day-to-day.* Like other successful business owners, Pollet says she is really trying to pull herself away from all the smaller decisions that have to be made every day, so that the business is not so dependent on her. When asked why, she remarked, "It's just good business sense."
- *Cash flow is a huge challenge.* Hadley learned about financial man-agement on the job. She says you must get a grip on your own cash flow, no matter whom you hire to help you, because "nobody under-stands your business like you do." She didn't anticipate this, and says that no one could've effectively warned her. Now, Hadley says, she'll "never stop looking at the bills" and she'll "always keep a close eye on finances." She says that for many women, discussing money can be humbling because it's not an area in which they're knowledgeable— "but that's all the more reason to learn about it."

The Role of the Owner:
Sales, Sales, and More Sales

On September 30 in year two of Direct Response Marketing's life, Anita Brattina wrote, "Money, money, money. I spend 99 percent of my energy worrying about the fact that I have so little of it. Solution: Go into sales full-time. I can't wait for these inexperienced salespeople anymore."[7]

When you start a company from scratch, you will quickly realize that no matter how good the products or services that you've developed are, the only way to pay the bills and keep the business going is to sell, sell, sell. You may enjoy this and consider yourself a good salesperson—if so, good. If you cannot imagine yourself in a sales role, you may want to reconsider entrepreneurship entirely.

That said, you certainly don't have to make every sale yourself. Figure out how to build a sales force that is appropriate for your industry and products. This may take the form of full-time employees, part-time employees, or commission-only salespeople who work on a contract basis. Hopefully, you'll find a way to take advantage of all the smart, skilled women out there who want to work part-time and can earn their keep.

For best results plus good morale, if you can afford it, I'd recommend offering in-house salespeople a low base salary plus a sales commission, rather than commission only. Set a goal for the salesperson—maybe 10 times their monthly expense to you. If they don't perform after a certain period of time (maybe three months), you may then be able to justify taking away the base salary (or turning it into a draw against future commissions). When figuring out commissions, be very clear about whether you are paying a percentage of revenues or of profits, and figure out the right percentage for your industry as well as for your company (there's no avoiding that profit and loss statement!).

One business owner I worked with had been paying her best salesperson a whopping 80 percent of what she thought was profits, only to realize much later that she was actually paying 80 percent of gross margins and, after accounting for overhead, was losing money on that business. Moreover, she sometimes paid the commission before she collected money from her customers, which is another no-no.

In your haste to grow your company, do not make the mistake of looking only at revenue growth. What good is it if your company has $1 million in sales if you are barely able to bring home a living wage? If you sell your company someday, what matters most is profit and cash flow, *not* gross sales.

Professionalize with Off-the-Shelf Technology

In this age of modern technology, there's no excuse for not using the outstanding, low-cost software tools that are widely available to professionalize your small business from the very beginning. I've met with many graying business sellers who cringe at the task of modernizing a business that was started long before these tools existed. I can eke out a little sympathy for them, but I privately delight at the low-hanging fruit dangling in front of the new buyer. Still, I have little patience for anyone who starts a business today without computerizing and professionalizing it from day one. It's so easy.

- *Get an accounting software program, and take the time to customize it.* Don't fall into the trap of thinking that Excel spreadsheets are adequate to keep track of your business finances. Use a software package meant for small businesses, like QuickBooks (www.quickbooks.intuit.com), and if you need help to customize your chart of accounts or invoices, get some advice early on. Train yourself in how to use it as you go, even if you hire a bookkeeper later. QuickBooks costs about $160 and is widely used.
- *Computerize invoices, accounts payable, and accounts receivable.* Go beyond just managing your profit and loss (P&L) on the computer. Computerize your invoices, accounts payable (A/P), and accounts receivable (A/R) so that you can keep good electronic records and not get overwhelmed by paper ones. Print your checks for a more professional look. QuickBooks can do all of these things for you.
- *Outsource payroll.* Even if you only pay two or three employees, this is worth it. As a small business owner, you do not want to deal with the legal headache involved in missing a payroll tax payment or a filing. Either use a payroll outsourcing service such as Sure Payroll (www.surepayroll.com) or use the feature available through your accounting software (again, QuickBooks offers it, and I've used it quite happily).

- *Set up a web site.* This is the fastest, surest way to appear professional and bigger than you are when small. If you're willing to use someone else's templates and tools, you need not pay a Web designer big bucks to create a professional site. Packages offering a domain name, e-mail addresses, Web hosting space, web site building tools, search engine optimization, 24/7 customer support, and even e-commerce tools, can be had for as little as $9 to $30 per month. Check out http://.geocities.yahoo.com, www.big step.com, and www.1and1.com. Do this early, because these services will help you decide on a company name in seconds by letting you see whether the domain name you want is available.

- *Print business cards and stationery.* Do this as soon as you can. You never know who you might run into who could become a customer, supplier, or advocate for you. If you want to use existing templates for stationery and business cards, try www .vistaprint.com. If you need a logo quickly, try www.gotlogos .com. If your business needs to have a very professional veneer, you may also want to consider using part-time business centers or virtual office services that you find locally. These business centers charge you only for the services and amenities you use, which can include a prestigious business address, conference rooms, mail handling and package receiving services, office machines, and voice mail. Even if you're the only one answering the phones, the right voice mail system can make you seem like a giant (try www.angel.com).

- *Get a corporate credit card, and accept credit cards from your customers.* One golden rule of business you should follow from day one is this: Don't comingle personal and corporate funds. Not only do lenders not want you to comingle funds, but it unnecessarily complicates financial record keeping. Even if you can't qualify for a corporate card, or if you don't want to lose out on frequent flyer benefits, get a separate card in your own or your business's name to conduct company business. In addition, set yourself up to accept credit cards from your customers. Many business owners find that receiving payment up front and avoiding the hassle of going after customers who haven't paid their bills more than pay for the service fees that credit card companies charge them.

- *Keep an annual tab of your company's worth.* Keep yourself honest about the value of your company by going through the private exercise of a do-it-yourself appraisal every year. As a start-up, you may not be able to afford a professional appraisal unless there's a real need for one, but you can still educate yourself about the rules of thumb that apply to your industry, and you can do some simple calculations (for example, a multiple of earnings) to get a feel for the value of your company. Create an Excel file, and update the model each year.

Seek Good Advice, Advisers, and Mentors

It's not just off-the-shelf technology that's cheap and available on the Internet. Good advice abounds too. One site I discovered that's chockablock with sage advice for small businesses is called All Business: Champions of Small Business (www.allbusiness.com). Not only can you find pertinent answers to many of your entrepreneurial concerns there, but you can buy many forms of legal documents (you may also attempt to find what you need for free at www.freebusinessforms.com). By all means, educate yourself, and come up with draft legal documents to help you get started. However, this will not take the place of professional advice.

At minimum, you'll need an attorney and an accountant, and possibly a banker. Also consider hiring a bookkeeper and using HR and insurance experts when the need presents itself. Referrals and recommendations are perhaps the best way to find the right advisers. However, if you don't have good connections to corporate attorneys with small business experience, consult the Martindale Hubbell Directory (www.martindale.com and www.lawyers.com). For accountants in your area, try www.cpafinder.com. Interview the candidates you find, and be sure to ask them what they spend the majority of their practice on. What size companies? What industries? The right fit is paramount because the right person will be able to advise you quickly and confidently, even if she is not the cheapest by the hour.

Attending educational conferences for women entrepreneurs, such as those offered by the Women's Leadership Exchange, can also connect you with business experts and other business owners (see www.womens leadershipexchange.com).

Occasionally, the right advisers can turn into incredible mentors for your business, and women I've interviewed are all in agreement about the value of good mentoring. Julie Hellwich is a great example of this, in no small part because her company's products get at the heart of what this book is all about.

START-FROM-SCRATCH PROFILE
Smart Women Products Find a Niche and a Mentor

Julie Hellwich might have been doomed to running a tiny, grassroots business forever if some women attorneys at Oppenheimer, Wolff & Donnelly in Minneapolis hadn't taken her under their wing. Her company's novelty and gift products, sold under the brand names "Smart Women" and "Good Guys," were being copied by bumper sticker sellers in other states, so she contacted a trademark attorney at Oppenheimer named Erika Koster. Erika came to visit Julie with two other female attorneys from her firm, including a senior partner. Not only did they help her fight the trademark infringement, but they also helped her get her corporate minutes together retroactively (pro bono, as a favor), and they introduced her to the COO of another company who helped Julie put together a good business plan and became her mentor. For Julie, who is the classic "accidental businesswoman" but nevertheless depends on her business income for survival, this was a godsend. She needed financial and business guidance, not to mention encouragement.

You can check out Julie's products at http://store.smartwomenstore.com. Smart Women products blend fun, functionality, and nostalgic design. The kitchen tool and household staple products are playful and practical, with uplifting messages that speak to the enduring strength, resourcefulness, and accomplishments of women. Examples include "Smart Women Light the Way" matchboxes and votive candles and "Smart Women Thirst for Knowledge" mugs and glasses. Julie's company has also been a vehicle for social activism, with products promoting women voters ("Smart Women Elect to Make a Difference") and publicizing an infertility support organization called RESOLVE ("Smart Women Have Resolve").

Now that Julie has great products and good mentors, she needs to focus more on growth and the bottom line. Julie is humble about her success thus far: "My business has succeeded in spite of me. I've made every mistake you can make, and I undervalued myself and my product. After five years in business, I'm only now writing a business plan. But believe it or not, I'm now money- and profit-oriented, and things are really looking up."

Get Inspired

When you're starting a business from scratch, you need all the inspiration you can get. It does help to read stories about women who started with nothing and grew to a large size or became a household name. One of my favorite inspirational stories is that of Sara Blakely, who started the hosiery and tights company Spanx. While working as a sales trainer by day and performing stand-up comedy at night, she came up with the idea of footless pantyhose that are slimming, comfortable, and can be worn with any style shoe. Against the odds, she found a mill to produce a prototype, came up with a bold and hip red package, and won over a buyer at Neiman Marcus by showing off her before-and-after panty lines in the ladies room. Now the company has $85 million in sales,[8] a new female CEO who's as interesting and impressive as the company's founder, and PR opportunities you'd die for, such as being featured on the Oprah Winfrey show.

Do get inspired by stories like Sara Blakeley's, and even Hadley Pollet's (who's hopefully on her way to being a brand as big as Spanx). But also take inspiration from those women and their businesses who aren't and will never be household names—Anita Brattina, Julie Hellwich,

Erin Hanlon, and all the other women in this book. Realize that you need to be in the right business for you and that you have some control over how big it gets or how small it stays. But be *smarter* than the average woman who starts a business from scratch. Then, pass on your tips to that average woman. Maybe with a little viral marketing, we women can help each other succeed in business like never before.

CHAPTER NINE

Smart Financing Strategies for Your Business

Perhaps the biggest initial challenge in financing women-owned businesses is to convince their owners to seek (or persist in seeking) external financing. Many women-owned businesses are poorly capitalized and as a result tend to remain small. Although women-owned businesses are the fastest-growing segment of the small business sector in the United States, did you know that only 2 percent gross $1 million or more annually, trailing the number of men-owned million-dollar businesses by a factor of eight to one?[1] Out of the approximately 10.6 million businesses that are at least 50 percent women-owned, that's only about 212,000 companies. (And speaking of size, $1 million in sales isn't huge; plenty of million-dollar businesses make enough to support just one or two owners.) Reluctance or difficulty in borrowing money is one of the main reasons for the low numbers.

To be sure, some women are very gung ho about raising money for their businesses and even seek to interest venture capitalists and private equity investors to buy into their concepts. However, the lion's share of investment capital still goes to men. Women who want to pursue high-growth businesses must learn the rules of this male-dominated game; moreover, they must be willing to grow at the pace demanded by outside investors, who want them to grow far beyond $1 million in sales.

This chapter can't possibly answer every question you may have about financing your business. You'll need to complete your education with networking, trial and error, other books, and online resources. You can also get a lot of help from the Small Business Administration (SBA). Amid the plethora of information you'll find, I'll offer you a few observations to help ground your thinking: (1) High-growth businesses and Main Street businesses are financed very differently; (2) the way you finance your business has a great deal to do with the character, feel, and pace of your company; and (3) sometimes the oldest, humblest financial products—such as loans from business owners and banks—meet your needs in ways that the glamorous and complex ones do not.

If your goal is to operate your business in such a way that it delivers the financial rewards you're seeking, use this chapter not only to hone your mind-set and business plans but also to educate yourself about your options. Inside, you'll find enough information on the following sources of money to decide where to go for further help:

- *Seller financing* (a great option if you decide to buy an existing business and can get the owner to finance your purchase).
- *Bank loans* (which include start-up, expansion, real estate, equipment, and working capital loans, and may be guaranteed by the SBA).
- *Microfinance* (organizations that specialize in lending small amounts—from as little as $500 to as much as $45,000—to women entrepreneurs and business owners, one notable example of which is the Make Mine a $Million Business™ program run by microlender Count-Me-In and OPEN from American Express).
- *Other common sources of financing* (credit lines, leases, trade credit, angel investors, and so on).

Why and When to Seek Outside Funding

I asked a rhetorical question earlier in this book: Why start from scratch if someone's done it for you? I could also ask this: Why stay in bootstrap mode if your idea or business plan is bankable?

Maybe you don't want to deal with outside investors—don't want the pressure, don't want to give up control. But have you considered that entrepreneurs and small businesses with good track records are eligible for favorable bank financing (or seller financing) that could offer you very good cash-on-cash returns? Did you consider that you might just be what the banks consider a very good credit risk (good business plan, good credit scores, smart, experienced, confident)? If you already have credit in the form of a home equity line, have you considered dipping into it to make starting or buying a business possible?

And here's another strange thought inspired by Jamie Walters, author of *Big Vision, Small Business*: Taking on debt may spur you to persevere through challenges that might otherwise cause you to quit or settle beneath your potential.[2]

According to Myra Hart, former chairperson of the Center for Women's Business Research, the vast majority of women-led firms with more than $1 million in sales achieved that level of revenues in less than five years of operations.[3] This indicates that they are doing something differently than the other 98 percent; in other words, it's not just that they've been around longer.

What some of them are doing differently is this: financing their business adequately from the get-go, in contrast to those who rely on bootstrapping. Bootstrappers use their personal funds, then their credit cards, and maybe they borrow from friends and family, but rarely do they think they can march into a bank and ask for a loan right off the bat. Plus, women tend to feel very uncomfortable about debt; we don't necessarily want to be on the hook to a lender. We know this may be irrational, but many of us are content to grow our little businesses without being beholden to outsiders, thank you very much.

Walters comments wryly in her book,

Whereas many people are perfectly comfortable borrowing tens or hundreds or thousands of dollars for a car or a home that could be reduced to scrap in a matter of minutes, or sitting in a classroom for several years to earn a degree that may or may not turn out to be useful, fewer are comfortable borrowing a fraction as much to build and learn through their business.[4]

Yet, if you want to improve the odds that your business will not only survive but also become a million-dollar business, *look for money before you need it.* That's the advice of Jennifer Williams, loan specialist at the Center for Women in Enterprise (CWE) in Worcester, Massachusetts, one of two SBA-sponsored educational resource centers for women entrepreneurs in the state (more on these centers later). Trained as a CPA, Jennifer began working at CWE long ago as a volunteer, helping women business owners with budgeting, forecasting, and tax planning. She joined the staff part-time about four years ago, and during that same time also acquired and now runs five day-care centers.

One of the biggest problems she sees in her work at CWE is that "Many people come to me just too darn late. They've got maxed-out credit cards, and their businesses are running losses. It breaks my heart." These women, who probably didn't want the stress of owing money to a bank, and who probably felt they were taking a less risky route in bootstrapping their businesses, are actually poised to lose everything because they didn't plan for their capital needs in advance.

This can happen even to the savviest of women. Suze Orman, personal finance guru, author, and television personality, admitted in a *New York Times* article entitled "Cleaning Up Messes, Friend to Friend" that after she started a financial advisory firm in the late 1980s she maxed out her credit cards, went deeply into debt, and suffered acute embarrassment. "I didn't want anybody to know, because if I was so great, how could I let this happen?" said Orman.[5]

One of the other common problems Jennifer Williams sees is that women don't know how much money to ask for, and often don't ask for enough. "The way we purchase homes makes people think that asking for a business loan is a similar process. I always have to drive home the point that you must ask for the *right* number, the realistic number," she says. If you can only get partway to your business goal with the money you've borrowed, you usually can't get more money from the bank, so Jennifer suggests using conservative estimates of your business's income and not making overly optimistic projections. She adds, "Banks are not easily fooled. They're wondering how they're going to get paid back, and how you're going to live." Their scrutiny can force you to be realistic in your own forecasts and prevent you from making overly optimistic assumptions.

Beth Polish, a frequent speaker and nationally recognized expert on business finance, adds the following rules of thumb: "If possible, a company should always have cash on hand to last about 12 to 18 months," and an entrepreneur or company "needs to allow at least three to six months" to obtain financing. Why be so prudent? Beth states, "Desperation makes the job of raising money so much harder and isn't attractive to funding sources of any type." (See Appendix J for information about Polish's financing and business plan primers.)

Thinking in Dollar Signs

While doing research for this book, I encountered a young man from a prominent business valuations firm who worked on many small transactions with business brokers. He was so enthusiastic about both the lifestyle and the favorable financing available to buyers of small businesses that he was constantly trying to lobby his friends in the white-shoe corporate world to "leave the rat race for the superior quality of life that certain small businesses are afforded."

For him, the clincher was that you can buy many small businesses with a cash down payment of only 15 to 30 percent of the purchase price, then finance the remaining 70 to 85 percent with an SBA-guaranteed loan. Theoretically, a good business purchased at the right price would throw off enough cash to make the annual loan payments and compensate the new owner; plus, it offers great tax advantages. Moreover, if you ran it well, you could sell it again some day. He enthused, "Look at the cash-on-cash returns! People would be all over a public company if it was priced this low! Buying a small company can be one heck of an investment!"

Do women commonly think about small business and entrepreneurial ambitions in number terms like this young man does? Do women search single-mindedly for cash-flow-positive businesses? In my experience, it's the rare woman who does. Should we? We absolutely should, although it shouldn't preclude us from other considerations. We must find a business we are passionate about, *and* we must ask what kind of return we can get for our money. Do lenders think in dollar signs? Frankly, yes—and most of those lenders are men.

Credit Risk and Personal Guarantees

Linda Stevenson is a senior vice president at National City Bank and the director of its Women's Business Development Program. She says that there's no conspiracy out there to lend less to women. On the contrary, she says, "In many cases, women don't even ask banks for financing. They look elsewhere. Women also tend to use their business cash flow to pay their bills instead of using a bank's money in the form of a credit line. We at National City believe we should enlighten women about the availability of funds and empower them to ask for them. It's not just the right thing to do, it's good business—women are a good credit risk precisely because they do pay their bills."

National City has put its money where its mouth is; Linda heads up an initiative to lend $3.5 billion to women-owned businesses across the country over a five-year period. Three years into the campaign, the bank has loaned $2.1 billion of that total to women, mostly for expansion of existing businesses.[6]

When I was putting together an offer to buy a basket-importing firm several years ago, the firm I wanted to buy with my partner was way too big to buy outright with cash. We knew we needed to borrow money to finance the purchase, and I had one thing on my mind: how to avoid giving a personal guarantee or using my house as collateral. That deal never moved far beyond the offer stage, but looking back on it, I know that I was being naïve about risk. I was comforted by the idea of a "limited liability" corporation and it didn't seem right to me that I would have to risk my personal assets to guarantee a loan. I felt lucky that our house was in my husband's name and was a legal "homestead"; the bank could never go after it—right?

Lisa Hodgen, a corporate attorney with Leisawitz Heller in Wyomissing, Pennsylvania, who has worked on many small business acquisitions, has seen many deals delayed or derailed by women who recoil at the idea of a personal guarantee. "Women feel that that's untouchable. They think, 'That's my family on the line.'" Linda Stevenson reinforced the notion that women are much less comfortable providing collateral for debt than are men. Says Linda, "Men tend to put up their personal assets without hesitating. They'll put it all on the line. Women are more cautious."

Yet, it's naïve to assume that a bank will bear all the risk of your business. Many small businesses are very dependent on their owners and have little in the way of hard assets and inventory to offer as collateral. Banks aren't in the business of operating or reselling small companies— if you default on your loan, they need something tangible that they can liquidate quickly to make up for the loss.

Risk-averse women and risk-averse bankers sometimes don't mix. That's a shame, because if you don't find a way to share risk with a bank (or investor), you'll be taking all the risk on yourself, and you may not have enough money or credit to turn your good business idea into a viable and profitable enterprise. While it may seem that the bank transfers all the risk to you if you sign a personal guarantee and pledge your house as collateral, that's not really true. It's a lot of work for banks to go after delinquent borrowers. If you're in default of your loan, a good banker will usually make a big effort to work with you, and only as a last resort will he attempt to repossess your house or, heaven forbid, eject your family onto the street. That said, if you need some strategies for waiving or modifying the requirement of using your primary residence as collateral, see Charles Green's *The SBA Loan Book*.[7]

Giving Up Equity

Under what circumstances should we raise money by giving up equity instead of taking on debt? Venture capital and private equity financing have become so glamorous in recent years that we tend to lose sight of the fact that the industry arose as a last resort for entrepreneurs who couldn't convince banks to lend them money. Business finance expert

Beth Polish says that equity investors are "not appropriate unless a business model has the capability to scale to something very large—in terms of revenue, profit, and overall valuation."

One upside to bringing on private equity investment may be the ability for the entrepreneur to minimize the risk of losing her personal financial assets, but for investors the stakes are high—and thus the pressure is on. There is definitely a trade-off between speed and scale on the one hand and control and lifestyle on the other. (See the profile of Ann Gray that follows for an innovative example of the high-growth model.)

Something to avoid is haphazardly selling shares in a venture in order to meet short-term needs for money. One woman business owner I interviewed for this book sold 45 percent of her company over time just to pay her bills. When she didn't have $2,000 for a graphic design bill, she gave a girlfriend who was willing to pay the bill 20 percent of her equity. Later, when her mom bailed her out with just $1,000, she gave her another 10 percent. She didn't consider going to a bank, she didn't foresee how her products would eventually take off, and she didn't realize the consequences of giving up that much equity for so little cash. Today, she feels chagrin about those decisions. She agreed to share her story so you won't make the same mistakes.

Those of us who aim to build more traditional businesses that aren't destined for a public stock offering don't have or necessarily want the option of giving up equity. We typically have to finance our businesses the old-fashioned way—by putting our own cash at risk or by borrowing money from a bank or retiring owner. This is not a bad thing, actually, so long as you know what you're getting into, what to expect. I believe it keeps us and our businesses honest and grounded.

ENTREPRENEUR COMPARISON

The Big Company versus Small Company Approach—Two Different Paths Illustrate the Value of Leverage

To buy small or to buy big? To borrow small or to borrow big? Those are the questions. Comparing and contrasting the story of two unrelated entrepreneurs will demonstrate the trade-offs. On the one hand, there's the story of Wendy Pease, a former director of international marketing for a large biopharmaceutical company, and on the other, of Ann Gray, a former professor at the Harvard Business School. Both decided to search for a business to buy after the end of their previous career phases. Both are quintessential, even elite, "smart women," and although one chose small and one chose big, both have been successful.

Wendy had four criteria when searching for a business: (1) It had to be in business-to-business services (B2B); (2) it had to be close to home; (3) she didn't want a business in which she personally had to both provide the basic service and market the company; and (4) it had to be small, to accommodate her other responsibilities (two children at home).

Ann also had two children at home, but her husband was willing to take on primary responsibility for kids and home for a finite period of time. Ann's criteria when searching for a business were somewhat different from Wendy's: (1) It had to be manufacturing-related (Ann is an engineer), (2) it had to employ at least 50 people ("because otherwise, you're doing everything yourself"); and (3) it had to be acceptable to both her business partner, Bill Rose, and to their financial backer, a buyout firm in Vermont called Green Mountain Partners that invests in profitable, mid-sized manufacturing companies. Ann and Bill weren't able to buy such a large company themselves, but they knew they could find a good acquisition target, get someone else to put up the cash to buy the company, and then run it. They wanted to be compensated with a combination of salary and equity.

Back to Wendy. On www.businessbrokers.net, Wendy found a language interpretation company for sale that fit her requirements (B2B, relocatable, outsourced labor, not too big). She herself spoke several foreign languages and loved diverse cultures, so she knew that she could get passionate about the business and take it to the next stage by creating a company web site and offering web site translation services. The business, Rapport International, was advertised at $60,000 and had $50,000 in annual revenues. She bought it outright for $35,000 ($25,000 at closing plus two payments of $5K later). The cash came out of her home equity line, a sensible choice for her because the interest rate was considerably less than going rates for an SBA loan. Within one year, she'd paid back the full amount to her home equity line and tripled the company's revenues, to $150,000. Her own income from the business was about 25 to 30 percent of gross receipts.

While very happy about her decision to buy Rapport, Wendy also realized that by buying a bigger business, one ought to be able to service debt with cash flow. She's now actively searching to buy complementary businesses to fold into Rapport and says, "If I came across another business like this one, I'd snap it up" (and, presumably, use debt to do it). Wendy started small but plans to use the leverage of debt to grow to her new optimal size.

Back to Ann. By joining forces with a seasoned business partner and a buyout firm with deep pockets, Ann was in a whole different world than Wendy: the world of midmarket companies and private equity. Private equity firms buy stakes in privately held companies at varying stages of growth (seed, expansion stage, and so on), hoping that they can exit a few years later and realize a large profit. Buyout firms typically buy 100 percent of their target investments and install new management. While Ann and Bill wanted to buy a company and run it, as did Wendy, because they chose to buy a big company, they needed a whole different model from hers. So Ann and Bill became what a buyout firm like Green Mountain calls *deal sponsors*. What this strategy boiled down to was the two of them fronting all the money for due diligence on their target company but investing none of their own cash.

Together, they found Fabrico, a multimillion-dollar precision metal fabrication company that needed to transition to a next-generation ownership and management team. Ann and Bill spent $150,000 on due diligence and legal fees, but Green Mountain Partners actually bought 100 percent of Fabrico at closing. Fabrico was one of a few companies that Ann and Bill would buy and run with Green Mountain's sponsorship (and they ended up with a 25 to 40 percent equity slice in each, plus management contracts). While Ann warns, "Don't assume that running a business will give you work-life flexibility, especially in the beginning," she also concedes that being big enough to afford a strong management team at Fabrico "has given me much more flexibility to balance work and family than I think I would have running a $2 million [revenue] business."

As you can see, answering the question of small versus big is a personal one, and it depends on many factors. However, both women leveraged the power of their own funds in some way and are continuing to do so.[8]

Is Seller Financing in the Cards?

Before we get into the topic of bank financing, I want to raise your awareness of the advantages of *seller financing*, an option potentially open to anyone who purchases a business rather than starting one. Here's a hypothetical example: Jane wants to buy a $200,000 medical records business and is able to make a cash down payment of $50,000. Rather than go to a bank, she's able to negotiate a note with the seller of the business to pay him the remaining $150,000 in fixed monthly payments of principal plus interest over seven years. Jane and the seller get along well, and he doesn't want to lose out on the right buyer at the right time. He's afraid that she'd get turned down for bank financing because of her lack of industry experience and divorce-related credit issues, but he's confident that she can manage his business, and he's willing to train her.

Owner or seller financing, often referred to as the seller "taking some paper," is often made available to the purchaser of a small business as a way to get a transaction done. Seller financing is easier to put in place than bank financing. It's also more flexible and negotiable. Like a bank, a seller usually will want to secure the loan with adequate collateral, but sometimes he'll agree to take the assets of the business as collateral, which a bank won't often do. A seller may want a personal guarantee, but he's less interested in the buyer's house than the bank would be. In many ways, it's easier for him to foreclose on the business than it is to foreclose on her house, because he knows how to operate it.

That said, a seller isn't very likely to foreclose on the business, because he really doesn't want it back (if he did, he wouldn't sell it to you in the first place). Moreover, sellers tend to be more forgiving than banks when buyers go through rough times and miss a payment or two, simply because they've gone through the same seasonal or competitive difficulties in the past.

Seller-financing ensures that the seller has a vested interest in your future business success and makes it less likely that he will set up a new, competitive business. Unless you intensely dislike the seller (which is a red flag and to be avoided anyway), seller financing can be a great opportunity to negotiate good borrowing terms and get the former owner to continue looking out for you. It's also an endorsement that the business really can pay for itself, since the departing owner knows that you must both support yourself and pay him back from the business's cash flow.

The only trouble is, many business sellers want to cash out, so seller financing isn't always an option (or if it is, it's only for a small portion of the purchase amount). Many sellers either need the sale money for some purpose or aren't eager to continue bearing risk for the business. But they may have to; it may be the only way to get the deal done with the right buyer. You may have to work to get the seller in the frame of mind to loan money to you. Make sure you emphasize how much the interest he'll receive will increase the selling price, and point out that the tax consequences of accepting a structured payout are more advantageous than those for an all-cash deal.

The bottom line: If you can get seller financing, take it. But don't neglect to write a business plan and do financial forecasting, just because no one's asking to see it!

Overview of the Bank Loan Process[9]

The difference in formality between personal loans and commercial loans is stark, as you'll see. Institutions in the business of lending money include banks (which hold federal or state charters) and nonbank finance companies (usually referred to as lenders, although this descriptive term applies equally to banks), and most have stringent documentation and due diligence requirements (especially if seeking SBA guarantees). There are thousands of niche lenders in the small business market. Likewise, there are many different kinds of loans, and borrowers should define the kind of money they need first and then approach the right kind of lender.

For example, there are business start-up loans, business purchase loans, business expansion loans, real estate loans, equipment loans, and working capital loans. Depending on the needs of your business, you may apply for a *term loan*, a *line of credit*, or both. A term loan is repaid through regular periodic payments; most business term loans run between 5 and 10 years, maybe 15 years or longer when real estate is involved.

A line of credit is a credit account that allows a company to borrow, repay, and reborrow up to a specified amount, much like a credit card (and quite similar to a home equity line). It helps smooth out your cash flows so that you can pay payroll and vendors on time, even if your customers owe you money. Ideally, the line should be paid down to zero once a year (many banks require this).

One other way of improving cash flows is to lease your fixed assets, such as industrial or computer equipment. A *capital lease* is like a loan with fixed payments, and it is secured by the assets you acquire with it.

If you're going to apply for a loan (or a lease or line of credit), it behooves you to submit a high-quality application that includes all the right materials the first time. Being turned down for a loan by a bank is a black mark that could hurt your chances with the next banker you approach, so spend a lot of time up front getting your materials together and researching whom to approach for the best chances of success.

What is a high-quality application? *One that clearly demonstrates your ability to repay the loan*. Not only will your business be critically evaluated on this criterion, but you personally will be evaluated. That's why it's best to look for money while your finances and credit history are healthy and intact, before bootstrapping gets you into trouble.

Are you in position to apply for a loan right now? Ask yourself the following questions, which all boil down to an assessment of your ability to repay a loan. If the answer to any of the questions isn't yes, do whatever you can to remedy the situation before you approach a lender.

- Do I have a good personal credit history?[10]
- Have I filed my personal and business income tax returns?
- Are my income taxes paid and up to date?
- Do I have any collateral to secure a business loan?
- Am I willing to personally guarantee a loan?

- Can I demonstrate that my business has the ability (or potential) to repay a loan?
- Can I contribute "owner's equity" of 10 to 30 percent of the total cash needed into the business?
- Do I have experience in the industry or in running my own business?
- How can I make a good first impression?

Expect lenders to closely evaluate the business for which you're seeking funding. They'll consider some of the following criteria:

- Whether it's a start-up or an existing business (obviously, start-ups are riskier).
- What type of industry you're in (banks have favorites).
- Historical and/or projected cash flow of the business.
- Value of any business collateral you can offer (e.g., equipment and inventory).
- Other indicators of business health, such as aging of accounts receivable, staffing concerns, any legal or financial liabilities.
- How much you're asking for and whether the amount is appropriate.
- The intended purpose of the loan.

All of this boils down to an indication of your *ability to repay.*

You'll be asked to submit a lot of personal and business-related documents with your application, without regard to how difficult it is for you to prepare them, and it's easy to feel overwhelmed by this task. The more you can understand and internalize what the documents (particularly the financial statements and implied ratios) are saying about you and your business, the better.

Personal documents to be submitted include your personal financial statement, your tax returns, your credit reports from credit agencies, and your personal resume.

There are several business-related documents that you will need, beginning with a *business plan*. This should include the following components:

- Executive summary.
- Company description and product detail.
- Description of your target market.
- Competition.
- Sales and marketing plan.
- Management team.
- Financing history.

You will also need financial statements and projections (which must be very strong for a start-up). If you are seeking financing for a start-up business, these documents should spell out:

- How you'll make money.
- Pricing strategy and defensibility.
- Costs to develop the product.
- P&L and cash flow projections.

For an existing business, expect to be asked to submit these financial documents:

- Income/P&L historical statements.
- Income/P&L projections.
- Balance sheet.
- Month-to-month cash flow statements.
- Accounts receivable and payable aging reports.
- A justification of your assumptions and numbers with research on competitors and industry averages.
- Business tax returns.
- Business credit reports.
- Business organization documentation.

Other documents pertinent to a business loan application include:

- A list of collateral and its value (note that banks will discount this value).
- Source and uses of funds (including owner's investment).
- Copies of leases and contracts.
- A list of professional advisers and their contact information.

A word of warning: After a loan is approved, closing and funding the loan can take months, and even more documentation will be requested. Be prepared for closing costs that can range up to several percentage points of the loan, including bank fees, legal fees, and the cost of independent reports (appraisers, engineers, surveyors, title searches, etc.).[11]

SBA Loans versus Regular Loans

The Small Business Administration (SBA) was established in 1953 to assist small business enterprises. The agency is most well-known for its loan guaranty program designed to benefit eligible small businesses, defined in most industries as either having under $5 million in revenue or fewer than 500 employees (see www.sba.gov for more detailed eligibility requirements).

Many people talk about *SBA loans,* but the term is widely misunderstood. The most important thing to realize is that the Small Business Administration does not do the actual lending—the lending institution does. It's up to you to find a bank or other lender willing to loan you money, and up to that lender to apply for SBA backing. What the SBA does is guarantee up to 85 percent of your loan, promising to reimburse the bank in case of default. In short, SBA products make it easier for banks to lend to someone risky.

You'll pay a little extra for this advantage in the form of a higher interest rate. Therefore, you don't want to get an SBA-backed loan unless you need one. Often your first business loan will be SBA-backed, but if you take out more loans in the future, your business and repayment history make you less of a credit risk, and you can get better financial terms without that guarantee. One expert I talked to had this advice: "Get away from SBA financing as soon as you can. Doing without it is much cheaper."

But in the beginning, an SBA loan may just be your lifeline, especially since SBA loans usually allow longer terms and lower down payments. Banks that won't be willing to lend to you outright will often be willing to do so if they can get SBA backing. This is especially true for start-up loans, the riskiest of all since the business doesn't have operating history.

The SBA offers two main loan-guaranty programs[12] in which it guarantees between 50 and 85 percent of the loan amount:

1. 7(a) Loan Guaranty Program—for business loans (start-ups, business purchases, expansion or renovation, construction of new facilities, purchase of real estate and capital assets, refinancing existing debt). Maximum loan $2 million; maximum guarantee $1 million. Fixed or variable interest rates are usually 2.25 to 4.75 percent over and above the prime rate.

2. 504 Loan Guaranty Program—business loans for purchase of major fixed assets such as land and buildings, real estate, or machinery or equipment for expansion or modernization. Cannot be used for working capital, inventory, debt repayment, or refinancing. Rates are pegged to an increment above the current 5-year and 10-year U.S. Treasury rates. The maximum guarantee ranges from $1.5 million to $4 million, depending on the project purpose (the SBA will classify it according to categories including job creation, community development, public policy, and manufacturing).

Who's Who? Shop Around

When considering which lenders to approach, local banks usually come to mind, but you should also consider the nonbank lenders that can make loans into any state, particularly if they have a special interest in your industry, personal or business demographics, franchisor organization (if applicable), or other business criteria. It's important to find out what kind of loan portfolios a lender currently has or wants to build. Here is a brief primer on who's who.

- *SBA lenders.*[13] Any chartered bank may apply to its district SBA office for a loan guaranty. A limited number of nonbank lenders, including Small Business Lending Corporations (SBLCs), also hold licenses to make SBA-guaranteed loans. Some lenders specialize in lending to small businesses and, because of the volume of loans they handle, are classified as "preferred SBA lenders" (in which the SBA approval is delegated to the lender and can be obtained within a day) or "certified SBA lenders" (in which the approval process is accelerated to within three days). All others are considered "general program lenders" (the approval process takes 5 to 21 days). When the SBA has preauthorized the lender to do its own underwriting, the process is streamlined. Without preauthorization, there's a chance that the SBA will not guarantee the loan even though the lender approved it.

- *Local versus national banks.* Even among banks, there is a huge variety of lenders. Says Jennifer Williams, "Banks are really interesting beasts. Each one has its own lending policies and guidelines, as well as its own tolerance for risk assumption. Also, keep in mind that these policies may change over time." Local, community-oriented banks are likely to be more interested in competing for your business. Nationwide banking institutions tend to be more risk-averse but may be a better fit if you're in international trade and want a line of credit. Some banks like start-ups, but some won't lend until you have at least six months of operating experience. A strong indication of whether a bank is a good source of small business funding is the size of the bank relative to its SBA loan portfolio. In *The SBA Loan Book,* Charles Green points out that a $70 million bank with a $15 million SBA loan portfolio is a better bet than a $2 billion bank with only $10 million in SBA loans.[14]
- *Nonbank lenders.* Nonbank lenders often offer a wider array of services than most banks: checking and savings accounts, online banking and payroll services, employee benefit packages, flexible leasing programs, and so on. The standard comment you hear about lenders is that they're expensive, but institutions that demand higher interest rates usually fund riskier deals.
- *Leasing companies.* If your business requires substantial fixed assets and equipment to operate, you will probably want to free up

cash by leasing those assets from a leasing company (or a bank). The SBA does not guarantee capital equipment leases, although it can guarantee equipment loans. Advantages of leases over loans include the ability to finance 100 percent of the capital purchase, the flexibility of choosing to own the assets or leave them off the balance sheet, and the willingness of specialized lenders to back the purchase of your specialized equipment when banks won't.[15]

- *Local government programs.* Some local and state agencies offer financing programs for the purchase of fixed assets, the development of high-tech businesses, and/or other special areas of interest. Ask your state senator or local SBA office.

- *Microlenders.* If you need only a small amount of money or have a mixed credit history, you want to look for a microlender. A *microloan* is a small loan of $35,000 or less, and it has historically been extended to people with limited means who otherwise would have no way to fund their business. Loans in this range are generally not financially attractive to traditional banks, so nonprofit organizations have stepped in to fill the void.

  The SBA has a microloan program, in which it funds certain qualified nonprofit organizations to act as intermediary lenders to new and existing small businesses. The loans are direct loans from the intermediary lender and are not guaranteed by the SBA; they have a maximum term of six years and rates that generally vary between eight and 13 percent. According to the SBA, the average size of a microloan is $13,000.[16]

  Count-Me-In for Women's Economic Independence. Cofounded by Nell Merlino, the creator of Take Our Daughters to Work Day in 1993, the online microlending program known as Count-Me-In deserves special mention (see www.countmein.org). It offers microloans of between $500 and $10,000, in addition to consulting and educational resources, to women who have nowhere else to turn for that first business loan. (The organization's Make Mine a $Million Business™ program, started in conjunction with OPEN by American Express and mentioned at the beginning of this chapter, offers loans of up to

$45,000, along with mentoring and marketing opportunities.) Count-Me-In charges an interest rate of between 8 and 15 percent, depending on credit history, business risk, and prior experience. Loan applications can be completed online. If approved, Count-Me-In sends the lendee a promissory note in the mail to sign and return. Count-Me-In's web site elaborates on its vision to offer women access to credit and capital:

> *Current criteria for gaining access to credit and capital does not fit the lives many women lead or the kinds of businesses millions of women start and own. Women tend to start smaller, service-related businesses, do not have traditional forms of collateral, have no credit or messy credit histories due to divorce or other life circumstances, and want smaller amounts of money to start a business.*[17]

Where should you start? Linda Stevenson recommends that you "look at all your options. Mix and match to meet your needs." Always ask what special financing programs are available in your state or local region. Go to your district SBA office, where there's a representative charged with looking out for the needs of women. (See http://www .onlinewbc.gov/wbors.pdf for a complete listing.)

You should shop around before you submit your loan proposal to a bank, and when you do you should probably submit it to more than one. If (and only if) you feel certain that you have a high-quality application, prepare multiple loan packages and submit them to different lenders at the same time. Let the lenders know you're doing this—they're more likely to act quickly and offer you competitive rates if they know you're shopping around.

BUSINESS BORROWER PROFILE
Buying and Revitalizing Shelter Island Gardens

Erin Hanlon couldn't have done what she did without an SBA-guaranteed loan from a local community bank. In April 2005, she purchased an existing landscaping, garden center, and nursery business from an owner who wanted to downsize to one location from two on the eastern part of Long Island. The $900,000 four-acre property with agricultural outbuildings was grandfathered for use as a nursery but otherwise could only be used for residential purposes. The business itself, which had annual revenues of about $600,000 per year, was barely profitable and had only one year-round employee (the rest were seasonal). It sold for $45,000, for a combined total purchase price of $945,000, including the real estate. Erin bought it for 15 percent cash down with the financial help of her fiancé (now husband) and financed the rest. She owns 51 percent, he owns 49 percent, and after several months of help from him in the beginning she now runs it on her own.

Erin, who is in her mid-20s, was trained as a landscape architect. She had worked for a nearby, competing nursery business for a few years before striking out on her own. Because her employer was going through difficult times while she worked there, Erin gained experience in all aspects of the business—design, estimating, client management, retail sales, property maintenance, even some financial planning and budgeting. Feeling disgruntled with the way the company was being run, she'd begun to think about going out on her own as a designer when it came to her attention that the owners of a nursery on nearby Shelter Island wanted to sell. She had what she describes as "an epiphany" and began to imagine the kind of community-oriented business she'd like to transform the property into if it were hers.

With nothing but an idea, Erin marched into the Stonybrook, New York, SBA office and asked them how she could make her dream happen. She left with paperwork, brochures, and an idea of which bankers in the area might be supportive. Then she hunkered down and wrote a business plan. (Erin's experience was unusual; typically, borrowers approach the bank first and have no direct contact with the SBA.)

Before she approached the seller, she did her homework. After doing some stealthy market research, Erin completed her business plan and met with Suffolk County National Bank (with a new SBA mentor by her side). After a lot of persistence, she was unofficially prequalified for both a "504" real estate loan and a "7a" business loan equal to 85 percent of the total amount she needed. In order to get the SBA guarantee, the bank insisted that she borrow 105 percent of the total deal price so she'd have leftover funds with which to do capital improvements. When she finally approached the seller with her offer to purchase, the negotiations went smoothly, and she closed in about two and a half months. The seller offered transition help in the way of client lists, pricing information, and vendor relationships.

Says Erin, "My bankers were very happy to lend to a women; they even said it would be easier if we'd been 100 percent woman owned." Obviously, this community bank was on a mission to increase its loans to females (not always the case!). Although Shelter Island Gardens doesn't have extensive operating history yet, Hanlon has already improved aspects of the business, and it's pretty clear, just based on property values, that she made a good deal. Not only could she not have afforded it without a bank loan, but she now has a solid business plan to work from, and her bankers actually check up on her regularly. (You can see her business plan in Appendix A.)

SBA Resources for Women

Is there any preferential treatment for women? I asked this question of Jennifer Williams (CWE Boston), Linda Stevenson (National City Bank), and Wilma Goldstein, Associate Administrator of the SBA Office of Women's Business Ownership. They all said no. However, Goldstein explained that "Over the years, SBA programs have stabilized the situation for women and created a level playing field." All three women concurred that banks won't make special concessions for a business just because it's woman-owned. But they also agreed that when women are educated and enlightened about issues of credit, risk, and debt, they'll be more prepared to borrow money for their businesses, and—all things being equal—have as good a chance at getting funded as men.

How do we know where to start? A good place to start poking around for financing help and education is the SBA's web site, www.sba.gov, and also www.sba.gov/women. How do we avoid going to the wrong lender for the wrong product and then getting turned down? The SBA has a network of nearly 100 Women's Business Centers (WBCs), educational resource centers designed to assist women to start and grow their small businesses (find one in your area at www.onlinewbc.gov). Often these offices and centers have good relationships with certain lenders and can make invaluable introductions. Some of them will actually work with you to prepare your loan application package, offering services similar to those of a professional loan packager.

Goldstein is in charge of the SBA's Women's Business Centers program. She told me that the centers serve two types of women. First and foremost, they're there to serve underprivileged women who need to establish economic self-sufficiency, often by setting up "micro-businesses" at home. These women have zero capital to fall back on and must usually keep another wage-earning job. The second group of women served by these centers have come there on their own initiative. Goldstein calls them "corporate refugees," women with professional experience who are looking to establish "lifestyle businesses" or otherwise do something entrepreneurial. Remarkably, both types of women need similar training, counseling, and mentoring, although the first group is more lacking in skills and sophistication. It's the second group that's more likely to seek help with loans from the center, although the women who start from humble beginnings often come back to these centers for further assistance building even bigger businesses.

Another program that is praised by women is SCORE (the Service Corps of Retired Executives), a valuable mentoring resource that operates as a partner organization to the SBA. Some SBA lenders will actually require that you work with a SCORE counselor, as did Isabella Califano's when she started her clothing line, Chickabiddy. There are more than 10,500 SCORE volunteers in 389 chapter locations who assist small companies with business counseling and training. It's fair to say, however, that the background of some of the volunteers is in big business rather than small, and few of the counselors are women. Isabella said that working with SCORE was a "very helpful process," despite her initial skepticism. According to SCORE's web site and online counseling initiative (see www.score.org), SCORE is the "best source of free and confidential small business advice to help you build your business—from idea to start-up to success." Did someone say "free"? Sign me up!

Alternate Sources of Financing

If you know that you're a good credit risk and that your business is on solid ground, taking on debt might be the safest, least risky growth option for your business.

But if you decide to pursue a financing model other than debt, such as equity financing from venture capital firms or angel investors, you're in a different ball game (and one beyond the scope of this chapter). I recommend reading *Clearing the Hurdles* by Brush, Carter, Gatewood, Greene, and Hart; and *The Old Girls Network* by Whiteley, Elliott, and Duckworth for tips.

There are multiple other creative ways to reduce the need for outside capital. Some not previously mentioned include:

- *Trade credit.* You may be able to get suppliers to extend interest-free credit for 30 to 90 days or more, once you become a regular customer. (Speeding up customer payments can also be helpful in freeing up cash.)
- *Factoring.* Consider selling your accounts receivable to a buyer at a discount. (This can be costly—rates of 25 to 30 percent are not uncommon—but it has the added benefit of eliminating a collections problem.)
- *Liquidation* of unneeded assets.
- *Bringing on a partner.* Business partners, whether silent or active, are a common source of capital for small businesses. See Chapter 10 for tips on dealing with multiple shareholders in a small company.

No matter what methods you consider, don't be shy about going out and talking to other businesswomen in your chosen industry. How did they finance their businesses? And would they have done it differently, knowing then what they know now?

CHAPTER TEN

You're Not Alone: Why Women Consider Business Partners

*I*t comes as no surprise that many women seek partners when they are planning a foray into entrepreneurial business. Many of us do not want to go it alone, and we recognize that we don't have the skills or knowledge to excel in every area. For some women who divide their energies between home and work, having a partner or at least a second-in-charge is absolutely essential to taking on the challenge of self-employment. Partnering with others can make the jump into entrepreneurship more palatable in terms of investment, overall responsibility, balance of talent and experience, or just camaraderie. With their excellent relationship skills, women may be particularly well suited to partnering.

No matter what might go wrong with partnerships, the fact remains that with a partner, you can achieve things you cannot do alone. You can try things you otherwise wouldn't attempt, take on challenges you otherwise couldn't afford. You have an imperfect union, but you're stronger together than you are alone—provided you can find a way to work together.

Even though I and many of the women I've interviewed have had mixed experiences with partners, I'm not soured on the idea of working with someone else to achieve my business dreams, and I would do it again. Those of us who have experienced partnerships that didn't live up to our expectations have learned from our mistakes, and most of us have poised ourselves to be better partners (or choose better partners) next time around. You're invited to learn from our mistakes, too, and consider all the benefits to business partnerships.

How Partnering Makes Your Work and Life Easier . . .

- You can share the financial burdens and risks.
- You have someone else to help you make the big decisions.
- You can pool your different skills, talents, and resources.
- You're more likely to have a faster-growing business with a partner than without.[1]
- You can cover for each other so that the business continues to generate sales and profits while one of you is fulfilling personal responsibilities or on vacation.

And Harder

- You must share the financial rewards and agree on whether to distribute or reinvest profits.
- You must achieve consensus with someone else on the big decisions, including the strategic direction of your company.
- You should present a unified front to employees, which isn't always easy.
- You must strive to maintain a professional environment rather than one that revolves around your own personalities and quirks.
- While it's easy to get into co-ownership situations, it's very hard to undo a partnership or extricate yourself from one.
- Your business partnership may create associated stress for your spouse (or whoever provides your support system).
- The costs of a failed partnership can be steep.

Share the Burden, Share the Spoils

The lone entrepreneur has to make every big decision alone. She has to do the impossible: put her customers first while not demoting her personal self or family to second priority. Simultaneously, she may have to put her family's financial assets at risk by personally guaranteeing a business loan or agreeing to a lien on her house. The lone entrepreneur has to step up to the plate when no one else is around and deal with the curve balls that are thrown her way every day in a small business, such as a surprise resignation of a key employee. While some women relish this challenge, many find that having a business partner to share these challenges is a gigantic relief. Other women, sometimes by necessity, are both single parents and lone business owners. So it can be done—the only question is, would you prefer to share both the risks and rewards with someone else?

Even when a business initially can't afford to support more than one person, partnerships are the chosen path for many hopeful women. Naturally, the expectation is that, through careful business decisions, the business will be able to support more than one owner. If your gut feeling or circumstances suggest that you'd be better off with a partner, choose a business that has the potential to grow and support you—and choose a partner you can envision growing with you.

Many women find that the trade-offs are worth it. Although you'll have to share the profits of the business with your partner, you may discover that your share of the jointly created profits is greater than you would have received if you collected 100 percent of the profits generated on your own. Partners often create—and share—a bigger pie! Sharing financial risks with another committed person can also be comforting, although sharing control and money requires a certain maturity and lack of avarice. Many partnerships start out rosy and then collapse when partners disagree over money matters. That's why many people have warned me: "If you can possibly do it by yourself, do it."

But I'm more inclined to ask, "How would it be possible, even preferable, to do this with someone else?" Maybe the answer is having a strategy for buying the other out if things go sour. Possibly the key is to choose a partner with strengths that complement your own. Drafting detailed job descriptions (and sticking to them) might prevent conflict. Maybe it's a good idea to set up an advisory board to help you when you're deadlocked on key business decisions. In some cases, it may be appropriate to structure a one-year trial period. Maybe all it takes to improve our chances for success is a lot of good planning.

Hope for the Best, Plan for the Worst

When you hear or read about unsuccessful partnerships, you hear about what the partners regret *not* doing almost as much as you hear what they regret *doing*. It turns out that cultivating a successful partnership requires a more deliberate effort than many people think. You can sum up most of the lessons learned from failed partnerships like this: You must *prepare yourself* for partnership success. If you're a planner, this is good news for you. If you're not, you'll have to draw upon your self-discipline to plan ahead or, alternatively, surround yourself with advisers who will do it with you. Mediation expert and partnership consultant David Gage recommends that potential partners spend time developing a structured conflict prevention plan called a "Partnership Charter" (see Appendix I). Gage wrote a book by the same name that I highly recommend.

Deciding to take on a partner is the easy thing. Planning for it properly is more difficult, and executing your plan, most difficult of all. Talking yourself into taking on business partners does not help you to (1) find the right partner (or the right business); (2) define your respective ownership, control, and legal rights; (3) define your respective day-to-day roles and responsibilities; or (4) ensure harmonious relations with your partner(s) now and in the future. Even the best of intentions, and the best of friendships, do not protect you from the perils of partnerships gone wrong. All the common sense in the world can't make you immune to emotional conflicts.

Although it may sound cynical, one of the best ways to prepare you and your partner for working together is to discuss ahead of time all the bad things that could possibly ever happen, while they are all still theoretical. Situations that you cannot imagine arising will. One of you may move away or lose interest; one may want to bring in a third partner, borrow money to expand quickly, change the business model, distribute as much cash as possible each year, or assume you'll both be working 60-hour weeks. A road map for handling some of these situations should be set in writing in a legal agreement between you and your partner (more on this later in the chapter). Additionally, discussion of all the things that don't belong in a legal agreement but that should be discussed in advance should be part of your preparation. How will you divide management duties? Who reports to whom? What are your working styles and how might they inadvertently cause misunderstandings? What role (if any) should your spouses play? And so on.

Many people fear going into partnership with others, and for good reason. The analogy business partners use most often is marriage, which we all know is not to be entered into lightly. (The analogy only goes so far, however, because you can sell a business, but no one has ever figured out how to sell a bad marriage!) But if you're lucky enough to be in a solid marriage, you don't want out, do you? Let's be honest: Most married couples prefer the imperfection of their team approach rather than the solitude of doing it all alone. Happy business partners say the same thing. One seasoned business woman I interviewed said she can predict how well people will handle business partnerships by examining how strong their long-term relationships are. She pointed out, "The capacity to give and take, an acceptance that things aren't always fair, the ability to make sacrifices for each other, and a refusal to 'keep score' are crucial qualities in both marriage and business."

So how will you find a partner who is suited, willing, and available to join you in starting or buying a business? Do you have someone in mind?

Finding the Perfect Partner

You may be disappointed to find that this chapter doesn't give you a magic questionnaire with which to screen people to see whether they fit your personal profile of a perfect partner. That's because doing so might lead you to reject potentially good partners; no one partner is really perfect. And don't forget, you may have a limited pool of people from which to pick because of geography, availability, financial situation, or other reasons. While some want to partner with other women who have similar life stage concerns and schedules, others would like to try working with their spouse or other family members, or with men and women who are complementary for a variety of reasons. What's the best answer?

David Gage reminds us that you don't have to be wholly similar in values and style, nor wholly different in skills and contributions. He writes, "It's a blessing when people are so different and the needs of the business are similarly diverse. . . . [But] when people come together with similar competencies, they can still find themselves slipping comfortably into very different roles."[2] The one thing you cannot compromise on, however, is the need to clarify roles, responsibility, authority, and accountability. What you want to achieve is a system for working together harmoniously, although, with time, partner dynamics sometimes change.

Though you may wish it to be true, having a lot in common personally with a business partner is not enough to make it work. Business partners need to have very clearly defined roles and responsibilities, and they need to have a roughly right combination of skills for their business. That said, the most successful small business people have the "jack of all trades" mentality that enables them to know just enough about the other's role to hold down the fort when she is out of the office, away on vacation or a business trip, or busy with something else.

Be honest about the primary reason you're seeking a partner, whether it is sharing the workload, needing an infusion of cash, making up for skill deficiencies, or wanting to work with a friend. Many modern women will admit to simply wanting someone else to share the burdens and time commitment. They choose to partner with someone who also needs and desires flexibility so that they can cover for each other but not resent the fact that neither is putting in 80-hour work weeks. That's fair. Just realize that being partners is far more involved than job sharing.

PARTNERSHIP MODELS
Four Stories and Their Lessons Learned

*Ex-IBMer Comes Up with Cool Idea,
Needs Savvy Business Partner to Bring It to Fruition*

Caryl Parker and Joanne ("Bobbi") Giudicelli played tennis at the same club, where Bobbi noticed that Caryl's racquet grip was wrapped in a cool, Hawaiian floral print overgrip. Although formerly in sales at IBM, Caryl had a real flair for design and had come up with a brilliant name for the product: Hip Grips. Caryl sourced the first batch of grips in Taiwan and shipped them to tennis shops all over the country. However, they were slippery and unusable, a problem that threatened to doom the small company before it took off. "I just don't have the energy to do this by myself," Caryl told Bobbi.

Bobbi, a veteran business owner and executive recruiter, took charge, and the two established a 50-50 legal partnership. Caryl's job was everything creative, Bobbi's job was everything else. Bobbi found a better manufacturer, mailed new samples to hundreds of tennis shops, and called on a connection at the Tennis and Education Foundation for an "in" at the U.S. Open. That connection opened doors at Wilson Sporting Goods, which offered to take over manufacturing and distribution in exchange for a licensing fee for the designs. Sales of their grips exploded, and their business model became simpler, less risky, and less work virtually overnight. Expansion to other products like softball bat grips seems like a no-brainer. Caryl and Bobbi made back their initial $35,000 investment in a matter of months and are hoping that their annual royalty stream from the racquet grips will top $100,000.

The lesson: This business wouldn't have thrived (and may not have survived) without both partners' input. Caryl couldn't have done it without Bobbi's talent in execution; Bobbi would have nothing to sell if it weren't for Caryl's idea and trademark.

* * *

Couple Purchases Multiple TCBY Franchise Outlets in 50-50 Partnership with Out-of-Town Group; Wife Runs the Businesses

Clara Bitter of Asheville, North Carolina, and her husband purchased and later sold six TCBY yogurt franchises over a 14-year period. The Bitters owned 50 percent, and the other 50 percent was owned by a consortium of three men who had bought the rights to 17 North Carolina stores in the early days of the franchisor's expansion.

This complicated partnership arrangement was very successful, according to Clara, for two reasons. First, she and her husband did not want to become minority shareholders, and they successfully resisted the group's attempt to own 51 percent. "What saved us was the 50-50 partnership agreement," says

Clara. Second, "Our partnership worked because I was the person in town running the business day-to-day. They brought expertise and money to the table, but kept their distance." Even Clara and her husband had separate roles—he let her take the lead running the stores on a daily basis, but was by her side for the big strategic decisions. The franchisor was also a partner of sorts.

The lesson: Good up-front planning can ensure the successful collaboration of multiple shareholders. Giving one party clear authority to manage daily operations, however, was key.

* * *

Former Engineer and Academic Buys a Company with an Older, Experienced Male Executive

Ann Gray, the former HBS professor and current president of a metal fabrication company whom you read about in Chapter 9, can't say enough good things about her partnership with Bill Rose. She explains, "Bill is in his mid-50s and his kids are grown. While we leverage each other and compensate for each other's weaknesses, the partnership has been particularly valuable to me because he's been very supportive of my effort to ensure I'm not sacrificing my kids for my career."

They're a good match not only in life stage but also core competencies—Ann's engineering and manufacturing expertise were complemented by Bill's deep management and leadership background. However, their wildly different styles clashed in the early months. "I was ready to kill him after about the first six months!" she says. They worked it out and got to know each other better. "You've got to give a partnership time," stressed Ann.

The lesson: Partners with different strengths and styles can complement each other well, especially when both are mature enough to take a long-term view.

* * *

Former Colleagues Start Fashion Business Together, Get Stuck Transitioning to Phase Two

When Eileen Chang started her jewelry design and manufacturing company, she went into business with an older woman with whom she'd worked at a public relations agency. They elected to run the business from their respective homes, in different states. Their business grew, and the brand attracted a real following, but the geographic challenges got harder when Eileen moved from Georgia to Florida (her partner had always been in Atlanta) and as the number of company employees grew.

The first four years of the partnership worked beautifully. At a certain point, though, the partners' needs and desires for their company diverged, and they struggled with their 50–50 structure and the geographic divide. Eileen considered using an arbitrator to help resolve their differences, but instead they were able to reach an agreement to sell their business to a third party. The deal didn't go through, however, because Eileen's partner had second thoughts just before the closing. Six months later and still at an impasse, they ended up shutting down the company, which had been profitable and debt-free.

The lesson: Working out a resolution would've been easier if they'd anticipated or planned for such worst-case scenarios at the beginning.

The Biggest Challenge: Interpersonal Relations

You may think the biggest challenges you'll face with a business partner are business related. *Think again.* Interpersonal relations with one's partners and colleagues take on an all-important priority in close quarters and in closely held businesses. No matter how good you are at business, be humble about how good you are with people. Stacy O'Reilly, who took over a large family business from her father, told me, "In business school, I learned ten times more math than I'd need in business, and only one-tenth of what I'd need to know about working with people."

Small businesses are personality driven. Let me say that again, because it's so important: *Small businesses are personality driven.* They are because *they can be.* Solo entrepreneurs go into business because they want the freedom to do things their own way, and so their businesses naturally reflect their personal styles. The business owner gets to hire and fire, create the company culture, and be the outside face of the company. Decisions do not need to be made by committee, as long as the customers, bank, or board (if there is one) don't balk. If an owner is gregarious, generous, and not particularly numbers oriented, the business may be sales oriented, very good to its employees, and financially disorganized. If an owner is introverted, technically precise, and financially conservative, the business may be low-profile, with excellent quality control, and growing modestly. If the owner is bold, with workaholic tendencies, and willing to take financial risks, the business may be ambitious and highly leveraged; the employees may be expected to put in long hours.

Many business owners indulge themselves in controlling their company's culture, as opposed to creating a professional atmosphere that adheres to certain peer-behavior norms. This type of behavior can retard a company's growth, especially after it reaches a certain size. Of course, as a small company grows it must become less dependent on its owner and any particular personal style. Some will lament this as a sacrifice of character and culture, and in many ways it is. Yet growth is better than stagnation.

If there's more than one owner in a business, the owners' personalities will somehow meld together to create the personality of the company. Having a style and skills that are different from your partner's may be nicely complementary for the business's objectives, but that does not diminish the need to focus on interpersonal relations with one's partner.

Women, who tend to appreciate consensus, sometimes hate to own up to the fact that they have different personal styles from their partners, or that these style differences can cause problems. But one key to working well with other people is not getting hung up on their individual quirks. A practical idea might be for you and your partner to take and share results from a personality test to evaluate each other's leadership styles. Well-known examples include the Myers-Briggs Type Indicator (MBTI) test and the DiSC Personal Profile System (*DiSC* stands for the four dimensions of dominance, influencing, steadiness, and conscientiousness).[3]

AUTHOR INSIGHT
How a Business Crisis Can Reveal the Fragility of a Partnership

When I experienced the devastating sudden failure of what I had known to be a successful business partnership with another woman, I was so shocked and hurt that it took months for me to understand what had gone wrong. I'd gone into business with someone who I knew had strengths and qualities that were different from my own assets and abilities, and we had dutifully planned for our partnership with the appropriate legal agreements. She valued my financial, strategic planning, and language skills, and wanted my help to grow the business she'd started several years earlier. I was impressed with her products, customer base, business model, and sales charisma. I wanted to help employees by standardizing pricing, sales, and other office procedures; she cared most about keeping employees happy and feeling that their contributions were valued. We figured that, between us, we'd be able to cover all the bases.

After going through an awkward but necessary period of negotiating my purchase of a stake in the business, drafting a buy-sell agreement, and putting employment agreements in place, we reverted to the comfort of dwelling on all that we had in common. Although we were pretty clear on how we'd divide the business responsibilities, at no point did we talk frankly about our respective personalities and working styles.

Early in our partnership, the business faced an unexpected challenge: a customer had inadvertently over-ordered some custom-made merchandise, and we had already paid to have it manufactured and shipped. The customer needed to renegotiate payment terms, but we were in a bind because we'd used our line of credit to buy the merchandise and were not going to be able to continue operating normally unless we collected the amounts due. My partner and I both turned our full attention to the problem, but

(Continued)

AUTHOR INSIGHT *(Continued)*

there was no easy solution to the situation, and we differed about how to handle the customer relationship (she wanted to avoid confrontation, and I wanted to take a more direct approach). Also caught in the middle was a long-serving employee who had landed the account and had historically been the customer's only direct contact. The cash flow crisis that ensued for the next several months put a strain on our partnership, especially because my partner was the only guarantor on the bank line. Aside from the customer crisis, putting the company's financial affairs in order generally was taking more time than I'd anticipated, and my partner began to resent the fact that I wasn't spending more time on sales. The tension in the office spread to our employees, and the warm and fuzzy culture she had nurtured was threatened.

I assumed that the mutual trust between us was inviolate, that we would get through the rough patches, the company would thrive, and our partnership would be stronger as a result. As the minority partner, I lost the battle—my partner, who had founded the company, decided that she wanted to be on her own again. She offered me a fair price for my shares, and I accepted her offer, but I left with a deep feeling of loss.

Looking back on it, I think we should've discussed our different styles up front. We should have been even clearer about our different roles and the reporting lines of our employees and advisers. Perhaps we could have given mediation a try instead of splitting up so suddenly. But one painful realization I came to is that some people don't really want business partners—they crave someone to share the burdens of their business, but at the end of the day they're not comfortable sharing control. Recognizing whether you yourself or the person you are going into business with is truly going to give partnership a fair try is critical to partnership success.

Essential Elements
of a Successful Partnership

Here is my own top-five list of the interpersonal factors that make or break a partnership.

1. *Attention to your partner relationship.* Nurture your relationship with your business partner(s) at all times. It's more critical to your success than your relationships with key employees. Don't assume that you have each other's unconditional trust. Instead, consider that you must continually earn your partner's trust through your actions. Talk over differences in style that could lead to misunderstandings, and talk about conflict as it occurs (but when you're calm).

2. *Open-minded evaluation of your partner's contributions.* Avoid measuring your partner's contributions to the business in petty ways; instead, look at the big picture of what you each bring to the table. Don't count and compare the hours you're each putting in, especially over the short term. The important thing is that your qualitative contributions are roughly equal over time, and that the business is performing well.

3. *Agreement on business and personal goals.* It's crucial to reach consensus with your partner about where you want the business to go, how it will get there, and how fast you want to travel. Many women's business ambitions are wrapped up with their personal ones, and they must be willing to reveal these to their partners. For example, you may want or need to sell the business (or your stake) by a certain point, when you envision big changes in your life. Or you may want to borrow or raise money to grow the company rapidly. These goals and interests *will* affect your partner, so you should be very clear and candid about them and remain open to how you will work out a joint strategy to meet the goals of all of the partners.

4. *No grudges.* You will face conflict with your business partner. Indeed, the first time you disagree on a business decision will be a test of the strength of your partnership, especially if it seems that

one of you won and the other lost. This inevitable situation will be easier to deal with if the partners see conflict as part and parcel of being as interdependent as partners are. Not holding a grudge is a key to long-term success. If you're a person who holds grudges, you should reevaluate whether it makes sense to have a business partner.

5. *Commitment.* In the end, much of this advice boils down to commitment. Give it time. Don't go into business with someone if you aren't prepared to take the downs with the ups, give it a real chance over a long period of time, proactively work through all the issues you may have with each other, admit your own failings, and be a good team player.

Ownership, Control, and Governance

Two major decisions await you when you decide to have a partner: (1) You must decide how you'll value and divide the shares of the company; and (2) you must decide who will have what roles, responsibilities, and authority. Making deliberate, careful choices about ownership and control before setting them in stone in legal agreements is smart. (If you haven't considered putting your ownership structure in writing, you should do so as soon as possible.)

When starting a company from scratch, two partners will often decide to split the ownership 50-50, only to discover later that they are deadlocked over a critical issue. A small business attorney I consulted for the book told me flat out that "the biggest problems come up with 50-50 partnerships. You really need to have one person in charge." However, that same attorney later stated that she "wasn't in favor of minority ownership." I suppose it's a matter of individual choice to rule out anything but a controlling position, but what exactly does that portend for the disadvantaged minority shareholder(s)? What if you cannot or don't want to own 100 percent (or 51 percent) of a company? There must be a workable, attractive solution to minority partners or investors. Learning how to get along with multiple stakeholders is what the vast majority of larger companies are all about.

No matter how you decide to structure your company, there are a couple of financial paradigms that I find useful when sharing control with others. First, *don't be greedy.* It's better to own a smaller piece of a successful enterprise than a bigger piece of a tiny or unsuccessful one. Second, *be willing to reinvest some profits back into your company* so that your business can grow, be less dependent on outside financing, and avoid cash flow crises that might tax your partnership.

Setting Up a Board of Advisers

When companies become large enough to be run by nonowner executives (that is, they're no longer managed by their founder or owners), a system of oversight or governance is used to help make sure that the company is being run in the best interests of its shareholders. The most common forms of governance are a board of directors and a board of advisers. Small companies sometimes create a board of directors as a legal formality but never hold bona fide meetings. After all, if one or two people own a company and personally manage it, what's the point of having a board? They have "board meetings" every day!

A more useful idea for closely held companies, especially those that are 50-50 or equal-thirds partnerships, is a *board of advisers.* Unlike boards of directors, boards of advisers do not have a fiduciary duty to oversee the management of a company, nor do they have control over the owners' ultimate decisions. Instead, they are there to offer expertise and advice, and to hear you and your partners out when you are having trouble agreeing on a particular strategy. An advisory board can include your attorney and accountant as well as independent businesspeople who have valuable insight about your business. No company is too small to have a board of advisers, and occasional meetings of these boards can get owners to think about their companies from a different, more strategic angle. It remains the owners' responsibility, however, to set an agenda for their board.

If you're serious about setting up an advisory board, you may want to apply to the ATHENA Foundation PowerLink program, which helps majority women-owned businesses expand profitably through the use of professional advisory panels appointed by the foundation. The Power-Link mentoring process links the businesses it selects with a volunteer panel of advisers recruited from the local community to serve for one year. These advisers help women gain a new perspective on strategic planning, financial analysis, operations, sales, and other critical business issues. Linda Stevenson, an executive with National City Bank, one of the funders of the program, comments, "Mentoring is one of the key elements that women-owned businesses need to grow. Women do best with a formal mentoring structure, in contrast to men, who tend to automatically and informally mentor and help each other." Go to www.athenafoundation.org for more details.[4]

Legal Documents: How Far Can They Take You?

Many people doing business together, especially those starting businesses from scratch, wing it when it comes to formalizing their relationship. Usually they see the need for putting things in writing well after they're in business together, when problems arise. Once you're in the thick of it, it's much more awkward to talk through sensitive issues. Don't fall into this trap. Draw something up early on.

I recommend beginning with a term sheet you write yourselves that spells out your agreement on the big issues (see Appendixes G and H). You'll then need an attorney to write it into the appropriate formal agreement(s). If you find it strange that I'm not advocating hiring an attorney from the get-go, remember that most of the big legal issues you'll be considering are essentially *business* decisions, and you should never leave business decisions entirely up to your attorneys. Don't make the mistake of glossing over terms in your agreements as merely legal mumbo jumbo.

Another consideration is that small businesses can't afford a lot of legal fees. I recommend hiring a really good small business attorney but limiting the work that he/she does. You can save money if you and your partner choose only one attorney to write up your mutual understandings, representing *your company* as opposed to either of you. But be aware that your corporate attorney cannot represent either partner personally if an issue arises between you. You'll each have to hire separate attorneys if that happens, and they'll be unfamiliar with your business.

Most states require corporations to have Articles of Incorporation; you may also be required to list the names and percentage ownership of each shareholder, member, or partner when filing your business entity with the Secretary of State or Division of Corporations. If you're just two women doing business together, you're not required to have a written contract. Yet, if you haven't documented your partnership in a "Shareholders' Agreement" or similar contract, pertinent state laws will govern your partnership (the specifics of which you may not be aware of and may not like). Although there's no legal requirement to file a partnership document with the state, it's to your own benefit to memorialize your collaboration and joint ownership in an agreement that goes by a name such as "Shareholders' Agreement," "Buy-Sell Agreement," "Joint Venture Agreement," and/or "Stock Purchase Agreement." Your term sheet can be turned into one or more documents like these.

Among the things that should be covered in the term sheet you hand over to an attorney are these:

- The number of shares in the company and amounts held by each partner.
- Any agreements on a future purchase of stock or redistribution of ownership, spelled out in as much detail as possible.
- Any agreements regarding borrowing rights, lines of credit, or cash calls.
- Buyout/exit strategy—spell out whether each partner can sell her shares to an outside party and on what terms. You'd be wise to set up a formula here for valuing the company and setting the purchase price of shares in the event that one of you wants to buy out the other or bring on another partner.
- What happens if one of the partners becomes seriously disabled or dies.
- How you prefer to resolve serious disputes (e.g., consulting advisers, mediation, arbitration).

If you and your partner(s) are all planning to work in the company (as opposed to being passive financial partners), you should put proper employment agreements in place. Being a shareholder is distinct from holding an operating position in the business. Your employment agreements (which should have a specified duration and should be reviewed and renewed regularly) should cover issues including the following:

- Duties, responsibilities, title.
- Term (i.e., duration) of agreement.
- Compensation (base salary, benefits, reimbursement of certain expenses).
- Ability to do work for a related business.
- Relocation—how you'll handle it if one of you moves away.
- General expectations as to working hours and vacation.
- Termination—usually a working business owner can only be terminated from her job for *cause* (generally defined as willful neglect of duties or doing something egregious or harmful to the business). Grounds for termination must be specified, and a warning period with the opportunity to cure the misbehavior can be given. As you can probably imagine, curing a certain misbehavior or gripe is often wholly inadequate in curing the ailing business partnership. Some partners require the company's board of directors' agreement to force a dismissal. But note that even if dismissed, a shareholder remains a shareholder.

This all sounds pretty formal, huh? Perhaps you and your partner are very close and don't want to pin all this stuff down. After all, that's why you left corporate America! I hear you, and I understand how you feel. But by not documenting these issues, you are significantly increasing the risk of future conflict. Misunderstandings and resentments can develop very quickly, even among the best of friends. "Many disputes among partners are essentially battles of memories," according to partner-mediator David Gage.[5] So do yourself a favor and write it down, at a point when it seems theoretical and not at all threatening, because the future may come sooner than you think.

Will the written word save you in all cases? It may infuriate you to know that no matter how much you put in your legal agreements, they may not do you much good. There *will* be circumstances and issues that you didn't foresee in your legal agreements, and you and your partners will probably make decisions or take actions that contradict the documents. In the event of a dispute, you will also have to consider whether you want to go to the expense of dissecting your agreements line-by-line with attorneys, rather than negotiating a solution to your problem yourselves or with the help of mediators. I know of a partnership where the first indication that a partner wanted to buy the other out was an attorney's letter to the other; the partners were never allowed to speak directly again. Madness? Maybe a little. Panic and poor advice, more likely.

When things go sour, it gets messy. Less messy if you've got written agreements in place, but messy nevertheless. Splitting up with your partners is sometimes inevitable, even when partners desperately do not want to split up and wish they could work things out. Wouldn't *conflict prevention* be a far better alternative? I can't say it loudly enough: *Yes!*

While you're writing your term sheet, consider going on a retreat to get to know your potential partner better. A structured exercise like David Gage recommends in *The Partnership Charter* is a good investment in the future and perhaps the best "partner insurance" you can buy (see Appendix I).

Formal Conflict Resolution

If, despite your best efforts, you and your partner really need outside help to move forward, you should strongly consider mediation as an alternative to hiring arbitrators or attorneys. The goal of mediation is to foster greater communication and collaboration between the parties, to find a way for them to creatively resolve their problems. Mediators are neutral parties who assist partners in negotiating a settlement. Typically, mediators meet with the partners together and separately until they agree to a settlement. They also meet in confidential separate caucuses so they understand any hidden agendas that may slow down or sabotage the process of reaching consensus.

Mediated settlements are usually less costly than settlements resulting from arbitration or litigation. While the mediation process is voluntary and the partners may stop it at any time, if they reach an agreement and sign it the resulting settlement is binding. Because mediated settlements are consensual and developed by the parties themselves, they are less often contested than settlements coming from arbitrators and judges.

Hopefully you'll never have to involve mediators, arbitrators, and litigators in your partner relations, but a word to the wise: At least spell out in advance the approach you and your partner(s) will take if disputes arise. It saves, time, money, and anguish to plan ahead of time for the worst that could happen—and then hope it never comes to pass.

Women's Natural Talent for Partnerships

I believe that women are natural collaborators, team players, and consensus builders. Women are intuitive and empathetic in relating to others. Many women—and even men—believe that women have superior communication skills. And, if I may be so bold, women are pretty good at keeping greed at bay and remembering all the many reasons they are in business for themselves. I really think that women have the tools to naturally build and maintain successful partnerships.

Just like anyone, though, women have to rise above petty grievances and catty complaints, reserve judgment, and restrain any volatile or control-freak impulses. Women also have to put their businesses first and choose partners as much for business reasons as personal preference.

Watching a company succeed and grow beyond what you ever could have done on your own, with a partner by your side, is a wonderful feeling. With a partner by your side, you can more easily defy that traditional wisdom about women-owned businesses—that they start small and stay small. More importantly, you can have fun at your job and enjoy close camaraderie with colleagues who are working toward the same goals. Doesn't that feel great?

CHAPTER ELEVEN

Don't Get Discouraged, Just Get Started!

$\mathcal{B}$y now you should feel on fire with all the possibilities for your phase two business career. Hopefully you have identified with some real life role models within these pages, and are beginning to think, "Wow, I could do that!" You're realizing how many different shades of meaning there are to the word *entrepreneur*. However, it's just as possible that you're feeling some form of information-overload and discouragement. Getting from A to B requires an energy and purpose you're not sure you can muster.

There's no need to be overwhelmed. Talk yourself out of it. Here's why: You've got everything going for you!

- Your prior work experience (and I don't mean for purposes of a resume).
- Your confidence and ability to juggle multiple roles.
- Your desire for independence and flexibility.
- Your "woman's intuition" and gut instincts.

That last item is the key to not feeling overwhelmed. Armed with the knowledge in this book, plus your natural excellent instincts, you will be able to figure out what's right for you once you start hunting around and unearthing possibilities.

Give yourself some time for a search. Go out and look at and compare specific entrepreneurial options. Write down your best start-up idea and what it might involve to pursue it. Go to www.bizbuy sell.com and do a search for available companies in your area of interest, geographic location, and price range. Go to a franchising web site and see if anything really piques your curiosity; meet with a franchise consultant if you want to explore specific opportunities. Consult for a friend's business for a while before you commit long-term to anything. Go observe a direct sales home party for a type of product you find appealing.

Talk to women business owners in your town or through your college alumni network. Share some of your ideas with your husband and your good friends. See if the person you think might make an ideal business partner is on the same wavelength. If applicable, talk to your father/mother/uncle about joining the family business. Take a look at your financial situation; clean up any credit issues and figure out what you could afford to put into a business. Keep your eyes and ears open for referrals to good small business attorneys and accountants. Read the business opportunities section in your Sunday paper. Do all this while you're still sitting at your desk in your safe corporate job, if you like.

After a few months of this kind of exploration, without committing to anything, you'll be amazed at how much more confident you'll feel about embarking on an entrepreneurial path tailored to your own skills, interests, and financial parameters. With some discipline, you can make sure you've cultivated the business mind-set I talk about in Chapter 1. With your gut instincts and intuition, it will be hard for you to go wrong. You can make an educated decision about which path, among the multiple options discussed here, seems right for you at this point in your life.

Even I, the humble author, plan to drink my own Kool-Aid and get out there and embark on another search to figure out my next business opportunity.

It's all right to pursue more than one of the options in this book, sequentially. Perhaps you'll use one of the ideas as a starter business to give yourself the confidence to attempt something bolder and riskier next time. Some of you may make a choice and realize part way into it that you've made a mistake, then need to salvage the pieces of what you've done and start again.

The Great American Labor Shift

I believe that you and I (and even our husbands and male friends) are part of an enormous labor shift in the American economy. The labor shift started with the huge wave of Internet start-ups in the 1990s. In the years since then, grassroots forces have legitimized new career models including freelancers in every industry, home-based businesses of all kinds, and a wide array of entrepreneurs who have reacted to the vanishing security of corporate jobs with pensions by taking their livelihoods into their own hands.

Most of those on the front lines of this labor shift care a great deal about quality of life, living and working where they choose, independence, flexibility—buzzwords for a new generation of workers. In fact, it's never been more socially acceptable than it is today to carve out one's own career path. You hear about people doing this all the time, and you can be one of them.

As this labor shift occurs, it's only natural that the half of the workforce that's female will be tweaking the new models to suit our gender-specific needs. The natural place for many of us to do so is in the huge world of small business. Finally, there is a dawning realization that women need different models for success at work than the strict 9-to-5 (or, more commonly, 8-to-8) grind of corporate career ladders and the linear, achievement-oriented resume. That model was made for men, and it's often not compatible with caring for families and pursuing what really matters to us.

This new labor market is made for self-starters. Government bodies and large corporations are not going to lead the way; at best, they're going to follow. That's why it's important not to waste too much time getting angry about what's lacking in our economy and our society.

Directionally Correct

I was describing and defending these new business and career models to my father recently, as I was in the throes of writing this book. Even though I emphasized that I'd interviewed many real women who had built successful careers on their own terms in the realm of small business, he had a skeptical look on his face, and I drew out of him a wise but conservative sentiment. The gist of it was this: "Ginny, you're making all these business options appear attractive and approachable to women in your book, but don't forget: Being self-employed is a grind, too. It's hard, it's intense, and it doesn't always work out. And this business about working part-time or setting your own hours in your own company—in my experience, it just doesn't work that way!"

I thought about what he said for a long time before replying, and I've thought about it a lot since. I couldn't really disagree with him, but I also knew I wasn't on the wrong track. So I said, "Yes, Dad, I know what you're saying, but I think the women I interviewed are onto something big. The trends I talk about in the book are—well, they're directionally correct." Directionally correct—yes. I kept repeating that phrase to myself.

Julie Hellwich's words actually help articulate what I couldn't quite express to my father: "Smart Women Thirst for Knowledge" and "Smart Women Light the Way." When I stumbled across Julie's products last summer, then called her about this book (see the latter half of Chapter 8), they resonated deeply with me. Now, to her many uplifting slogans, I can add a few practical mantras:

- Smart Women Explore All Their Options.
- Smart Women Do Their Homework.
- Smart Women Dare to Borrow Money.
- Smart Women Use Good Advisers.
- Smart Women Work Smarter, Not Necessarily Harder.

No Regrets

There's no question in my mind that pursuing small business ownership is the right choice for millions of midcareer business-oriented women. I also know and admit that doing it successfully is in many ways more difficult than reporting to a job five days a week. But the evidence is there that women can express themselves successfully through the medium of business. The evidence I saw is the near-total absence of regret among the women I talked to. Despite some regret over particular business decisions, they all said they wouldn't for the world change what they'd done, and most of them said they had no desire to go back to their old careers.

So what else is left to say? Smart women of the world, unite! Have fun! Do good! And make money.

APPENDIX A

Sample Business Plan—
Revitalizing Shelter
Island Gardens

EXECUTIVE SUMMARY

Shelter Island Gardens ("SIG") is the only full-service garden center and nursery on Shelter Island, New York, a 12-square-mile island lying between the north and south forks of Long Island (the "Hamptons") and accessible by fast commercial ferries. Although ownership has changed twice, SIG has been continuously operated since 1949.

Under the current ownership of Coastal Landscape Partners, the business has seen combined sales growth of more than 30 percent over the last three years. However, Coastal Landscape Partners' primary business is farming an 80-acre nursery elsewhere in the Hamptons. The principals' modest experience in landscape design and

---

This is an actual business plan used by one of the female entrepreneurs profiled in the book, Erin Hanlon, to purchase and revitalize an existing business. Hanlon successfully used this plan (edited here for length) to secure $985,000 in SBA-backed loans from Suffolk County National Bank. The corporate name of the prior owner of the business has been changed to protect the privacy of the individuals involved.

high-end retail, coupled with the inadequate amount of time they've been able to devote to the Shelter Island property, have proved to be limiting factors to the business. The principals are therefore offering to sell the four-acre commercial property and related business operations for a total of $945,000.

We, the prospective buyers, are currently seeking funding in the amount of $1,200,000 to cover the costs associated with the purchase of this commercial property and the revitalization of the related business. We have approximately $165,000 in funds to invest toward this total. SIG will be owned and operated by its co-principals, Erin Hanlon and Sean McLean, who each have extensive experience in landscape design, nursery operations, and site construction and management.

SIG intends to capitalize on a growing and captive market for landscaping services in an exclusive island community. Shelter Island has become one of the country's most exclusive second-home communities, benefiting from its isolation and limited available land. Our team's expertise in the luxury retail and design markets of the south fork, and our intimate knowledge of the Shelter Island community, will allow us to provide a level of service currently not available to "Islanders."

SIG's experienced sales staff will offer trees, shrubs, perennials and annuals for sale in the yard as well as planting supplies, pottery, garden tools, garden furniture and ornamental accessories in the garden center. Other services include landscape design and planning, landscape construction, and project management. Shelter Island Gardens will sponsor community and educational programs creating an enriched social atmosphere promoting the very reason our clients are on Shelter Island— the outstanding beauty of its natural environment.

Over the last several decades, the fields of landscape design and gardening have shown significant growth on the east end of Long Island, as well as on Shelter Island itself. The operation of a quality landscape nursery, garden retail facility, and landscape service provider is necessary to the community of Shelter Island. Under our ownership, Shelter Island Gardens will reach its full potential.

STATEMENT OF PURPOSE

It is our intent to present this business plan to a local lending institution for the purpose of obtaining approximately $1,000,000 in funding. This amount, together with the principals' investment of $165,000, will pay for the purchase of the commercial property and business opportunity. A portion of the monies requested will be used for renovation of the existing facilities to create a more functional retail center. Please see the attached sources and uses of funds spreadsheet for more detailed information. A loan term of 20 years is requested; $50,000 of the money requested should be in the form of a credit line.

BUSINESS LOCATION, DESCRIPTION, AND HISTORY

Formerly known as "Shelter Island Nursery," Shelter Island Gardens has operated as a garden center and nursery at 29 Saint Mary's Road, Shelter Island, New York, since 1949. Shelter Island lies between the north and south forks of Long Island in the center of the Peconic Bay, is comprised of 12 square miles, and has more than 15 miles of coastline. SIG is located 1,000 feet from Route 114, Shelter Island's main commercial and travel corridor, with 440 feet of street frontage along St. Mary's Road for displaying retail nursery stock.

Within this centrally located four-acre property lies a 2,500-square-foot main building with retail showrooms, office, and storage/work areas. Additional structures include an equipment/storage building of 1,500 square feet and a greenhouse facility of 3,800 square feet.

PRODUCTS AND SERVICES

SIG aims to create an enjoyable, sociable, and educational environment for the residents and visitors of Shelter Island. This business will form a partnership with the community to educate them about the ecology, biology, and viable plant life of Shelter Island, while empowering and enabling the community to make a tangible difference in their own backyard landscape.

SIG will offer diverse products and services to its customers:

- In the *garden shop*, the experienced sales staff will work to provide customers with the highest level of customer service. SIG will offer garden ornamentation and furniture, pottery, garden tools, local artistry, planting supplies, and plant health care solutions.
- In the *yard*, our staff will lead guests through a collection of quality trees, shrubs, perennials, annuals, as well as unusual plant selections of exceptional quality and native species.
- For the experienced home gardener SIG will offer our unique *"Express Planting" program*. This program will allow knowledgeable customers to handpick their trees, shrubs, vines, and so on at our nursery, and we will provide delivery and planting services to them within five business days.
- For the novice home gardener, the Garden Shop staff will introduce customers to SIG's *design and planning services*. This program offers on-site consultation and estimates without obligation. The design and planning team can provide clients with conceptual sketches and complete landscape master plans, through manual drafting or computer-aided design. The design professionals will also offer project phasing to meet clients' individual needs and budget.
- The *landscape construction services* at SIG will include landscape design, installation, project management, and customized property care. We will work closely with local developers, real estate agents, contractors, pool and masonry companies, and the like, to develop a signature "Shelter Island Style" landscape to a new or updated property.

Every day will bring a mixture of meeting new clients and getting to know their landscape needs, then filling those needs to the best of our staff's capabilities. Quality of our plant material will be important, of course, but our primary focus will be on service to our customers. Immediate individual response to each client will set Shelter Island Gardens apart from any "off island" competition.

MARKET ANALYSIS

SIG has served a unique and captive gardening community for over 50 years. Although Shelter Island comprises a smaller market than other neighboring East End towns, the island has benefited from the extremely robust real estate market that has prevailed here and in other nearby premier Long Island communities. Improved market conditions have led to the sale of many remaining vacant parcels and the redevelopment of older or underutilized properties, therefore creating increased demand for on-island design and landscaping services. One undeniable indication that this demand exists is that SIG's combined sales have grown more than 30 percent over the last three years.

We feel that the current owners have not reached the fullest potential possible in this market. After surveying several related businesses and former or current clients, the number one complaint was a lack of service to the island. We feel that our growth numbers shown in the attached pro forma are quite conservative.

The department of planning for Suffolk County estimates that the seasonal home owner population on Shelter Island could increase by up to 80 percent over the next 10 years. This fact, in addition to the current considerable and growing turnover of existing properties on the Island, indicates that SIG is poised for substantial growth.

If the level of customer service is increased we believe the loyalty of the Island will come back to Shelter Island Gardens. "Islanders" like to support local business. They are, however, wealthy and discerning home owners. They will hire off-island companies if the local businesses can not provide adequate service and quality. However, no major companies on the north or south fork have thus far been able to corner the market on Shelter Island.

To help grow the business, SIG will work with local clubs and organizations such as the Gardening Club to hold community events, womens' teas, educational lectures, local artist shows, and other seasonal special events. These events will help to cement new support and loyalty

for a truly local business. In addition, future owners Erin Hanlon and
Sean McLean plan to move to Shelter Island, demonstrating their commitment to the island and their business.

GROWTH ASSUMPTIONS AND STRATEGY

Our current forecast is for gross sales of $634,000, $760,800, and
$912,960 in years one, two, and three, representing a growth rate of 20
percent in each of the latter two years.

Net profit before taxes is estimated to be a modest $30,840 in year
one but to grow to $109,552 in year two and to $200,947 by year three.
This is in addition to a working owner's salary of $43K in year one, $45K
in year two, and $47.6K in year three.

Debt service at $77,400 per annum is included in the projections. If
financed as planned, the business should be able to service its debt, pay
the working owner (Erin Hanlon) a modest salary, and produce a
healthy profit that will grow over time.

For comparison purposes, the following table was compiled from reference sources that give historical industry ratio information from other
private companies within our U.S. Standard Industrial Classification
(SIC) code:

*Average Sales, Expense, and Profitability Figures for U.S. Small
Businesses in "Retailing—Building Materials & Garden Supplies"*

Total Revenue (Sales)	$634,000	100.0%
Total Expenses as Percent of Revenue	$568,095	89.6%
Net Income to Owner as Percent of Revenue	$ 65,905	10.4%

Detail of Expenses (as Percent of Revenue)

Cost of Goods Sold	$391,681	61.8%
Salaries and Wages	$ 41,178	6.5%
Advertising	$ 7,853	1.2%
Auto and Truck Expenses	$ 14,692	2.3%
Depreciation	$ 9,585	1.5%

Employee Benefits	$ 1,093	0.2%
Home Office Business Expenses	$ 354	0.1%
Insurance	$ 8,275	1.3%
Interest Expense	$ 9,764	1.5%
Legal and Professional Services	$ 2,005	0.3%
Meals and Entertainment	$ 1,415	0.2%
Office Expense	$ 3,235	0.5%
Retirement Plans	$ 80	0.0%
Rent—Equipment	$ 3,583	0.6%
Rent—Office and Business Property	$ 7,186	1.1%
Repairs	$ 7,362	1.2%
Supplies	$ 5,539	0.9%
Taxes—Business and Payroll	$ 13,784	2.2%
Travel	$ 2,150	0.3%
Utilities	$ 9,574	1.5%
Other Expenses	$ 27,708	4.4%
Total Expenses as Percent of Revenue	$568,095	89.6%

MANAGEMENT AND STAFF

Erin Hanlon, Co-Owner and Senior Manager of Shelter Island Gardens. Erin holds a bachelor of fine arts/landscape architecture from Rhode Island School of Design (RISD). Erin has been a successful landscape designer and landscape account manager in the exclusive resort area of the "Hamptons," New York. Erin's past clients include the likes of Martha Stewart, Calvin Klein, and Steven Spielberg. In 2004 Erin designed and managed the landscape reconstruction of the outdoor sculpture garden at East Hampton's exclusive Guild Hall Museum and Theater. In addition, her design was used in the construction of the "Hamptons Designer Showcase House" located in Wainscott, New York. As Principal, she will manage all aspects of the garden center, direct and evaluate the management team, supervise all daily programs and activities, insure adherence to state/local health and safety requirements, and implement company policies and procedures. She will manage SIG's finances, develop and screen new clients, and liaise with associated organizations. Erin will also function as the on-site landscape design consultant.

Sean McLean, Co-Owner. Sean holds a master's degree in real estate development from New York University and a bachelor of arts in psychology from Princeton University. He has over five years of site construction and development experience. As a senior project manager for McLean Contracting he has managed more than $30 million of construction projects, including the construction of an 18-hole golf course, $6.8 million worth of landscaping for over 1,200 homes, and a 35-acre Town Park with 7.5 soccer fields. Mr. McLean is also a founding principal in Dionysus Company, a small consulting firm founded in 1998 specializing in the development of real property. Projects of note that he has worked on are (1) Heritage Square at East Moriches, a 420-unit senior resort property on Long Island; and (2) Sweden Town Center, a master planned community (currently in the planning stage) which will consist of approximately 1,000 residential units and 250,000 square feet of retail, commercial, and hotel/entertainment space in Rochester, New York. As Principal, Sean will act in an advisory, rather than day-to-day management, capacity. His responsibilities include the overall management of the proposed site and building improvements at the nursery. In addition he will oversee property management and maintenance. He will be intimately involved with the company's financing and development.

Ken McGuiness, Retail Garden Shop Manager. Ken will remain employed by Shelter Island Gardens after the purchase. Ken was hired in spring 2004 and helped to increase the gross income of the retail garden center by almost 50 percent. Ken, a Long Island native, has had a 20-year career in the high-end retail garden center business. Most recently he supervised the Annuals and Tropicals Department at Martin Viette in East Norwich, New York. He also served as general manager at Woodstock Farms in Oyster Bay, New York, serving from its start-up to its establishment as a full-service garden center. His responsibilities at SIG will include managing all retail sales personnel and all retail sales functions. These operations include purchasing, inventory management and merchandising. He will direct the sales team, develop new clients and provide continuity to maintain existing client relationships. He will report directly to Ms. Hanlon.

Equipment Operators. Two part-time operators will return to work for the landscaping division of Shelter Island Gardens. They have extensive knowledge of all heavy machinery used for production.

Laborers. Five part-time laborers will return to work for the nursery this spring. They are experienced in all aspects of landscape construction and maintenance. Additional labor will be sought from a more than adequate construction pool on the east end of Long Island.

ADDITIONAL MATERIALS
SUBMITTED WITH THIS BUSINESS PLAN
(not shown)

1. Shelter Island Demographics, a table taken from www .neighborhoodscout.com.
2. Garden Market Forecast—a summary of a current market research report from Unity Marketing detailing the $41 billion industry; the fast-growing garden hardware and accessories business; the prevalence of middle-aged, affluent garden center customers; and the trend toward "reconnecting with nature."
3. Photographs of the property before the purchase.
4. Financial projections:
   a. Sources and uses of funds.
   b. Pro forma cash flow statement, years 1, 2, and 3.
   c. Pro forma income statements, years 1, 2, and 3.
   d. Pro forma balance sheets, end of years 1, 2, and 3.

Start-Up Business Plan Outline

A proper business plan is composed of an executive summary (2 to 4 pages) and the plan itself (usually 20 to 25 pages). Even if you will only use it for internal purposes, it's best to write for an outside audience. Include ample background information, portray your business dynamically, and analyze it dispassionately. At some point, you'll need or want to use the business plan with financiers, employees, or professional advisers. When that time comes, you may tailor the contents for your particular audience, but you'll have a base from which to start.

The following outline for a start-up business plan is exemplary because it makes one think, rather than just recite.

I. **Company Description and Product Detail**
    a. Describe your product or service.
    b. Why is it unique, or better, or cheaper, or faster?
    c. Why will you be a market leader?

The outline in this Appendix comes from the "Tool Kit" at the back of the book *Clearing the Hurdles: Women Building High-Growth Businesses*, by Candida Brush, Nancy M. Carter, Elizabeth Gatewood, Patricia G. Greene, and Myra M. Hart (Upper Saddle River, NJ: FT Prentice Hall/Pearson Education, 2004), 183–184.

    d. How does the product address your customer's need or solve a particular problem?

    e. Describe the stage of your company's development (i.e., concept stage, prototype, launch).

II. **Description of Your Market**

    a. Describe the target market for your company's product or service.

    b. Drill down to the specific segment within the market that you are targeting.

    c. How large is the market segment? How fast is it growing and what factors drive this growth?

    d. Project a realistic estimate of what share of the market you can capture.

    e. Provide detail on your customer base: who, how many, how they make purchasing decisions.

III. **Competitive Landscape**

    a. What is your competitive advantage (i.e., proprietary technology, new design, better pricing)?

    b. Are there barriers to entry?

    c. How does your product differ from the competition, and why?

IV. **Revenue Model and Assumptions**

    a. How do you make money?

    b. Outline your pricing strategy and defensibility.

    c. List the costs to develop your product and bring it to market.

    d. Give a minimum of three (maximum five) years' projections for revenue, expenses, and profits.

    e. When will you achieve breakeven and cash-flow-positive positions?

V. **Sales and Marketing Strategy**
   a. Strategy for taking product to market; how your product will be positioned.
   b. Distribution plans (i.e., direct sales, distributors, strategic partnering).
   c. Implementation plans and timetable.

VI. **Management Team**
   a. Why are you the right management team to build this company?
   b. Provide brief bios and profiles of yourself and other key members of your management team.
   c. Highlight specific experience that lends itself to this enterprise.

VII. **Financing Details**
   a. How has your company funded itself to date? Describe outside capital raised, if any.
   b. What milestones have you achieved to date?
   c. How much capital are you looking to raise? Give a brief description of the offering (i.e., debt or equity). Don't put a dollar valuation of your company's worth in these documents.
   d. How will you spend the new capital you raise (i.e., sales and marketing, product development, technical support)?
   e. Describe your exit strategy.

Top 10 Reasons to Contact an Attorney When Starting a Business

10. *Contracts.* Businesses execute or generate contracts for most business transactions, including purchases, sales, and services. Companies also have agreements between partners, investors, employees, and independent contractors.

9. *Licensing.* Some business entities are required to register with the state in which they do business in order to be recognized and obtain certain licenses or permits.

8. *Who's in Control?* The choice of business entity often dictates the manner in which the business is operated and who will be in control of it. This is especially important for multi-owner businesses.

7. *Intellectual Property.* The choice of business name and other trademarks should be vetted to make sure that you will not infringe on someone else's trademarks. Inventions may need to be patented.

This appendix was provided in its entirety by Lisa Hodgen of Leisawitz Heller in Wyomissing, Pennsylvania.

6. *Conformity with State Law.* Failure to maintain your business form in conformity with state law may cause you to lose the law's benefits and protections.

5. *Money.* Businesses need to raise money, keep financial records, and behave in a fiscally responsible manner. Different business entities may require different procedures for raising capital and making distributions to the owners.

4. *Which Entity?* In addition to the challenge of choosing the right legal entity for your business, there are options within these entities that determine taxation of the entity and its partners and potential liability for the acts of partners. The preconditions to forming and conducting a business entity in one state may not be accepted in another.

3. *Decisions by Default.* When forming a new business entity, the things you don't decide are decided for you. State law will fill in the gaps for business entities where their charters, by-laws, and other organizing documents are silent. You may be subject to a whole set of laws and regulations that you don't even know exist.

2. *Taxes.* Different business forms provide different tax advantages and disadvantages. The only thing more crucial to a new business is limited liability.

1. *Limited Liability.* Different business forms provide different protections and risks to the business owner/investor. While a business entity can minimize your personal liability, it will not necessarily eliminate it. Personal liability means that your business puts everything you own at risk (personal guarantees are common when securing bank financing). An attorney can help you minimize the risk that your business may compromise the economic well-being of you and your family.

APPENDIX D

Choosing a Legal Business Entity

Type of Entity	Main Advantages	Main Drawbacks
Sole Proprietorship	• Simple and inexpensive to create and operate • Owner reports profit or loss on his or her personal tax return	• Owner personally liable for business debts
General Partnership	• Simple and inexpensive to create and operate • Owners (partners) report their share of profit or loss on their personal tax returns	• Owners (partners) personally liable for business debts

(Continued)

This appendix was provided in its entirety by Lisa Hodgen of Leisawitz Heller in Wyomissing, Pennsylvania. This form is provided for informational purposes only and is not intended to be used as legal advice, nor is it a substitute for professional legal advice.

Type of Entity	Main Advantages	Main Drawbacks
Limited Partnership	• Limited partners have limited personal liability for business debts as long as they don't participate in management • General partners can raise cash without involving outside investors in management of business	• General partners personally liable for business debts • More expensive to create than general partnership • Suitable mainly for companies that invest in real estate
Regular Corporation or "C" Corporation (named after Subchapter "C" of the Internal Revenue Code)	• Owners have limited personal liability for business debts • Fringe benefits can be deducted as business expense • Owners can split corporate profit among owners and corporation, paying lower overall tax rate	• More expensive to create than partnership or sole proprietorship • More paperwork • Separate taxable entity • Compliance with legal formalities (e.g., board meetings, state filings) required to preserve limited liability

Type of Entity	Main Advantages	Main Drawbacks
"S" Corporation (named after Subchapter "S" of the Internal Revenue Code)	• Owners have limited personal liability for business debts • Owners report their share of corporate profit or loss on their personal tax returns • Owners can use corporate loss to offset income from other sources	• More expensive to create than partnership or sole proprietorship • More paperwork than for a limited liability company which offers similar advantages • Income must be allocated to owners according to their ownership interests • Compliance with legal formalities required to preserve limited liability • Owners must be U.S. citizens
Limited Liability Company (LLC)	• Owners have limited personal liability for business debts even if they participate in management • Profit and loss can be allocated differently than ownership interests • IRS rules now allow LLCs to choose between being taxed as partnership or corporation	• More expensive to create than partnership or sole proprietorship • Some states aren't LLC-friendly and may tax LLCs as corporations • Can be difficult to administer or explain

Business Information Sheet

Name of business: _____

Where listed/source of ad: _____ Date first seen: _____

Broker representing seller: _____

Business address: _____

Reason for selling: _____

_____

How many years has business been in the hands of this owner? _____

What is the owner's day-to-day involvement? _____

How many employees work in the business? _____

What were gross sales in each of the last four years?

_____   _____   _____   _____

What was the owner's discretionary cash flow in each of the last four years?

_____   _____   _____   _____

What is the asking price for the business? _____

How did you arrive at the asking price? _____

_____

Is the seller willing to finance some portion of the purchase? _____

Is the seller willing to stay on for a transition period? _____

What are the ways that a new owner could grow and improve this business?

_____

NDA signed _____ Selling Memorandum requested _____

_____

This form was inspired by a similar one created by Marcia Rosman of BusinessBroker Services, Braintree, Massachusetts.

Sample Business Valuation— Main Street Florist

$\mathcal{V}$aluing small businesses, particularly those under $1 million, is more of an art than a science. *Fair market value* is defined as "the cash or cash equivalent price at which property would change hands between a willing buyer and a willing seller, neither being under a compulsion to buy or sell and both having reasonable knowledge of relevant facts." Still, math is important. There is one number more important than all the others in valuing small businesses: *seller's discretionary earnings* (SDE), which is synonymous with *seller's discretionary cash flow* (SDCF).

> SDE = pretax income + discretionary cash add-backs, including depreciation + amortization + interest + owner's compensation + owner's noncash benefits + any nonbusiness or nonrecurring expenses passed through the company

---

Much of the introductory information in this appendix was based on discussions on October 5, 2005, with Darren Mize, one of the founders and principals of Gulf Coast Financial, a Tampa-based business valuation firm. The sample appraisal report of Main Street Florist excerpted here was also provided by Gulf Coast Financial.

Example calculation:

SDE (2005) = $37,857 in pretax income + $6,298 in depreciation and
amortization + $17,194 in interest expense
+ $75,998 in owner's salary, perks, and benefits
+ $20,163 in above-market rent collected by owner
for lease of personally owned premises
+ $12,500 in unnecessary furniture expenses
= **$170,010** in seller's discretionary earnings

(As you can see, the calculation is meant to give a more realistic picture
of the cash flow that a new owner could expect, compared to just pretax
income.)

Applying a multiple: Comparing multiples of SDE is the most common way to value small businesses in most categories, but appraisers often use and compare multiple valuation methods in an appraisal, as
you'll see in the sample in this Appendix. While the typical valuation
range for companies worth less than $1 million is 1.5 to 3.0 times SDE,
an actual fair market value depends on many factors, among them:

- Size.
- Financial strength–quality and consistency of financials.
- Dependence on owner; personal goodwill.
- Ability to retain key employees or former owner.
- Customer concentration.
- Quality and loyalty of vendor/supplier base.
- Location.
- Industry.
- Ease of transition.
- Longevity of the company.
- Historical trends—steadily rising, steadily dropping, flat, or
  volatile.

Experts can help you value businesses, but depending on the size of
the business you're acquiring, this may not be an affordable option. You'll

pay many thousands of dollars for a comprehensive valuation analysis that is defensible in a court (often necessary in a divorce, partner dispute, or other specific situations). A medium-priced solution might be a "restricted use limited appraisal report" for $1,000 to $5,000. You can do some of your own homework by paying a one-time fee ($99 to $150) for market comparables from sources like BIZCOMPS or Pratt's Stats. Some businesses for sale may have already obtained valuation reports from appraisers and may be willing to share them with you in order to justify their asking price.

I obtained a sample limited appraisal report for a florist from Darren Mize of Gulf Coast Financial, a Tampa-based business valuation firm. Excerpts of key sections from the 48-page appraisal follow.

Appraisal of Main Street Florist, Inc.
(Excerpts)
By Gulf Coast Financial
January 2, 2005

General Business Information

Name of Business:	Main Street Florist
Address:	123 Beverage Lane, Tampa, FL 33609
NAICS Code:	453110
Type of Business:	Florist
Type of Statements Used:	Tax Returns
Type of Entity:	S Corporation
State of Incorporation:	Florida

Financial Information

Last Full Year Revenue:	$598,741
Last Full Year EBITDA (adjusted):	$ 69,885
Adjusted Book Value (valuation date):	$125,000 (furniture, fixtures, equipment, and inventory)

DESCRIPTION OF THE BUSINESS

The Company was originally founded over 30 years ago by the current owner. It has been a family-owned business since inception. The Company operates as a full-service florist located in Tampa, Florida. Approximately 50 percent of total sales relate to fresh flowers, 30 percent relate to green and blooming plants, with the remaining 20 percent being generated by balloons, gifts, and other items. Currently there are three full-time employees and three part-time employees; all have been with the Company for at least five years and will stay on after the acquisition. The business is located near the USF campus in a strip mall with a strong anchor.

STRENGTHS AND WEAKNESSES

The Company's main strength is its history and name in the community. They have many repeat customers. The primary weakness would be the threat of competition as there are currently several stores within a five-mile radius.

ASSETS AND LIABILITIES INCLUDED IN SALE

Items included in our estimate of value are as follows:

Inventory	$ 25,000
Fixed Assets	$100,000
Cash	$ 0
Accounts Receivable	$ 0
Other Current Assets	$ 0
Other Assets	$ 0
Real Estate	$ 0
Assumption of Liabilities	$ 0
Total Assets/Liabilities Included in Sale	$125,000
Goodwill	To be determined

Main Street Florist Adjusted Cash Flow

	Tax Returns 2002	Tax Returns 2003	Tax Returns 2004	Projected
Revenue				
Gross sales	$512,410	$556,412	$598,741	$621,410
Pretax Profit				
Unadjusted pretax profit	57,647	65,127	69,928	75,705
Nonrecurring Items				
Depreciation and amortization	5,641	6,654	7,410	8,141
Interest expense	2,124	2,321	2,547	2,695
Officer compensation	25,000	25,000	25,000	25,000
Family salaries and benefits	0	0	0	0
Officer insurance	0	0	0	0
Officer auto	0	0	0	0
Personal expenses	0	0	0	0
Other add-backs	0	0	0	0
Historical rent	0	0	0	0
Fair market rent	0	0	0	0
Total add-backs	32,765	33,975	34,957	35,836
Calculation of Cash Flow				
Pretax profit +	57,647	65,127	69,928	75,705
Total add-backs	32,765	33,975	34,957	35,836
Seller's Discretionary Earnings (SDE)	**90,412**	**99,102**	**104,885**	**111,541**
Less replacement salary	(35,000)	(35,000)	(35,000)	(35,000)
EBITDA	**55,412**	**64,102**	**69,885**	**76,541**
As percentage of sales	10.81%	11.52%	11.67%	12.32%
Cash flow weight	0	0	1	1
Weighted SDE	**$108,213**			
Weighted EBITDA	**$ 73,213**			
Weighted Revenue	**$610,076**			
Weighted EBIT	**$ 65,438**			

Main Street Florist Summary of Valuation Methods

	Value	Weight of Valuation Method Used	Extension
Cost Approach to Value			
Tangible asset value (inventory and equipment)	$125,000	0%	0
Market Approach to Value			
Price to SDE	$270,533	20%	54,107
Goodwill to SDE	$287,320	20%	57,464
Comparable transaction method	$243,587	20%	48,717
Industry method	$291,032	10%	29,103
Income Approach to Value			
Capitalization of earnings	$313,881	20%	62,776
Discounted future cash flow	$323,484	0%	0
Excess earnings method	$306,193	10%	30,619
Enterprise Value		100%	$282,787

Based on the information contained in the report that follows, it is our estimate that the enterprise value of Main Street Florist, Inc., as of December 31, 2004, can be reasonably stated as $282,787. The value considerations herein are contingent upon the analysis and limiting conditions as set forth in the body of the report.

Sample Term Sheet for 100 Percent Asset Purchase of an Existing Business

Background Notes

When purchasing a company, a buyer will either purchase the *equity* of the company, including its assets and liabilities (a "stock sale"), or just the *assets* of the business, with or without assuming any specifically identified liabilities (an "asset sale"). It is usually in the buyer's best interest to pursue an asset sale, since there are tax advantages to doing so and she may avoid lawsuits from inherent corporate liabilities. Even in the context of an asset sale, however, she may choose to acquire certain liabilities, such as real estate leases and customer contracts, that would be helpful for a seamless transition between owners. The seller, on the other hand, would

---

Lizette Perez-Deisboeck, partner at Goodwin Procter in Boston, Massachusetts, contributed to this document. Goodwin Procter LLP provides pro bono legal counseling services to qualifying women served by the Center for Women in Enterprise in Boston, Massachusetts. This document, however, does not constitute legal advice. Some of the terms in this Appendix were drawn from Russell Robb's *Buying Your Own Business* (Holbrook, MA: Adams Media Corporation, 1995), 174, 184, 234–237.

usually prefer to sell stock, because not only are there tax advantages to the seller in doing so, there's also a clear transfer of all of the liabilities of the business from seller to buyer. For more comprehensive details on stock sales versus asset sales, see Robb's *Buying Your Own Business*. An asset sale example was chosen for this Appendix because that deal structure is not only more common but is often also more advantageous to buyers.

The term sheet that follows is written in layman's language; the final legal documents would be longer and more precise. In addition, depending on the circumstances, additional terms may be included. Typically, a "Term Sheet" or "Letter of Intent" (LOI) is explicitly nonbinding and represents the intentions of the parties until they draft, negotiate, and sign a "Purchase and Sale Agreement." Executing a nonbinding document makes sense because, among other things, (1) a brief, preliminary document such as this one will not be able to cover all relevant issues in appropriate detail; (2) in the event that you uncover major surprises or obstacles during the completion of your due diligence, you need to be able to get out of your commitment to buy; and (3) from the seller's perspective, it is important to keep options open until there is a firm and specific commitment from the buyer. The Term Sheet or LOI may be used as the basis for an "Offer to Purchase," or it may serve the purpose of documenting the parties' verbal negotiations in writing, so as to frame the discussion on the specific terms without straying too far from the intended business deal. In this fictional example, even though the buyer is an individual, she has set up an S-corporation to buy the assets of the business.

Term Sheet

1. *Parties' intent and form of purchase.* Red Lantern Solutions Incorporated ("Buyer") proposes to purchase all of the assets of Green Light Technology Consulting Corporation ("Seller") of Waltham, Massachusetts, including goodwill, customer lists, and all other intangible and balance sheet assets, to be substantially the same as those set forth on the balance sheet of Seller as of December 31, 2005 (Exhibit A), as well as to assume certain contractual liabili-

ties of Seller. The name Green Light Technology Consulting, or any derivation thereof, is not transferable in the sale.

2. *Purchase price and structure.* The purchase price for the assets will be $300,000, payable as follows:

   a. $10,000 as a good faith deposit ("Deposit"), to be paid on the date that this Term Sheet is executed and held in escrow by Lifestyle Business Brokers of New York, New York, to be applied to the cash payment in 2 (b)(i) at closing.

   b. $180,000 (60%) in cash
      i. $90,000 (30%) as a cash payment from the Buyer
      ii. $90,000 (30%) as a cash payment with proceeds received by Buyer from a lending institution to be determined.

   c. $90,000 (30%) in the form of a Promissory Note ("Note") of Buyer payable to the Seller, secured by a second lien on the assets of the business as well as a personal guarantee from Buyer. The Note shall be payable over five years at an interest rate of 6.75 percent, in equal monthly payments of $1,771.51 per month. No prepayment penalties shall apply to such Note. The obligations of Buyer under the Note may not be assigned.

   d. $30,000 (10%) in the form of an "earnout" contingent on future performance of the business, based on milestones and targets to be determined by the parties.

3. *Consulting agreement.* In addition to the above, Seller will enter into a Consulting Agreement with the Buyer and will receive aggregate payments of $30,000 for providing comprehensive transition and training activities to the Buyer for a period of six consecutive weeks following the closing and for an additional nonconsecutive 10 business days within the 12-month period following the closing, upon reasonable request and prior notice. The specifics of the consulting services to be provided, including the timing of the payment for such services, will be more fully described in the Consulting Agreement.

4. *Brokerage fees.* Buyer and Seller agree that Lifestyle Business Brokers, Inc. shall be paid a commission equal to 8 percent of

the purchase price ($24,000) at the closing. Payment of such commission shall be the sole responsibility of the Seller.

5. *Lease of building space.* It is agreed that Seller will use its best efforts to transfer the lease to Buyer, with the landlord's prior approval, at current or market rental rates as permitted by the lease.

6. *Timing for completion.* The closing shall take place 60 days from the signing of this Term Sheet, at which time a Purchase and Sale Agreement, the initial draft of which shall be provided by the Buyer's attorney, shall be signed. This Term Sheet shall expire 60 days from the date of signature if the Purchase and Sale Agreement has not been signed by that time, and at such time the good faith deposit shall be returned to Buyer. Buyer agrees that, provided all contingencies in paragraph 12 below have been met prior to expiration of this Term Sheet, if she should fail or refuse to complete this transaction, the Deposit shall be forfeited and, at the Broker's option, shall be split 50 percent to Seller and 50 percent to Broker. This deadline may be extended by the mutual agreement of the parties in the event that due diligence, bank financing arrangements, or other issues delay the closing. Seller agrees to negotiate exclusively with the Buyer during this 60-day period and to effectively take the company (and its assets) off the market during this exclusivity period; a breach of this commitment could cause Buyer to sue the Seller. Seller agrees to inform Buyer of any offers it may receive, including the details of that offer, during the exclusivity period.

7. *Closing costs and the responsibilities of buyer and seller.* Except for the brokerage fees described above, Buyer and Seller shall each pay their own expenses, including legal expenses, up to the time of the closing. The cost of due diligence shall be the responsibility of the Buyer. Attorneys' fees for closing costs shall be borne equally between Buyer and Seller, but the closing day's business shall belong to the Seller. The following adjustments and pro-rations shall be made at the closing: rent, payroll, security deposits, inventory transactions, utilities, etc. Prior to closing, permission for any nonordinary expenses shall be sought from Buyer.

8. *Noncompetition agreement.* Seller and its principals agree not to compete, directly or indirectly, with the business of Buyer nor to solicit or hire Buyer's employees for a period of three years after closing. Seller further agrees to disclose during the due diligence phase any outstanding noncompete agreements or obligations with third parties.

9. *Confidentiality.* With certain exceptions such as where information of Seller is already publicly known and known to Buyer's advisers, Buyer promises not to disclose information of Seller to outsiders and not to disclose that negotiations are under way.

10. *Access to books and records, key customers, and key employees prior to closing.* Subject to the confidentiality obligations in paragraph 9, Seller will make available to Buyer and Buyer's representatives reasonable access to the office, books, records, and assets of the business and will furnish to Buyer financial and operating data and such other information as Buyer reasonably requests as part of Buyer's due diligence investigation of the business. Buyer shall not communicate with employees or key customers of the business without Seller's prior permission.

11. *Insurance.* Seller shall offer Buyer proof of business insurability during the due diligence phase and shall specify what will happen to the existing corporate insurance policies.

12. *Contingencies.* This purchase shall be contingent on the following:

    a. Buyer's securing of satisfactory bank financing as described in 2 (b)(ii).

    b. Buyer's completion of satisfactory due diligence on the Seller (including financial information, condition of equipment, merchantability of inventory, and review and approval of any key contracts held by the business) and Seller's completion of satisfactory due diligence on the Buyer (including background and credit checks).

    c. Buyer's review and acceptance of terms for a lease as described in 5.

13. *Representations and warranties.* The Seller warrants that (i) it has clear and marketable title to the business being sold, and that no consents are required for transfer; (ii) the financial information provided to Buyer represents the actual financial condition of the company at the time of sale; (iii) at the time physical possession is delivered to Buyer, all equipment will be in working order and the premises will pass all inspections necessary to conduct business. Seller agrees to indemnify Buyer if any of the above representations and warranties are not true.
14. *Nonbinding.* This Term Sheet is a nonbinding agreement and contains the entire understanding between the parties.

Multiple Shareholder Legal Questionnaire

$\mathcal{T}$his questionnaire is designed to aid multiple shareholders of a single company in planning formally for possible future scenarios such as (1) the decision by a shareholder to sell her shares in the corporation; (2) the death or serious disability of a shareholder; (3) a shareholder competing with the corporation; or (4) a shareholder's declaration of bankruptcy. The terms on which such person's shares would be purchased or transferred, if at all, are to be agreed upon in advance in a legal agreement called a "Shareholders' Buy-Sell Agreement." The questionnaire should be used by stockholders to give advance consideration to these issues before engaging an attorney to draft specific terms of an agreement.

This questionnaire is based on an actual client questionnaire prepared by Lisa Hodgens, an attorney with Leisawitz Heller in Wyomissing, Pennsylvania. Hodgen specializes in small business transactions and is the co-owner of a family business run by her husband.

Issues to Be Considered

1. Option/Obligation to Purchase Shares
   a. Is the corporation required to purchase the shares of a deceased shareholder? (This is customary.)
   b. Should the corporation be obligated to purchase shares of a shareholder if such shareholder retires, becomes permanently disabled, competes against the corporation, or declares bankruptcy? (An option to purchase, but not an obligation, is customary.)
   c. If a shareholder desires to transfer his or her shares to a person or entity other than the corporation, should that shareholder first offer to sell such shares to the corporation and the other shareholders? (This is customary.)

2. Death of a Shareholder
   a. In the event a shareholder dies, should either the corporation or the remaining shareholders be *required* to purchase the deceased shareholder's shares? If so, which entity or persons should be the required purchaser?
   b. In lieu of a sale or redemption of shares, should a deceased shareholder be permitted to transfer his or her shares via estate planning documents?
   c. Should the corporation and/or the remaining shareholders have the right but not the obligation to purchase the shares owned by the estate of a deceased shareholder?

3. Disability
   a. Do you want to require a shareholder to sell his or her shares if and when the shareholder becomes permanently disabled?
   b. How long must a person be disabled to be deemed "permanently disabled?"
   c. How do the shareholders want to define "disability"?

4. Employment/Age
   a. Do you want to require a shareholder to sell his or her shares if his or her employment is terminated by the corporation?

b. Do you want to impose a mandatory discount on the value of the shares being sold if a shareholder's employment with the corporation has been terminated for cause? What about a shareholder who merely resigns?

c. Do you want to impose a mandatory retirement age for shareholder-employees? Do you want to allow shareholder-employees the right to require a buyout of their shares when any such shareholder reaches a certain age?

5. Valuation

a. How will you value any shares to be sold by a shareholder? What methodology is most appropriate for your company? (For example, a multiple of earnings, plus inventory at book value.)

b. Will you consider valuing the company according to a certain formula on an annual basis? (For example, you can execute on an annual basis a "certificate of value" that will set forth the total value of the corporation's assets and the current value of each shareholder's shares. If a shareholder's shares are to be transferred and the corporation's most recent certificate of value has been signed within one year prior to the date of the proposed sale, the purchase price for the shares shall be the value stated for such shares on the certificate. If the most recent certificate of value is more than one year old, and the parties cannot otherwise agree to a purchase price for the shares, the selling shareholder and the purchasing entity may each retain a qualified and experienced appraiser to prepare a valuation of the fair market value of the shares to be sold. If the two appraisals are the same, the purchase price shall be the appraisal price. If the two appraisals vary by less then 10 percent of the lower valuation, the purchase price shall be the average of the two appraisal values. If the appraisals vary by more than 10 percent of the lower valuation, the two appraisers shall pick a third party who shall review the two appraisals and pick one of the two appraisals as the purchase price.)

6. Payment Terms
   a. How will payment for shares be made? (For example, should there be a three-year payment plan, and if so, should required payments be made in annual, quarterly, or monthly installments? Or should the purchase price be paid in full at closing on the sale of the shares?)
   b. Do you want to use a valuation methodology for calculating the value of shares other than the previously described method?
   c. What interest rate should be applied to any judgment note ("Note") delivered under the agreement?

7. Ownership of Shares
   a. Should the purchaser acquire ownership of shares upon the delivery of a Note to pay for the shares or upon making the final payment pursuant to the Note? Alternatively, should the purchaser acquire title to a prorated number of shares in installments tied to the amount of each payment under the Note?
   b. While shares are being purchased under a Note, what activities of the corporation, if any, may not be undertaken without the consent of the selling shareholder?

8. Insurance
   a. In case of the death or disability of a shareholder, will the purchase price for either the redemption or sale of shares be prefunded via the purchase of life insurance or disability insurance on the lives of the shareholders?
   b. Will each shareholder purchase life insurance on the lives of each of the other shareholders?
   c. If a shareholder dies and there is a life insurance policy in effect to purchase the deceased shareholder's shares, who shall receive any remaining life insurance proceeds after the purchase price for the deceased shareholder's shares has been paid?

9. Reciprocal Rights

   Do you want to impose the transfer restrictions on each shareholder or do you want to exempt certain shareholders from any or all shares transfer restrictions?

10. Valuation Discounts

    a. Do you want to impose a predetermined minority interest and/or lack of marketability discount(s) on the value of each shareholder's shares? If so, what will be the terms and the amount of the discount(s)?

    b. If you do not want to impose such discounts each year, do you want to allow the accountant that regularly represents the corporation to impose such discount(s) when the shares are valued?

11. "Drag-Along" and "Tag-Along" Rights

    a. If the majority shareholder decides to sell all of his or her shares, do you want to allow such shareholder to require the other shareholders to sell their shares to the same buyer on the same terms?

    b. If a majority shareholder wants to sell his or her shares, do you want to allow the minority shareholders to have the right to participate in such sale on the same or similar terms?

12. Competitive Activity

    a. Do you want to allow shareholders to engage in business activities that compete with the activities of the corporation?

    b. Do you want to require shareholders who engage in such competing activities to sell their shares? Do you want to merely give the corporation and/or the other shareholders an option to purchase shares in this situation?

    c. If so, what discount, if any, should be imposed on the value of such shares?

13. Dispute Resolution

    a. In the event of any dispute relating to the interpretation of the agreement and/or the rights/duties of any party thereto, should the parties resolve their differences by mediation, binding arbitration, or some other alternative dispute resolution process?

b. If so, which dispute resolution method should be used?

14. Management of the Corporation

What decisions affecting the corporation, if any, must be approved by a supermajority of the shares or the unanimous consent of the shareholders?

15. Antidilution Rights

Do you want to require the corporation to offer newly issued shares to existing shareholders so as to prevent the dilution of each shareholder's equity interest in the corporation before issuing such shares to new shareholders?

APPENDIX I

The Partnership Charter Process

A partnership charter is a tool either for people contemplating becoming business partners or for existing co-owners who are facing transitions or other challenges. The partnership charter is in part a road test. It carefully steers people through a thicket of topics that most partners either don't know about or avoid because of the sensitivity of the issues (e.g., power, money, ownership percentages). If you each "pass the test" (i.e., complete the charter), then you know you're good to go. The process can be undertaken by the partners themselves, or they may choose to have someone facilitate it.

Partners who complete the charter process end up with a 20- to 30-page document that records their understandings and serves as a guide for working together closely day in and day out. While one partnership or shareholders' agreement may look strikingly like another, no two partnership charters will ever look much alike. A partnership charter captures

---

This Appendix was contributed by Dr. David Gage, a psychologist, mediator and business school professor who wrote the book, *The Partnership Charter: How to Start Out Right with Your New Business Partnership (Or Fix the One You're In)*, and co-authored *The Partnership Charter Workbook* with Dr. Edward Kopf. Information about the book and the workbook are available on the web site www.BMCassociates.com. The idea of a charter that thoroughly covers both the business and interpersonal sides of being partners originated with Dr. Gage.

partners' intentions, dreams, expectations, and agreements—their collective reality. It defines who they are as partners and defines what the vague word *partners* means to them. Partners who complete the charter process also end up with a high level of confidence in themselves because they have successfully examined their plans for operating as a team in a way very few partners have ever done.

An important side benefit of creating this in-depth partnership document is that many partners who are starting their ventures hand over their charter document to their attorneys, who use it to help them draw up partnership, or shareholder, agreements as well as buy-sell agreements and other legal documents.

Not all people who dive into the depths of partner planning pass the road test. Some decide the idea to band together is a mistake and abandon it—an appropriate outcome for some people because they may not be suited to become partners. Figuring this out sooner rather than later saves everyone a lot of grief, even though it usually also feels disappointing.

The end product is a signed document but not one written in stone; it's a *living document* that changes as the business environment, individual partners, and the partnership itself change. Partners must make a commitment to review it periodically and revise it as needed. The periodic reviews help ensure that partners attend to changes that are taking place before it's too late to do anything about them. A charter cannot totally preclude the possibility of destructive conflict, but it is an effective way to minimize it and simultaneously build greater confidence in the partnership.

The outline presented here contains guidelines and exercises for reaching agreement on 12 different business and interpersonal topics that have proven, in the author's 20 years of mediation experience, to have caused the most problems in partnerships. The partnership charter drills down into the nitty-gritty details of how people plan on working together because, when the relationships among partners fall apart, 9 times out of 10 it's over the details—personality quirks, amount of time off, the time a partner comes into the office in the morning, the way money is handled, the way a partner dresses, or how slow someone is to make decisions.

An Outline of a Partnership Charter

I. Introduction
   A. *Preamble*
      1. Partners lay out their goals for the charter process.
      2. They explain to one another, among other things, why they want to have partners generally, and why these partners specifically.
   B. *Partners' Vision and Direction for Their Partnership and Their Business*

   Here, partners delve into their visions for both their partnership and their business. Surprising as it may be, people who start businesses together often have different ideas about the exact nature of the business they want to build. Sometimes the differences aren't terribly significant; other times they are. One famous co-founder, Steve Jobs of Apple Computer, once said, "It's okay to spend a lot of time arguing about which route to take to San Francisco when everyone wants to end up there, but a lot of time gets wasted in such arguments if one person wants to go to San Francisco and another secretly wants to go to San Diego."

II. Interpersonal Issues
   A. *Personal Styles*
      1. Most people taking on partners are not naïve to the challenge of having personalities that mesh reasonably well. Everyone wants to get along, but what can people do to improve their odds in the murky world of individual quirks? Plenty, it turns out, starting with gathering some useful data.
      2. Using an instrument such as the Personal Profile System (DiSC), people can get 15 pages of feedback on their personal style. Information from the test helps them better understand how they operate in close quarters. They can share that information with one another.

3. Most importantly, every two people in the partnership can make specific agreements with one another *based on the information from their tests* that can help them have more effective working relationships.

Example: Two of the agreements that Margaret (a perfectionist) made with her soon-to-be partner, Barbara (a results-oriented type) were to "provide opportunities to review and discuss your achievements" and "support you in accomplishing your objectives." A few of the agreements that Barbara made with Margaret included being patient "in drawing out your goals," giving her "time to adjust to changes," and "provide you with assurances that no surprises will occur."

B. *Personal Values*

1. Personal values are the underpinnings of people's decision making and frequently a source of conflict; therefore people need to understand their own and their potential partners' personal values. The challenge is to know which values to discuss and how to measure them. Just talking about values abstractly doesn't help.

2. We recommend that each person take a test that gives feedback on eight personal values that are relevant to being partners and running a business together. You can obtain the Personal Values test from BMC Associates' web site, www.BMCassociates.com. The eight personal values in the test are Power-Seeking, Individualistic, Spiritual, Materialistic, Theoretical, Ritualistic, Humanitarian, and Aesthetic.

3. Each partner creates agreements with each other co-owner based on the results of the values test.

Example: In a start-up company with four co-owners, two of the people developed an agreement that reads like this: "Barry and Julie differ on many fronts. For one, Julie is power-seeking, spiritual, and materialistic. Barry, on the other hand, is aesthetic, theoretical, and humanitarian in his values. While this may cause some tension in mapping out a strategy for the company, both share characteristics that make them able to work well together. For one, both Barry and Julie value teamwork and cooperation, and thus should be able to set aside personal difference in management styles for the greater good of the group. Both Julie and Barry like to lead by example. The key to this relationship is for both of us to focus on communicating with each other and understanding the other's motivation for thinking one way or the other. Both must realize that the business will entail compromises in management styles and both must be willing to bend to the other's needs and wishes while maintaining the integrity of the partnership."

III. Business Issues
   A. *Contributions and Rewards*
      1. There are partners who make $200,000 each, but feel cheated, when two years earlier they both felt blessed to make $50,000. That math may not make sense, but if you look closely at the issue of fairness, it can make perfect sense. People, usually unconsciously, compare what they are putting in (contributions) with what they are taking out (rewards). Furthermore, they compare what they are putting in and taking out with what their partners' contributions and rewards are. In all of these comparisons, perceptions reign over facts.
      2. People can tolerate their "interpersonal equity balance sheets" being in the red for a period of time. But if perceived inequities persist for long, they will inevitably take steps to correct the imbalance.
      3. It is wise for people joining forces in business to be aware of what each of them is contributing to their venture and what each of them hopes to get out of it. Having this awareness goes a long way toward raising partners' feelings of satisfaction with their arrangement, regardless of how much they are making.

4. Some examples of people's contributions:
   - Personal networks and connections
   - A book of business
   - Reputation in business and legal communities
   - Finance expertise
   - Political acumen
   - Published articles
   - Experience running an $80M company
5. Some examples of people's rewards:
   - $300,000+ compensation
   - Opportunity to acquire more authority
   - Ability to come in only in the afternoons
   - Ability to retire by age 50

B. *Roles, Responsibilities, Authority, and Accountability*
  1. When partners step on each other's toes or experience turf battles, these are symptoms that partners have not divvied up their roles and responsibilities with sufficient clarity. Power struggles also break out when people are looking more at their own personal needs than at the needs of the business.
  2. Many business owners do a reasonably good job at holding employees accountable for performance, but holding a fellow partner accountable for her performance is much more challenging.
  3. Some partners try to get around the discomfort of being one-down with a partner by making themselves co-presidents. It is doubly important for these partners to be clear about their duties and who is responsible for what.

C. *Money*
  1. People starting businesses need money, and most entrepreneurs gather their money from credit cards, personal lines of credit, and of course, friends and family. People need to discuss their different money styles and agree on where the money will come from.
  2. Start-ups don't usually generate money, they consume it. It might seem premature, therefore, for people becoming

partners to spend time thinking about how to get money out of the business. Nevertheless, this is a subject over which many partners fight.

3. Are partners going to pay themselves the same amount? If they are, then they had better be sure they'll value their respective contributions equally.

D. *Ownership*

1. How people determine who will own how much of a company is a fascinating issue, and one that is almost never discussed in public, or in private, despite the significance of the issue.

2. People customarily resort to the "magic numbers," which are 50-50 and 51-49 (or their variations, such as 25-25-25-25), without fully appreciating what it means to be equal or majority-minority partners.

3. Many partners think they have a single decision to make relative to money, decision making, governance, and ownership, namely, "What percentages of ownership will we each have?" They believe that from those numbers, everything else will fall out.

4. People becoming partners have much more flexibility in these matters than they realize. Partners have the ability and freedom to apportion each of these rights (e.g., the right to a share of the profits, the right to approve borrowing) as they see fit. They can customize their partnership by developing financial, managerial, governance, and ownership structures that fit their particular circumstances, and there are advantages to doing so.

E. *Governance*

1. A governance body—a board of directors—is not a pressing matter for many people when they are forming a company. Beginning partners are more apt to consider having an informal advisory board. It is advisable for people to have a meeting of the minds about what the different possibilities are, what would be useful, and when it should be instituted.

2. Who will serve on a board and how they will be selected are also issues to consider.

IV. The Future of the Business and the Partnership
  A. *Expectations*
    1. Co-owners in failed businesses relationships will often complain, "My partner didn't meet my expectations." If asked whether they ever told their partner what their expectations were, they will admit they did not. The things some people expect of their partners are 180 degrees different from what other people expect. There are few, if any, right and wrong expectations. The trick is for people to be open and honest about what they expect and for their partners to either accept or reject those expectations.
    2. People can clarify their expectations of themselves and one another with the following exercise. Each person lists her expectations in the following categories and then shares her list with her partners: (1) expectations I have for myself, (2) expectations I think my partners have of me, and (3) expectations I have for each one of my partners.

Examples of expectations some people have for their partners:
- "You will think of us as collaborators."
- "You'll never criticize me in front of our employees."
- "If you have a problem with something I'm doing, you'll tell me right away."
- "You'll give me the benefit of the doubt about my professional capabilities."
- "You will provide social introductions for me at our country club."
- "You won't talk with employees about what happens between us."
- "You won't refer to me as 'the new guy.'"

B. *Fairness*
   1. The fundamental question each partner needs to ask is, "Does the totality of the relationship we've arrived at seem fair to each of us?"
   2. At the end of the charter process, partners must step back and look at the whole pie, individually and then collectively. A partner may reach the conclusion, for example, that while it seemed to make sense to compromise about her authority and give in on the percentage of ownership she had hoped for, the combination now doesn't feel fair. It helps to think of the analogy of negotiating to buy a car. Even if you got the exact model, price, extras and delivery date you wanted when you negotiated the deal, you have to step back at the end and ask yourself, "Am I really happy with this whole package? Is this the car I want?"

C. *Scenario Planning*
   1. Anticipating the unexpected is a powerful way to lessen the risk inherent in partnerships. While the majority of the work on the preceding topics could be called anticipating the "expected," the goal of scenario planning is to anticipate the "unexpected."
   2. Partners brainstorm about what could happen to them as partners and to their businesses that would put a real strain on them as a team. They then create and agree upon guidelines for dealing with the hypothetical scenarios.

D. *Conflict Prevention and Resolution*
   1. Today, most businesspeople realize there are alternatives that can keep partners out of costly and destructive litigation, but few people, or their advisers, plan in advance for a multiple-step procedure for resolving conflict among partners.
   2. Step one is negotiation. In this step, partners sit down as soon as possible and try to discuss and negotiate their differences by themselves.

3. Step two is mediation. With mediation, partners turn over control of the process to third-party neutrals who are trained to help people collaborate and resolve deadlocks. The partners remain solidly in control of the outcome. Any resolutions arrived at are consensual, signed, and binding on the parties.

4. Step three is arbitration. Because mediation is always voluntary (i.e., seeing it through to an agreement), there needs to be a back-up procedure if the partners cannot reach an agreement through mediation. When neutral arbitrators take over, they are in charge of both the process and the outcome. An arbitrator's job is not to help the partners reach a mutually satisfactory outcome; it's to determine who is right and who is wrong. Specifying arbitration as the final step keeps people from going to court to resolve their differences and is in most instances faster, more efficient, and more economical than litigation.

Books Worth Reading

BUYING AND VALUING BUSINESSES

Joseph, Richard A., Anna M. Nekoranec, and Carl H. Steffens. *How to Buy a Business: Entrepreneurship Through Acquisition.* Chicago: Dearborn Financial Publishing, 1993.

Robb, Russell. *Buying Your Own Business.* Holbrook, MA: Adams Media Corporation, 1995.

West, Tom. *The 2006 Business Reference Guide: The Essential Guide to Pricing a Business.* 16th ed. Wilmington, NC: Business Brokerage Press, 2006. (available at www.bbpinc.com)

FRANCHISING

Birkeland, Peter M. *Franchising Dreams: The Lure of Entrepreneurship in America.* Chicago: University of Chicago Press, 2002.

Bond, Robert E. *How Much Can I Make? Actual Sales, Expenses, and/or Profits on 137 Franchise Opportunities.* 4th ed. Oakland, CA: Source Book Publications, 2004.

Kowalski, Gary M. *The Franchise Ratings Guide: 3000 Franchisees Expose the Best & Worst Franchise Opportunities.* Lincoln, NE: iUniverse, 2006. (available at www.iuniverse.com/bookstore/index.asp)

Seid, Michael, and Dave Thomas. *Franchising for Dummies*. Foster City, CA: IDG Books Worldwide, 2000.

DIRECT SELLING

Christopher, Doris. *The Pampered Chef: The Story of One of America's Most Beloved Companies*. New York: Currency, 2005.

CONSULTING

Biech, Elaine. *The Consultant's Quick Start Guide: An Action Plan for Your First Year in Business*. San Francisco: Jossey-Bass/Pfeiffer, 2001.
Fishman, Stephen. *Working for Yourself: Law and Taxes for Independent Contractors, Freelancers, and Consultants*. Berkeley, CA: Nolo, 2004.

FAMILY BUSINESS

Francis, Anne E. *The Daughter Also Rises: How Women Overcome Obstacles and Advance in the Family-Owned Business*. San Francisco: Rudi Publishing, 1999.
Lansberg, Ivan. *Succeeding Generations: Realizing the Dream of Families in Business*. Boston: Harvard Business School Press,1999.

STARTING A BUSINESS FROM SCRATCH

Brattina, Anita. *Diary of a Small Business Owner: A Personal Account of How I Built a Profitable Business*. Chicago: ATHENA Foundation, 1996, 2003.
Friedman, Caitlin, and Kimberly Yorio. *The Girl's Guide to Starting Your Own Business: Candid Advice, Frank Talk, and True Stories for the Successful Entrepreneur*. New York: HarperResource, 2003.
Timmins, Jeffrey A., and Stephen Spinelli. *New Venture Creation: Entrepreneurship for the 21st Century*. New York: McGraw-Hill–Irwin, 1995, 2003, 2006.

FINANCING AND BUSINESS PLANNING

Brush, Candida, Nancy M. Carter, Elizabeth Gatewood, Patricia G. Greene, and Myra M. Hart. *Clearing the Hurdles: Women Building High-Growth Businesses*. Upper Saddle River, NJ: FT Prentice-Hall/Pearson Education, 2004.

Green, Charles H. *Financing the Small Business: Raise Money for Your Business at Any Stage of Growth*. Avon, MA: Adams Media Corporation/Streetwise, 2003.

Green, Charles H. *The SBA Loan Book: Get a Small Business Loan—Even with Poor Credit, Weak Collateral, and No Experience*. Holbrook, MA: Adams Media Corporation, 1999 (or see the 2005 revision).

Polish, Beth. *Business Plan Power: Creating a Tool That Works for Your Company*. New York: DROOM™ Books, 2006. (available at www.businessplanpower.com)

Polish, Beth. *DROOM™ in the Market for Money Primers*. New York: DROOM™ Books, 2005. (available at www.inthemarketformoney.com)

Whiteley, Sharon, Connie Duckworth, and Kathy Elliott. *The Old Girls Network: Insider Advice for Women Building Businesses in a Man's World*. New York: Basic Books, 2003.

PARTNERING WITH OTHERS, JOINING EXISTING BUSINESSES

Gage, David. *The Partnership Charter: How to Start Out Right with Your New Business Partnership (or Fix the One You're In)*. New York: Basic Books/Perseus Books, 2004.

Watkins, Michael. *The First 90 Days: Critical Success Strategies for New Leaders at All Levels*. Boston: Harvard Business School Press, 2003.

WORK-FAMILY CONFLICT, WOMEN IN BUSINESS

Heffernan, Margaret. *The Naked Truth: A Working Woman's Manifesto on Business and What Really Matters*. San Francisco: Jossey-Bass, 2004.

Hewlett, Sylvia Ann. *Creating a Life: Professional Women and the Quest for Children*. New York: Hyperion/Talk Miramax Books, 2002.

Nash, Laura, and Howard Stevenson. *Just Enough: Tools for Creating Success in Your Work and Life*. Hoboken, NJ: John Wiley & Sons, 2004.

Warner, Judith. *Perfect Madness: Motherhood in the Age of Anxiety*. New York: Riverhead Hardcover, 2005.

SMALL BUSINESS, LIFESTYLE BUSINESSES

Schine, Gary. *How to Succeed as a Lifestyle Entrepreneur: Running a Business without Letting It Run Your Life*. Chicago: Dearborn Trade Publishing, 2003.

Walters, Jamie. *Big Vision, Small Business: 4 Keys to Success without Growing Big*. San Francisco: Berrett-Koehler Publishers, 2002.

INTERNET AND eBAY BUSINESSES

Collier, Marsha. *Starting an eBay Business for Dummies*. 2nd ed. Hoboken, NJ: John Wiley & Sons, 2004.

NOTES

CHAPTER ONE   The Business Mind-Set: Your Key to Success

1. Sharon Whiteley, Connie Duckworth, and Kathy Elliott, *The Old Girls Network: Insider Advice for Women Building Businesses in a Man's World* (New York: Basic Books, 2003), 4–5.
2. Sylvia Ann Hewlett, *Creating a Life: Professional Women and the Quest for Children* (New York: Hyperion/Talk Miramax Books, 2002), 289.
3. Gary Schine, *How to Succeed as a Lifestyle Entrepreneur: Running a Business without Letting It Run Your Life* (Chicago: Dearborn Trade Publishing, 2003), 7.
4. See Harvard Business School professors Laura Nash and Howard Stevenson's book, *Just Enough: Tools for Creating Success in Your Work and Life* (Hoboken, NJ: John Wiley & Sons, 2004) for further discussion of models for success.

CHAPTER THREE   Why Start from Scratch If Someone's Done It for You?

1. For an excellent compilation of recent statistics about women's business ownership, see the National Women's Business Council web site, www.nwbc.gov, "Fact Sheet: Women Business Owners and Their Enterprises," March 2005.
2. Center for Women's Business Research, *"Key Facts about Women-Owned Businesses, 2005 Update,"* pamphlet, April 2005. This statistic pertains to businesses with annual revenues of $1 million or more.

3. Whiteley et al., *Old Girls Network*, 3.
4. Based on a database of 3,800 transactions in the BIZCOMPS database, as analyzed by Toby Tatum in his book, *Transaction Patterns*, and cited/summarized in Tom West, *The 2004 Business Reference Guide*, 14th ed. (Wilmington, NC: Business Brokerage Press, 2004), 312.
5. West, *2004 Business Reference Guide*, 15–17.

CHAPTER FOUR   Finding the Right Business for You

1. For example, Mom Corps matches accounting, legal, marketing, and IT professionals with U.S. companies seeking contract or project talent (www.momcorps.com); Aquent offers a way to find contract jobs in specialized recruiting services, marketing, and healthcare consulting (www.aquent.com); and The Hired Guns matches independent marketing, PR, web design, writing, and other professionals with interim project needs at hiring companies (www.hiredguns.com). All these companies are small and growing, but none specializes in working for small businesses.
2. www.vrbusinessbrokers.com/pages/about/index.jsp, accessed October 24, 2005.
3. Ibid.
4. West, *2004 Business Reference Guide*, 44.
5. A quick way to analyze a target company relative to its industry is to use Risk Management Association (RMA) Annual Statement Studies, which are available in most business libraries. Find a closely matching Standard Industrial Code (SIC) for your target company and then look up the RMA (or Dun & Bradstreet) ratios compiled from voluntary submissions from private companies. Compare your target company's profit margins, liquidity ratios, days of inventory, and other benchmarks to industry averages, usefully sorted by sales volume and asset value.
6. Author interview with Darren Mize, Gulf Coast Financial, October 5, 2005.

CHAPTER FIVE   Franchises and Direct Selling Companies

1. Direct Selling Association web site, www.dsa.org, accessed December 8, 2005, "Frequently Asked Questions."
2. Direct Selling Association, "2004 Direct Selling Growth & Outlook Survey Fact Sheet," available at www.dsa.org.
3. "Franchise Leaders Send Largest Delegation to Capitol Hill," International Franchise Association press release by Terry Hill and Amy Bannon, September 14, 2005, available at www.franchise.org/article.asp?article=1220&paper=93&cat=297.
4. Interview with Scott Evert, Director of Franchise Sales and Re-sales for Sunbelt Business Advisors Network, March 22, 2006.
5. Ibid.
6. From a handout provided by Evert, March 21, 2006.
7. www.franchisesolutions.com/index.cfm/fa/read/resource_id/13/, accessed December 8, 2005.
8. As cited by Perri Capell in "Franchising Insight: Women Franchisees Seem Few and Far Between," WSJ.com/DowJonesStartupJournal .com, November 11, 2004.
9. Peter M. Birkeland, *Franchising Dreams: The Lure of Entrepreneurship in America* (Chicago: University of Chicago Press, 2002), 101–102.
10. Ibid., 91.
11. From the International Franchising Association's online course "Franchising Basics: the Official IFA Course," subheading "Franchising Regulation," available at www.ifa-university.com.
12. Ibid.
13. Michael Seid and Kay Marie Ainsley, "Use a Franchise Broker: The Risks of Using an Online Broker May Outweigh the Supposed Benefits," *Entrepreneur* magazine, July 9, 2001.
14. Direct Selling Association, "2004 Direct Selling Growth & Outlook Survey Fact Sheet," available at www.dsa.org.
15. Ibid.

CHAPTER SIX   A Piece of the Pie—Working for, Consulting for, or
Partnering with Existing Business Owners

1. "The Best B-Schools," *BusinessWeek*, October 18, 2004, as cited on
   the www.catalyst.org web site, "Quick Takes—Women MBAs," accessed September 21, 2005.
2. Business Valuation Resources, LLC, "Valuing Small Businesses
   Worth Less than $1 Million," transcript of pay-to-join teleconference
   held on December 16, 2004.
3. Ibid.
4. Michael Watkins, *The First 90 Days: Critical Success Strategies for
   New Leaders at All Levels* (Boston: Harvard Business School Press,
   2003), 74.

CHAPTER SEVEN   The Family Business Advantage (for the
Lucky Few)

1. Anne E. Francis, *The Daughter Also Rises: How Women Overcome
   Obstacles and Advance in the Family-Owned Business* (San Francisco: Rudi Publishing, 1999), 77.
2. As cited in "Facts and Figures on Family Business" at the Family
   Firm Institute web site on February 27, 2006, http://www.ffi.org/gen-Template.asp?cid=186#us.
3. Francis, *Daughter Also Rises*, 30.
4. Ibid., 119.
5. Ibid., 194.
6. These ideas are taken in part from Francis, 70.
7. See Francis, 178 and 180.

CHAPTER EIGHT   If You're Sure You Want to Start a Business

1. Anita Brattina, *Diary of a Small Business Owner: A Personal Account
   of How I Built a Profitable Business* (Chicago: ATHENA Foundation, 1996, 2003), 202.
2. Ibid., 1–2.

3. Ibid., 30.
4. Ibid., 120
5. Ibid., 13.
6. Ibid., 204.
7. Ibid., 26.
8. As mentioned by Laurie Ann Golden, CEO of Spanx, at a presentation to Harvard Business School alumni in Atlanta, Georgia, on February 15, 2006.

CHAPTER NINE   Smart Financing Strategies for Your Business

1. As cited in "'Make Mine a $Million Business'™ Program Aims to Propel Women-Owned Businesses Past the Million-Dollar Barrier," a press release issued on March 14, 2005, by Count-Me-In for Women's Economic Independence, a not-for-profit organization dedicated to increasing women's access to credit and capital; the Women's Leadership Exchange (WLE), an educational and networking company that conducts conferences for women business owners across the United States; and OPEN from American Express™. The statistic about the number of small businesses that are at least 50 percent women-owned (10.6 million) comes from the Center for Women's Business Research "Top Facts About Women-Owned Businesses" (see www.cwbr.org).
2. Jamie S. Walters, *Big Vision, Small Business* (San Francisco: Berrett-Koehler Publishers, 2002), 179.
3. As cited in "Women Demonstrate They Have What It Takes to Build Million Dollar Firms," a research summary from the Center for Women's Business Research (see http://www.womensbusiness research.org/milliondollar/), undated but archived on July 26, 2005.
4. Walters, *Big Vision*, 177.
5. "Cleaning Up Messes, Friend to Friend," *New York Times*, March 5, 2006, BU 5.
6. On the National City Bank web site, there is a listing of "professional women business advocates" within the company whom women are

encouraged to contact directly with loan requests. See www.national city.com/smallbusiness/solutions/WBOAdvocates/default.asp and click on "Local Advocates."

7. See Charles H. Green, *The SBA Loan Book* (Holbrook, MA: Adams Media Corporation, 1999), 90–91.

8. Both women were referred to me by the intermediary/brokerage firm that sold them these companies, Carpenter Hawke & Co. of Boston.

9. This section is based on both (1) a presentation offered by the Center for Women in Enterprise in Boston, Massachusetts, entitled "How to Obtain Bank Financing for Your Start-Up or Existing Business," obtained from Jennifer Williams in November 2005, and (2) information from Green (1999).

10. To order credit reports, contact: (1) Equifax, www.equifax.com, 1-800-685-1111; (2) Experian, www.experian.com, 1-888-397-3742; (3) Transunion, www.transunion.com, 1-800-916-8800.

11. See Green, *SBA Loan Book*, Chapter 6, "Getting the Loan Closed."

12. This section is based on a presentation offered by the Center for Women in Enterprise in Boston, MA, entitled "How to Obtain Bank Financing for Your Start-Up or Existing Business," obtained from Jennifer Williams in November 2005.

13. Green, *SBA Loan Book*, 19, 27.

14. Ibid., 27.

15. Charles H. Green, *Financing the Small Business* (Avon, MA: Adams Media Corporation, 2003), 318.

16. www.sba.gov/financing/sbaloan/microloans.html, accessed July 5, 2006.

17. www.countmein.org/what/index.html, accessed December 6, 2005.

CHAPTER TEN   You're Not Alone: Why Women Consider Business Partners

1. See David Gage, *The Partnership Charter: How to Start Out Right with Your New Business Partnership (Or Fix the One You're In)* (New York: Basic Books, 2004), 3–4. Gage analyzes *Inc.* and *Entrepreneur* magazines' listings of fast-growing companies and finds that the ma-

jority were started by partners. Academic research from Marquette University and other studies also confirm that entrepreneurs who pool their strengths rather than operating solo grow their businesses faster.

2. Gage, *Partnership Charter*, p. 92.
3. In chapters on personality styles and personal values, David Gage says it's important to understand similarities and differences, but even more important to use that information to develop written agreements regarding how partners will interact day to day.
4. The PowerLink program was originally started in 1992 in Pittsburgh, Pennsylvania, by Barbara Moore and Ilana Diamond, two friends of entrepreneur Anita Brattina, whose book *Diary of a Small Business Owner* is featured in Chapter 8. Brattina's business was the very first to participate in the PowerLink program. The program was scaled nationally in 1998 through a partnership with the ATHENA Foundation and is now funded by National City Bank and the Ewing Marion Kaufmann Foundation.
5. Gage, *Partnership Charter*, 45.

ACKNOWLEDGMENTS

*T*o all the "smart women" I interviewed, whose examples are on display throughout this book, I am deeply grateful for your willingness to share the meaningful details of your small business experiences. You are the female role models with whom our readers will identify and whom they will emulate, and you are the essence of this book.

To those who encouraged me to write this book, I owe special thanks, especially to my husband Alex, who offered me support, strategic insights, and critical backup at home during the entire process of writing it. Having written two books himself, he inspired me to have faith that I could complete a project like this in less than a lifetime.

My friend and fellow author Ruth Stevens pointed me in the right direction from day one, explaining how to write a winning book proposal and making valuable introductions. I am grateful to Al Reyes and Pam Yatsko, both authors and dear friends, for steering me toward this esteemed publishing company, John Wiley & Sons.

Laurie Harting, my editor at Wiley, offered the perfect mix of constructive criticism and confident encouragement, while her assistant Brian Neill took care of many important details, and both the production team (including Linda Witzling and Cape Cod Compositors) and marketing staff did an excellent job of ensuring that the book was professionally produced and presented. I also extend thanks to those who commented on early chapter drafts and helped me refine them, especially my twin sister and talented writer Ann Davis Vaughan, my parents John and Jeannie Davis, Deborah Moore (Sunbelt Business Advisors), David Gage (BMC Associates), Lizette Perez-Deisboeck (Goodwin Procter), Kendra Wilde, and Gregg Lestage.

Those who provided more than just editing help include Deborah Moore, Erin Hanlon (Shelter Island Gardens), Lisa Hodgen (Leisawitz Heller), Darren Mize (Gulf Coast Financial), and David Gage, who contributed, respectively, the Preface and several original appendices — thank you.

Other experts in their fields who spared some of their valuable time to speak with or help me include Brace Carpenter (Carpenter Hawke & Co.), Scott Evert (Sunbelt Business Advisors), Wilma Goldstein (U.S. Small Business Administration), Myra Hart (Harvard Business School), Susan Kezios (American Franchisee Association), Betsy Myers (formerly with the SBA and now the executive director of the Center for Public Leadership at Harvard's Kennedy School of Government), Beth Polish (Critical Junctures / DROOM Books), Linda Stevenson (National City), Kathy Tito (Franchise Solutions for Women), Austin Webb (Gulf Coast Financial), and Jennifer Williams (Center for Women in Enterprise, Worcester, Massachusetts).

Thank you also to my friends Maisie, Lamia, Kendra, Gina, Julia, Rachel, and others who took my book idea seriously and encouraged me to proceed. Madelyn Yucht, whom I interviewed for this book and whom I've known for almost 10 years, deserves special mention for being the first person ever to inspire me to consider buying, rather than starting, a business. It was also through her that I was introduced to former and current heads of women's programs at the U.S. Small Business Administration.

Thank you, all.

INDEX

Index

ABOUT THE AUTHOR

*G*inny Wilmerding is a small business consultant and former small business owner. Her business background includes senior executive roles at small private enterprises and Internet startups in the Boston area as well as leadership positions in large corporations in the United States and China (Lucent Technologies Inc., AT&T Corp., and Hutchison Whampoa Ltd.). She is a former research associate at the Harvard Business School. Ginny has negotiated the purchase of small businesses and has professionally authored business plans, private equity placement memorandums, and business cases. She graduated summa cum laude with a degree in East Asian Studies from Princeton University in 1991. Originally from Asheville, North Carolina, she now lives in Brookline, Massachusetts, with her husband and two children. She may be contacted at gwilmerding@rcn.com. Readers are also encouraged to visit the author's website at www.smartwomen-smallbusiness.com for book excerpts and useful links.